Franchise Operations and Antitrust

Donald N. Thompson
Harvard University
and
The University of Alberta

Heath Lexington Books
D. C. Heath and Company
Lexington, Massachusetts

Table of Contents

vi

vii

List of Tables and Figures

Preface

The writer of a study encompassing as many disciplines as does this one is indebted to many persons, directly and indirectly. Many of them will be found mentioned in the footnotes.

I would like to express deep gratitude to Dr. E. T. Grether, University of California, who provided constant guidance and encouragement in the research and writing of this work. It was Dr. Grether who suggested the broad formulation of purposes and objectives of the study; and it was Dr. Grether who prodded me incessantly to keep a reasonable balance among the managerial, economic, and legal sides of the study.

Grateful acknowledgement is also due to Dean Richard H. Holton and Dr. David A. Clarke, Jr., both of the University of California, for their careful scrutiny of the text and their many insightful comments on it.

I am also tremendously indebted to Dr. Roger Dickinson of Rutgers University for the many hours he spent reading and criticising the first draft of the manuscript and for his encouragement in the development of the early parts of the work.

This research was supported in part by a grant from the Marketing Science Institute (MSI). It constitutes part of an ongoing MSI research project on governmental constraints upon marketing decisionmaking. My thanks are extended to Dr. Wendell R. Smith, former President, and Patrick J. Robinson, former Director of Management Studies at MSI, for their advice, encouragement, and their patience.

A sincere appreciation is expressed to the many individuals, both inside and outside of the franchising industry, who discussed franchise system problems with me, who supplied me with source materials, data, and opinions, and who answered my many letters. Many of them remain, by request, anonymous. Others are identified in the text. My research correspondence is several times the volume of this study, a tribute to the sympathetic response that my queries received.

Unfortunately, I cannot shift the blame for any errors, mistakes, or omissions onto anyone but myself. It was I who made the final decision in all cases, and it is to me that all criticisms should be directed.

Cambridge, Mass.   **Donald N. Thompson**

**Franchise
Operations
and
Antitrust**

1 Introduction

Franchise systems, and the contractually integrated marketing systems of which they are a part, have grown more rapidly in recent years than either their wholly owned or administered system counterparts. This development may prove to have been one of the most significant trends in distribution in the postwar period. By the end of 1969, it is estimated that the franchise industry had reached $124 billion in annual sales. There are over 500,000 franchised businesses in the United States—about one business enterprise in nine in the nonfarm sector—with new franchisees being added at a fairly constant rate of 13,000 per year.

For a number of reasons this dramatic growth has received relatively little attention: the many new kinds of franchising, the stable number of franchises in the traditional areas of automobile retailing and soft drink wholesaling, and the wide diversity of product and industry groups involved. There have been several attempts to study the managerial side of franchising in a comprehensive way,[1] but no very extensive study of the public policy aspects of franchise systems.

While it is common to apply the term franchising to a whole range of different economic and legal relationships, the contractual bond of interest is one in which an organization, the franchisor, develops a pattern or formula for the manufacture and/or sale of a product or service, and extends to other firms, the franchisees, the right to carry on the business, *subject to* a number of restrictions and controls. In almost all the cases of significance, the franchisee operates using the franchisor's name as a trade name.

There are two quite distinct classes of franchise systems, one involving a product or service, the other revolving around trademark licensing arrangements. These two break down further into six identifiable types, designated by kinds of market supplier and franchisee. Thus, a franchise agreement may exist between manufacturer and retailers in the case of Chevrolet and Mary Carter Paints; between manufacturer and wholesalers in the case of Coca Cola; and between wholesaler and retailers in the case of Western Auto or Walgreen's. A trademark owner-franchisor may contract with manufacturers in the case of Fruit of the Loom fabricated textiles; with wholesalers or retailers in the case of Hertz or Kelly Girl; or with franchisees on the same level of distribution as the franchisor in the case of Sealy Mattresses.

The central issue in franchising today is emphasized in the above definition which states that the right to carry on business under the franchisor's

1

trade name and style of operation is granted to the franchisee ". . . subject to a number of restrictions and controls." Franchise contracts frequently require agreement by the franchisee to limit his sales to specified territories or to a stated group of customers; to use that equipment or deal only in that merchandise furnished him by the franchisor or by a supplier named by the franchisor; to sell only at prices dictated by the franchisor; and to advertise, hire employees, keep records, or landscape the premises only in accordance with the franchisor's rules and restrictions.

Recent decisions have confirmed that the courts and federal and state enforcement agencies are inclined to condemn a variety of these controls in the name of the "rule of competition." Because franchising contributes significantly to the ability of small businesses to compete effectively with larger organizations and counters the trend towards concentration of economic power, it has been suggested that these extensive regulations fail to recognize the values of the franchise system and penalize legitimate and valuable business arrangements.

Federal regulatory agencies such as the Antitrust Division of the Department of Justice and the Federal Trade Commission have become involved in the controversy through their concern with the trend toward both horizontal and vertical integration and the relationship of franchising to this problem. Both the Antitrust Division and the Department of Commerce have indicated concern with the development of appropriate criteria for determining when a franchisor has gone beyond permissible limits in imposing rules and restrictions on franchisee behavior.

The courts have recognized that the successful operation of a franchise system requires that the franchisor control certain activities of his franchisees. The courts have also stated, in no uncertain terms, that in maintaining this control the franchisor is under a duty to avoid violating the antitrust laws.

To date, franchisors have made little effort to justify the controls they seek to impose in the light of the managerial and economic requirements of modern distribution. When they have been asked to defend these controls, their responses have concerned the necessity of their actions to remain in business; assertions of the difficulty of objective proof; and claims of their need as small businessmen to do things which their larger competitors find unnecessary.

The courts and regulatory agencies have given franchisors specific warnings that these claims are inadequate and that more realistic appraisals will be required. In the *White Motor* case,[2] the Supreme Court demanded more information from both parties regarding the economic factors involved in franchising before it would rule on the propriety of current practices. In its most important ruling on vertical territorial restraints, the Supreme Court suggested it may not be sufficient to demonstrate sound business reason and intent on the part of a franchisor who would impose controls. Assuming nonpredatory motives and business purposes, it may also be necessary to demonstrate that the impact of the control in the marketplace is procompetitive.[3]

Thus, there is a real need to evaluate the controls placed on franchisees in the light of the realities of franchising—the special needs of the franchisor and franchisee, and the place of franchised business in the economy. The more restrictive the control, the more persuasive the proof must be. The case of customer or territorial restrictions probably requires the highest degree of proof—proof not only that the restriction is desirable and helpful, but also some indication that, without it, the franchisor's ability to compete would be impaired. In *White Motor* in 1963, the Supreme Court suspended judgement on this issue. In the 1967 *Arnold, Schwinn and Co.* ruling, the Court seems to have applied a rule of *per se* illegality which repudiated the rule of reason interpretation of *White Motor*. By a 5 to 2 majority, the Court said that franchisees must be permitted to resell to unfranchised dealers. Since the majority decision leaves franchisors free to use territorial and customer restrictions in conjunction with agency, consignment, or other distribution plans, the final impact of the ruling on franchised business is not clear.

Tying arrangements, the requirement that the franchisee purchase the franchisor's products, are as difficult to justify as territorial restrictions. Only where the tying agreement can be demonstrated to be no more restrictive than necessary to facilitate a worthwhile goal, can the franchisor feel secure from an antitrust attack (or from the kind of inquiry which Congressional Committees have directed to practices of the major oil companies in their TBA relationships with their franchisees).

My principal intent in this study is to contribute to the evaluation of the major controls contained in franchise agreements. I have tried to indicate the economic and social context of franchise systems by beginning the study with a detailed look at the history, nature, growth, and scope of franchising.

Chapter 2 discusses interpretations of franchising from managerial, academic, and legal sources; develops a working definition of franchise systems for use in the study; and describes the major types of franchised business.

Chapter 3 traces briefly the development of franchising in several industries and presents data on the quantitative contributions of franchising in terms of the size, growth rates, and failure rates of franchised business. The chapter concludes with a discussion of the qualitative contributions of franchising to the economy.

Chapter 4 discusses the relationship of franchising to other forms of vertical market organization. There is a discussion of the use, by franchisors, of contractual and noncontractual distribution restrictions in franchise systems. The chapter concludes with a consideration of conflict and cooperation within the franchise marketing channel.

Chapter 5 provides an overview of the legislation (and judicial or administrative agency interpretation) applicable to the controls found in franchise systems. Legislation on franchise systems includes the Sherman, Clayton, and Federal Trade Commission Acts, special legislation such as the "Dealer Day in Court" statute concerning automobile industry franchise agreements, and state legislation on special forms of marketing and selected industries. The reader who is interested primarily in the economic aspects of franchise systems may skip this chapter without loss of continuity in the study.

Chapters 6, 7, and 8 discuss economic and managerial aspects of the most important franchise system controls: tying arrangements, territorial and customer confinement of franchisees, and exclusive franchising and exclusive dealing. The three chapters point up the business justification for these controls in relation to their current legislative and regulatory status. Is the control necessary, in the sense of being reasonably ancillary to a necessary function of the franchisor,[a] or in the sense of being necessary to the existence of the system as a whole? The idea of "least necessary restraint" is introduced as a set of criteria against which franchise system controls may be weighed and evaluated.

One caveat is in order. The writer, although currently located at a school of law, is by training an economist and not a lawyer; the distinction is reflected throughout the study. Antitrust law, like other human institutions, is undergoing development, clarification, and change as experience accumulates, and particularly as economic and social conditions vary. A lawyer looks at the cases in a series, especially where they stand unchallenged, as representing the state of the law. I have tried to look at the cases mentioned as indications of first gropings with a problem, rather than as presenting its final solution even in the state in which they were found. A lawyer, in interpreting a case, looks to the two questions: "What are the significant categories of facts and what are their significance to the court?" and "What differences in facts or in procedural set-up produce differences in the court's action when the situations are otherwise alike?" I have tried to look at a third question: "Given these categories and the procedural set-up that the court *chose* as significant, what trends are suggested as being of significance for the future?"

---

[a] The rule of reasonably ancillary restraints was spelled out in *United States* v. *Columbia Pictures Corporation*, 189 F. Supp. 153 (S.D.N.Y. 1960), at 178, as follows: "Where challenged conduct is subservient or ancillary to a transaction which is itself legitimate the decision is not determined by a *per se* rule. The doctrine of ancillary restraints is to be applied. It permits, as reasonable, a restraint which (1) is reasonably necessary to the legitimate primary purpose of the arrangement, and of no broader scope than reasonably necessary; (2) does not unreasonably affect competition in the marketplace; and (3) is not imposed by a party or parties with monopoly power.

. . . It permits . . . business arrangements of benefit to the parties, and perhaps to the public, which have no injurious effect in the sense of antitrust policy."

2 The Nature of Franchising

Definitions in the Literature

The term "franchise" is derived from an old French word "francher" and the more modern "affranchir," both meaning "to free," and used to express a freedom from servitude or restraint. The term gradually acquired the meaning of a privilege conferred on an individual by a sovereign. It was adapted to the form of business organization to indicate the granting of a positive right to do something, most commonly the right to use a name or form of operation that belonged to someone else, this time by a commercial organization.

In the hundred or so years in which the term has been in use to describe a commercial relationship, there has been in economic and legal discussions a tendency to avoid an explicit definition of a franchise or franchise system. However, there has been no shortage of descriptions by writers in all fields of what franchising means to them.

With few exceptions, writers from within the franchise industry[a] have shown a lack of conception of the scope and essential characteristics of franchising by either considering it to be so broad as to defy definition — or by defining it very narrowly and in terms of the experience and needs of their own franchising organizations. In explaining to a Senate hearing what is meant by franchising, one franchisor whose admitted most pressing problem was the recruitment of franchisees, described franchising completely in terms of its attraction for those people:

The following general features are common to many [franchise] arrangements. The franchisor undertakes to assist one who desires to enter his business [and] passes on . . . know-how to the franchisee, thus reducing the franchisee's risk of failure in starting and running his own business. . . . The franchise system permits a chain-type operation which, so far as the individual franchise is concerned, is only possible through the franchisor . . . a readymade reputation built up by the franchisor and his existing franchisees is transferred to a new franchisee . . . There is an identity of trade names, frequently of buildings, and other distin-

---

[a] The term "franchise industry" is used to indicate the strong community of interest which, despite their diversity of forms and backgrounds, exists among franchisors. According to Grant Mauk, President of Duraclean Company, "I would say that we have more in common with other franchising firms, regardless of their industry, than we do with nonfranchising firms in our own industry. Our problems of motivation, training, business development of franchisee-franchisor relations are not shared by firms that simply sell their products to a totally independent operator or deal with employees in company-owned outlets."[1]

5

guishing features which characterize all the franchise locations . . . all franchisees maintain quality standards . . . products and services which are standardized and of high quality. . . .[2]

The popular press and trade literature have tended to explain franchising in a highly simplified manner and have shown extraordinary similarity in their approaches to a definition:

A franchise . . . is a contract to distribute and sell goods or services within a specified area. A franchise business is owned by an individual and operated by him as part of a national, regional, or local chain of businesses. The franchise agreement gives the franchise holder the right to sell for or represent the parent firm in an area. In return for this exclusive privilege of distributing an established product or service, the holder contracts to pay either a sum of money [a franchise fee] or a commission on gross sales, or to buy equipment or supplies from the parent company — or a combination of these considerations.[3]

The approach taken by the Small Business Administration, and by all government agencies in their approach to defining franchising, has been to clarify the term by identifying the provisions of the franchise agreement, often at some length. There has evolved one basic definition which is being used by several government agencies:

While it . . . appears . . . fashionable to apply the term [franchising] to a multitude of different legal and economic arrangements, the contractual relationship we are interested in . . . is one whereby a firm, the franchisor, which as developed a pattern or formula for the manufacture or sale of a product or a service, extends to other firms, the franchisees, the right to engage in the business subject to certain restrictions and controls. In virtually all the cases . . . the franchised activity represents the major, if not the sole, business of the franchisee. More often than not, the franchisee is identified as a member of the franchisor's family.[4]

It is the legal profession which has been perhaps most interested in defining and classifying the franchising form. In general, their efforts have led to the conclusion that the franchise system cannot be classified under the usual forms of business organization. While there is agreement as to the legal classification of the franchise relationship, that agreement is a negative one; the relationship is not one of either employment or of agency. Also, to the extent that a franchisor restrains his franchisees as to the methods and conditions under which the franchise may be operated, the relationship does not fit within the traditional legal definition of an independent contractor relationship. Although it has definite characteristics of each of the legal forms of employment, agency, and independent contractor, and might well have been considered as a hybrid of all of these, it fits so badly into any of these traditional classifications that it has generally been considered as being *sui generis*. The unique legal character of the relationship has arisen largely because it incorporates a trademark license, with the licensor actively aiding the licensee in the exploitation of the trademark and the know-how of the licensor.[b]

There exists some disagreement in the literature as to whether a franchise agreement is in fact a contract. The agreement typically includes the nature of the relationship; its duration; the terms of renewal, or of cancellation (in the case of an agreement without expiration date); the operating controls under which the franchisee agrees to function; and the financial and other contributions to be made to the system and to each other by the parties to the agreement. Most of the legal literature takes the position that a franchise agreement is not an ordinary business contract. The courts have classified franchisees as agents for some purposes and as independent buyers for other purposes. The terms of the franchise agreement are in general not a result of independent bargaining by two parties. The alternatives open to the franchisee are to accept the terms offered him by the franchisor or to choose some other business. We may thus in general consider the franchise agreement to be a unilateral control device, not necessarily contractual in nature, but best classified as *sui generis*. (It is clear that many franchise agreements are not meant to be valid legal contracts and are intentionally drawn so as to be unenforceable as contracts.)

An Operational Definition of Franchising

The preceding collection of definitions helps describe what franchising does and illustrates the diversity of meanings of the term in different sectors of the economy and of society. The problem remains to define exactly what it is we are to be concerned with in this study; to identify the characteristics of the franchise concept which make that concept unique; and to find a definition which permits a derivation of the boundaries of the franchise form, and which does so in a way which satisfies both the public and the legal conception of franchising. I have adopted a definition of franchising which includes several features from the definitions above, but which centers on four aspects of the franchise concept which make that concept unique and identifiable. The four aspects are:

1. Although the franchisee may be economically dependent on the franchisor, he is a legally independent member of the franchising system;

---

[b] In legal litigation in the area of automobile franchise agreements, neither the courts nor the legal literature has been in agreement as to a proper legal position. Charles Hewitt, Jr. indicates that the positions of vendor-vendee, mixed principal-agent and vendor-vendee, principal-agent, and *sui generis* have all been advanced, with a trend for the judiciary to treat automotive franchise agreements as being *sui generis*.[5]

2. The franchisee's business is operated with the advantages of name and standardization of the franchisor accruing to the franchisee;[c]

3. The franchisee's business came into being in its present form (although not necessarily physically), with the expressed purpose of marketing the franchisor's products or service;[d]

4. A formal agreement, most commonly called a "franchise agreement" or "franchise contract," is in existence. The agreement calls for a continuing, although not necessarily indeterminate, relationship.

The franchise system itself may be defined as an organization, composed of marketing, production, and/or research units, created and administered by a franchisor (or group of franchisees in the role of a franchisor), as a medium for expanding and controlling the distribution of a good or service.

This definition is in agreement with both public and legal concepts of a franchise system. The reasons for the seemingly restrictive interpretation of the franchising form will become apparent with a consideration of the multitude of arrangements which have or should have been termed as franchising. (The early common law established the legal principle that courts have the power to classify legal relationships according to substance rather than form. The fact that parties label their legal relationships as one thing does not preclude the court from ruling that the actual legal relationship is something entirely different.)

The first requirement, of legal independence of franchisee from franchisor, eliminates several forms of vertical integration in which the distributor has contracted away virtually all of his freedom to his principal. In particular, there are a large number of people, within and without the petroleum industry, who believe that the restrictiveness of the contractual relationship between the service station operator and the contracting oil company eliminates the service station business from being included as part of franchising.

The second requirement, that the franchisee's business be operated with the advantages of name and standardization of the franchisor accruing to the franchisee, eliminates most franchised departments or product lines such as those found in the electrical appliance, liquor, clothing

---

[c]There is one exception, the horizontal trademark licensing case, which is discussed later in this chapter. In the normal case, the franchisee uses both the trademark *and* trade name of the franchisor. Where both franchisor and franchisee exist on the same level of the marketing channel, and where the franchisor organization is comprised solely or primarily of members who are also franchisees, the franchise agreement may cover only the trademark, with the franchisee doing business under his own (and usually unpromoted), trade name. In this horizontal trademark licensing case, we have a franchise system even though the name provision, in the sense of a trade name, may not apply.

[d]This aspect follows from the previous one that the franchisee adopts the franchisor's name. Again, an exception exists in the horizontal trademark licensing case.

and furniture industries. Here dealers normally operate under their own trade names rather than being identified as members of a group. While such retailers may identify themselves to purchasers as franchised dealers, the term "authorized dealer" is probably more appropriate. The contracts involved, if any, are normally only statements of the intention of the manufacturer to supply the dealer with a product or product line. Many suppliers simply provide a window transfer or sign bearing their name, and the words "franchised dealer" or "authorized dealer" for the merchant to display. This second requirement is obviously met by organizations such as Ben Franklin Stores, Chicken Delight, Howard Johnson Motor Lodges, Hertz, and Mister Donut, all of which operate under a common trade name and have physical features of the business which are both distinctive and common to the whole organization. The merchandise or services sold and the internal operating procedures of each organization are also standardized to a considerable degree.

The third requirement, that the franchisee's business come into being with the expressed purpose of marketing the franchisor's products or services, recognizes one of the unusual aspects of franchising; it is perhaps the only form of business organization that, by its very nature, tends to create new business units. When the franchisee joins the franchise system, his new trade name, the acquisition of a distinctive business appearance, and the standardization of products, services, and operating procedures lead to the birth of a new enterprise for the express purpose of marketing the franchisor's products or services.

The fourth requirement, of a formal agreement, recognizes that franchise systems are based on a relationship under which the responsibilities of all parties are spelled out. If only because of the legal requirement that the franchisor control the usage of trademarks and trade names which he owns, we can say that any system which does not include an agreement controlling such use is *not* a franchise system.

The Components of Franchising

The remainder of this chapter discusses two distinct classes of franchising, with six identifiable types. Each type shows a reliance on certain kinds of controls in the franchise agreement, and each encounters somewhat different antitrust implications in its operation. In each area, dollar volume through franchised outlets represents a significant percentage of total product or service sales.

I.   Product and Service Franchise Systems
    1. manufacturer-retailer systems
        (a) franchising an entire retail outlet (autos, paint)
        (b) franchising a single department (soft goods)
        (c) franchising a single product line (liquor, clothing)

    2. manufacturer-wholesaler systems (beverage syrups)
    3. wholesaler-retailer systems (cooperative and wholesaler-sponsored groups)
II.   Trademark Licensing Franchise Systems
    4. trademark licensor-manufacturer systems (fabricated textiles)
    5. trademark licensor association-association member systems (bread, milk, mattresses)
    6. trademark licensor-retailer systems (rental automobiles, restaurants)

Product and Service Franchise Systems[6]

Manufacturer-Retailer Systems. In the first of these, manufacturer to retailer systems, manufacturers may franchise an entire retail outlet, a single department within a retail outlet, or a single product or product line within an outlet. Virtually all the cases of importance involve entire retail outlets, including producers of automobiles and trucks, petroleum products, farm equipment, earth-moving equipment, paint, and shoes. Almost all new automobiles and trucks, and more than 90 percent of all retail petroleum products are sold through franchised outlets. There is some disagreement, mentioned earlier, as to whether service stations should be considered franchise outlets because of the restrictiveness of the contractual relationship under which the franchisees operate. The arguments, while of interest from an antitrust standpoint, will not be discussed in this study; I will assume throughout that the oil industry markets the bulk of its consumer products through a franchise system.

The franchising of single departments occurs in some department stores and specialty shops, particularly in soft goods lines and liquor, while franchising of single product lines occurs with appliances and radio, television, and high fidelity sound equipment. In most cases, arrangements concerning single departments and single product lines do not qualify as franchise systems under the definition given earlier. The classifications are included only because there do exist cases of a franchised single department or product line, most apparent in professional areas such as optical goods or beauty salons. These carry the trade name of the franchisor (as well as that of the retail outlet), use a standardized format developed by the franchisor, and are viewed by the public as part of a franchise system rather than as an integral part of the retailer's operation.

Manufacturer-Wholesaler Systems. The most important examples of manufacturer to wholesaler franchise systems exist in the beverage industry with soft drink syrups and with beer. All national manufacturers of beverage syrups, including Coca-Cola, Pepsi-Cola, and Seven-Up, franchise independent bottling companies which in turn service local retail and institutional accounts. In the case of the Coca-Cola Company, beverage syrup and concentrate is produced in 36 principal company plants around the world and sold to some 1,800 franchised bottlers (800 of them abroad), some of which also serve as jobbers in reselling syrup for use at soda fountains. Franchised bottling plants account for more than 90 percent of soft drink sales and have since the inception of the industry in 1891.

In the past, automotive and some appliance manufacturers have also used franchised wholesalers, but in recent years the practice has almost disappeared as direct sales from factory to dealer become more common. Under a recent Supreme Court ruling on a franchise program operated by Arnold, Schwinn & Co., a bicycle maker, the Court may have effectively disallowed one kind of manufacturer-wholesaler franchise system by ruling that Schwinn could not distribute bicycles solely through franchised wholesalers who were restricted to reselling them only to franchised retailers approved by Schwinn.

Wholesaler-Retailer Systems. Franchise programs include two kinds of wholesaler-to-retailer arrangements. In cooperative programs, retailers group together to form or purchase wholesale organizations, then set standards under which new members may join the retail cooperative. While some cooperatives are merely loose buying federations, the majority have adopted detailed standards and merchandising programs for their members. In wholesaler-sponsored programs, the franchisor-wholesaler recruits independent retailers on a voluntary, but contractual basis. These groups may be either national or regional in scope, and include organizations such as Butler Brothers, Western Auto Supply, and Super Valu Stores, Inc. The largest organization of this kind is the Independent Grocers Alliance (IGA) chain.

In a frequently quoted article, Leonard Konopa has raised the question of whether voluntary chains, either cooperative or wholesaler sponsored, should be included in the definition of franchised business. His approach is to compare the origins and practices of voluntary organizations and of recognized franchisors to "determine if significant differences do exist which warrant continued segregation rather than a synthesis of these terms."[7] While Konopa concludes that voluntary chains are sufficiently different that they should be considered separately, it is not clear that this alters either the economic or legal status, or the public image of these organizations as being part of franchising. For the purposes of this study, there seems no reason to differentiate voluntary wholesaler-retailer franchise systems from others so long as they qualify on the definitional bases of legal independence; operation with the advantages of name and standardization of the franchisor accruing to the franchisee; the form of the business coming into being with the advent of the franchise agreement; and a formal agreement being in effect between franchisor and franchisee.

Trademark Licensing Franchise Systems

While product and service franchise systems are well known and highly visible to the public, trademark licensing franchise systems[e] are far less widely recognized and understood. Several writers discussing franchising have failed to distinguish trademark licensing systems, while others have failed to recognize their special nature by grouping them under omnibus headings such as "service sponsor to retailer franchising." It also appears that a number of people, both within and without franchise systems, have failed to understand the special characteristics of trademarks and the conditions under which they can be used by other than the registered owner. Thus, before specifically discussing the last three types of franchise systems, it seems useful to include a short discussion of trademarks and the growth of trademark licensing.

The growth of national advertising and national branding of consumer products, and the increased mobility of consumers has had the effect of enlarging the market share of nationally advertised goods. The trend has threatened local or regional producers in some industries with economic demise. This is particularly true with products which, because of their ratio of shipping cost to value or because of rapid spoilage, cannot be transported over large areas in order to utilize national advertising and promotion. Mattresses are an example of the former, and milk or bakery products of the latter. For such products to be marketed without excessive costs, they must be produced in many local areas. Even in these areas, consumers are increasingly demanding the product reputation that comes from national advertising.

Virtually all service businesses dealing with the general public have the same problem. In the hotel-motel industry, the locations and often the ownership are local, but the traveller (and especially the inexperienced traveller) looks for the standards of service and the known cost of accommodation inherent in a nationally recognized and promoted trade name.

In virtually every industry where local operation is advantageous but national reputation and promotion are important, franchising systems have been created. Organizations of independent local businesses come into being by contractual means, either in the franchising form or through cooperative and voluntary chains as discussed earlier. In many of these industries, the alternatives facing independent operators have clearly been those of a synthesis with some sort of national group with continued independent operation, or ultimate demise in favor of nationwide chains

---

[e]Trademark licensing franchise systems will be referred to as "trademark franchising." Note that *all* franchising involves a trademark or trade name. Trademark franchising refers specifically to those systems in which the trademark or trade name, rather than a product or service, represents the chief contribution of the franchisor.

of manufacturing or service establishments as has occurred in food stores, hotels, dairy plants, and breweries, to name a few.

Until the beginning of this century, American courts would not allow such groups to use trademark licensing, the practice of permitting a person other than the owner of a trademark to use it on goods not manufactured by the owner of the mark. The prevailing theory, originating in common law and with a long legal precedent in Great Britain, was that the function of a trademark was to indicate the source of a product, and that permitting the use of a mark by more than one person violated that function. With the development of national markets, mass distribution, and mass media, the theory gradually evolved to recognize that trademarks performed an additional function, that of guaranteeing the consistency of quality of the product identified by the mark. Under the guarantee theory, the function of the trademark was held to be to assure the consumer of a consistent level of product quality rather than simply to designate the source. One result of the new theory was the idea of an implied guarantee that all products bearing a given trademark would be of like quality and composition. A second result was to allow a trademark to be used as a competitive tool by persons other than the owner, to expand markets for branded products in geographical areas where the owner could not or would not expand for reasons of financing, production facilities, or lack of interest. A third result was that local small businesses could band together to produce in accordance with an established set of standards, utilizing one common trademark, and through standardized advertising and promotion provide regional and national competition to the corporate chains that already operated on these principles. In 1946, the guarantee theory was recognized in Section 5 of the Lanham Trademark Act, which stated that a trademark could be used by "related companies," with such use inuring to the benefit of the trademark owner. A "related company" is one that is controlled by the registrant as to the nature and quality of the goods or services with which the trademark is used. The requirement of quality control is necessary to retain the validity of the trademark license and of the trademark itself at common law, and is consistent with the guarantee theory.[8]

Because of a widespread misunderstanding of Section 5 of the *Act*, a number of practices have mistakenly been undertaken under the name of trademark licensing. Some manufacturers have entered into trademark "license" agreements with all their wholesalers and sales agents, with the latter considering themselves "licensees" simply because the product they resell is trademarked. Wholesalers and retailers who resell a trademark owner's goods in the original package, or who merely repackage them are *not*, either legally or economically, "licensees," nor are they "registered users" under the Act. Nor, of course, are they franchisees, unless they also satisfy all the conditions set out earlier.

A second misunderstanding arises in situations where a trademark owned by the manufacturer of a product is used as part of the trade name of a dealer, for example in the name of a television dealership: *Fadda's Magnavox Center*. This does not represent a true trademark licensor-licensee relationship, since the dealer does not use the Magnavox trademark to identify or distinguish his own product, but only to advise potential customers that he sells this particular brand.

A third misunderstanding exists where the trademark identifies a product manufactured by the trademark owner and the product is used as one component of a finished good. In the textile industry, where a trademarked fabric is incorporated into finished garments, there is not normally a trademark licensor-licensee arrangement, because the fabric trademark owner is not responsible for the quality of the finished product. There is one case, discussed below, where quality control *is* exercised by the fabric trademark owner over the manufacture of the finished product, a licensing arrangement does exist, and a franchisor-franchisee relation is possible.

Even with the misunderstanding surrounding them, trademark franchising systems offer substantial potential benefits to franchisor, franchisee, and the public. The trademark franchisor is able to penetrate markets for his products and services that would otherwise be beyond his reach either financially or geographically and to offer competition to ownership integrated companies operating on a regional or national basis. The franchisor achieves an income from licensing with a minimum of capital investment, and little managerial responsibility other than maintaining the quality and other standards under which the trademark is used.

Individual franchisees without the financial, research, or production resources to expand on their own are enabled by trademark franchising to utilize the franchisor's operating and/or engineering expertise and his national advertising and promotion.[9] Trademark franchising allows a group of small or regional producers to compete against larger or national producers with nationally advertised brands.[10]

Trademark franchising may have adverse competitive effects if it serves to discourage innovation by either franchisor or franchisee, if it discourages the entry of new firms to a field where trademarks are well established, or if it disrupts a number of local or regional markets through entry of a well advertised and promoted national trademark in competition with small local or regional companies. There is also the possibility that, under the justification of quality control, the trademark franchisor may attempt to control the retail price of goods produced by the franchise, that he may impose exclusive dealing requirements on the franchisee, that he may illegally seek to divide territories among franchisees, or require franchisees to purchase some or all of their requirements from the franchisor or from franchisor-approved sources.

Trademark Licensor-Manufacturer Systems. The fourth type of franchising, and first of the three types of trademark franchising systems, is that between a trademark licensor and manufacturers. Here, the trademark franchisor neither manufactures goods nor performs services himself, but develops a product and selects a trademark, establishes quality standards and production specifications, plans regional or national promotion campaigns, and develops standardized accounting and control techniques. The trademark franchisor then franchises one or more firms to produce the product under his quality control and to market it under his trademark within stated geographic areas. The arrangement is exemplified by BVD garments and Fruit of the Loom or Forstmann fabricated textiles. As mentioned earlier, there exists a case where a trademark identifies a component manufactured by the trademark owner and the component is used as one input of a finished product. In the textile industry where a trademark fabric (with labels identifying the fabric) is made into a finished garment, there is not normally a trademark franchising arrangement, because the fabric trademark owner is not responsible for the quality of the finished product. If the fabric manufacturer does exercise quality control over the garment manufacturer, and if the finished good is sold under the fabric trademark as one result of this quality control, then a licensing arrangement exists; and if the other requirements are met, a franchising relationship is possible. For a number of reasons, primarily the desire of manufacturers depending on technology from outside sources to build up a market position under their own trademark, licensing to manufacturers has not been a significant area of franchising expansion.

Trademark Licensor Association – Association Member Systems. The fifth type of franchising is that between a trademark licensor association and the members of that association. In this situation, the franchisor licenses only a trademark, and the franchisee continues to do business under his own trade name. Normally, trademark licensing which does not cover the trade name is excluded from the definition of franchised business. Otherwise, it would include the common licensing of names for use on unrelated products, for example Mickey Mouse balloons and Daniel Boone caps. However, where franchisor and franchisee exist on the same level of the channel of distribution, where the franchisor organization is comprised solely or primarily of members who are also franchisees in the system, and where the franchisee uses only the licensed trademark and continues to do business under his own trade name, this arrangement should also be considered a franchise system, both in the common use of the word and in terms of the application of legislation and regulation.

Trademark licensor association – association member systems play an important, if not dominant role in the mattress, bread, and milk industries. A group of established local or regional manufacturers of a product join to pool their financial resources and technical abilities; to develop a trademarked product for national distribution in competition with national companies; to organize a company to develop and promote the trademark;

to carry on product research and development; and to provide national advertising and promotion for the resulting product. The umbrella corporation, in the role of franchisor, licenses each of the participating companies, which most commonly are members of the original group, to act as franchisees and use the trademark only on those goods manufactured to the quality standards of the franchisor organization.

Some of the details and advantages of such arrangements are illustrated by the following quotation from Walter J. Schob, President of Honorbilt Products of Philadelphia, a franchisee of the Serta group in the mattress industry:

Each . . . licensee contributes funds to Serta on an annual basis for use primarily in (a) national advertising; (b) local advertising; (c) maintenance of a central office, staff, and showroom; and (d) research and maintenance of standards. They are licensed to sell the Serta line in separate territories. The Serta line sold must conform to the specifications developed by Serta Associates, Inc.

The individual factories (franchisees) in Serta have benefited from the parent company in many ways. Chiefly, they found that they could compete with other nationally advertised brands. They could get expert advice on specifications and manufacturing techniques. Each licensee found that, collectively, national advertising, which was completely impossible in a single operation, had become feasible.

. . . the consumer has also benefited. We can literally pick the brains of our 40 members, and through interchange of ideas and production methods we have been able to improve the product and to effect savings in manufacturing to help offset constantly increasing costs in labor and material.[11]

An example of the cooperation between a franchise licensing association in the baking industry and one of their members is seen in the efforts to perfect the first continuous dough mixing process in the industry. Members of the Quality Bakers of America cooperative expressed interest, in the early 1950s, in the potential of the new process but no one baker could afford either the cost or the risk of adopting it. In 1952, all QBA franchisees agreed to share the risk of underwriting one franchisee in adopting the new process. The franchisee would pay for the unit if successful, the franchisor group would share the cost if it were a failure. By spring of 1954, the pilot operation had proven the process feasible and members of the QBA group were able to buy up all existing machines and secure a lead of several years on the rest of the baking industry, which was so concentrated that the eight largest ownership chains of wholesalers did 41.5 percent of the business in the industry.[12] Quality Bakers developed and registered the trademark "Batter Whipped," advertised it widely, and enjoyed considerable success in using it.[f]

---

[f]The three major groups, Quality Bakers of America, American Bakers Cooperative, and Independent Bakers, together account for 21.4 percent of wholesale business in the industry.

Trademark Licensor-Retailer Systems. The sixth and final type of franchising is that between a trademark franchisor and a franchisee-retailer. Here, the typical franchisor manufactures goods or provides services in one geographic area, but cannot or will not expand into other areas, usually because of financial or personnel limitations. He authorizes one or more franchisees in other geographic areas to market goods or services with his trademark *and* trade name, and to his quality control standards. This represents the fastest growing area of franchised business. The most common arrangement involves a service originated and developed by the franchisor. A product, often a food or beverage, may also be involved. While the product may be supplied by the franchisor through a tying arrangement, the source of the product is usually secondary to its sale under the trademark and trade name. Included in this category are businesses such as auto rentals, with Hertz and Avis; part-time help agencies, with Kelly Girl and Manpower; specialty food stores such as Tastee Freeze, Mister Donut, and Chicken Delight; restaurants such as Howard Johnson's and Cobbs; motels such as Holiday Inn and Congress Inn; and the new "celebrity franchise" operations such as Mickey Mantle's Country Kitchens. Several of these, notably Howard Johnson's and Tastee Freeze, have grown through franchising to become the largest national chains in their industries.

Similarities and Differences

What are the similarities and differences among these six types of franchising? In the three product and service franchise systems, the franchisor is the producer, and the franchisee the distributor. Where trademark franchising is concerned, the franchisee may be either a producer or a service operator. The three trademark franchising cases share a common interest in the question of quality control imposed by franchisors over the products made or the services rendered by their franchisees. All six types involve trademarked commodities, and in all six both franchisors and franchisees exhibit a common interest in protecting and developing the trademark.

Economic aspects such as the methods of compensating the franchisor for his contributions, the amount of initial entry capital required by the franchisee, and the degree of contractual power held or utilized by the franchisor over the franchisee will differ among the six types as well as within each type. From the standpoint of both economics and public policy, the similarities within each of the six are more important than their differences; it is for this reason that they have been so categorized.

3 The Development and Contributions of Franchised Business

Development of Franchised Business

Franchising before 1900

Franchising in one form or another dates back many hundreds of years. During the Middle Ages important persons, often high church officials, were granted by the local government a franchise conferring the right to collect tax revenues and special levies. In return, the franchisee paid his franchisor a lump sum of money, plus continuing personal services and other considerations. This early form of franchising (which was really that, and not an agency or brokerage arrangement) ended around 1562, when the Council of Trent demanded a reform of tax collection procedures and an end to the system of patronage in government.[1] As late as the eighteenth and nineteenth centuries, franchises of a different kind were being granted in England by royalty or by legislative bodies. These involved the right to a monopoly in some form of trade or commerce over a long period, with a single cash payment and continuing obligations to the franchisors being contributed by the franchisee.

As might be anticipated, franchising in the business form that we recognize today also has a long history as a method of distribution. The Singer Sewing Machine Company developed an extensive franchise system just after the Civil War, so franchising has been an integral part of the marketing structure of the United States for almost one hundred years. Not much is known of the early Singer experiment, except that it was gradually phased out over about two decades.[2]

The use of the franchise form that we know today was not to expand again until the adoption of a franchise system by the automobile companies in the period after 1910, and its adoption by the integrated oil companies during the 1930s. The real franchise boom has come only since the early 1950s, with the increase in service franchising and trademark franchising systems.

Franchising in the Automobile Industry

Since the establishment of the first franchised dealership for electric cars in 1898, a major portion of all passenger cars and trucks have been sold through franchised outlets. In 1967–68, 94.8 percent of total passenger car sales were made through such outlets.

Contrary to widely held belief, the automobile industry did not develop the first franchising plan, nor was the plan it adopted an innovation at the time, nor has the industry exhibited innovation in franchise systems over the period of its existence. But franchise systems did achieve their first substantial dollar volume and strategic importance as a result of the growth of the automobile industry and its importance in total economic terms. It is of interest to compare the difference in motivations leading to the beginning of franchising in the automobile industry and later in the petroleum industry with those underlying the current franchise boom.

From 1900 to 1910, virtually all automobile manufacturers sold their cars directly to the ultimate user. Many manufacturers solicited business by mail. Some sold cars to agents on a consignment basis. Others utilized travelling salesman, while some even sold through large department stores. Charles Mason Hewitt, Jr., who has carried out an extensive study of the structure of the early automobile industry, concludes that ". . . virtually every type of distribution device was experimented with during this [1900–1910] period."[3]

It was into this confused pattern of distribution that the device of franchised agencies was introduced. The honor of being the first franchised dealer has been attributed to William E. Metzger of Detroit, who established a dealership to handle steamers in 1898. Automobile franchising had become fairly common by 1906, with wagon dealers, bicycle retailers, hardware store owners, and men from all types of business being drawn into the early dealerships.

In adopting a franchise system, the automobile manufacturers sought the solution to a number of distribution problems. By granting exclusive territories, thus protecting their dealers from intrabrand competition, the manufacturers were able to attract a high grade and financially strong group of franchisees. In restricting the number of franchisees, the manufacturer could guarantee each one sufficient volume to require in turn that each handle only the products of that manufacturer — and thus elicit a more vigorous and concentrated selling effort. By selling to only a few franchisees, each manufacturer could reduce his selling and transportation costs through fewer customer calls and larger individual shipments. Similarly, each manufacturer could obtain more accurate estimates of future demand from franchisees operating in a protected market — and thus improve his own production scheduling control. Finally, by having fewer and financially stronger retail outlets, it was possible for each manufacturer to require more extensive investments in buildings, inventories, and equipment from franchisees, improving the image and prestige of the manufacturer's products and providing more assurance that adequate consumer service would be rendered after sale.

The combination of these advantages suggests why an automobile manufacturer might utilize a restrictive franchise system, rather than simply selling to any dealer who would maintain adequate facilities and pay cash for the product on delivery. It does not explain why, as some of the major manufacturers acquired the necessary capital resources, they did not turn to a policy of general distribution, or to a system of manufacturer-owned retail outlets.

As was true with the beginning of automobile franchising, the answer to why the franchise form has been perpetuated seems to have been primarily economic. A financially independent franchisee can be forced to absorb part of the costs of overproduction or styling errors made by the manufacturer. These costs would have to be borne by the manufacturer in a system of manufacturer-owned outlets. Franchised dealers absorb the first impact of any price fluctuations at the retailing level, as the manufacturer's price fluctuates much less frequently and less strongly than do retail prices. The problem of used car trade-ins and resale introduces further financial uncertainties that are borne by the franchisee rather than by the manufacturer. There are additional state taxes and fees to be paid where a nationwide manufacturer-owned retail system is involved. Also, branch managers are not felt to have the same degree of motivation to succeed as the independent franchised dealer who has both his income and business investment to lose in case of business failure.[4] Finally, franchised dealers are felt to have a stronger attachment to and rapport with the local community than would salaried employees of a manufacturer.

The continuation of the franchise system in automobile distribution can be partially explained by the immense amount of capital that would be required by a franchisor who wished to buy back franchisees and establish a wholly owned system. *Business Week* estimated that in 1955, franchised automobile dealers had a total of $4 billion invested in land, buildings, equipment, and inventory.[5] According to a study by the National Automobile Dealer's Association in December, 1951, franchised dealer's aggregate investment in that year had exceeded the aggregate investments of all automobile manufacturers combined. Based on a per-dealer investment of $300,000 and 36,200 franchised dealers, that figure today would be $10.8 billion. Even if the major automobile franchisors could raise this immense sum, the rate of return on capital invested in the distribution system might well be less than if it had been invested in other manufacturing opportunities.

Franchising in the Petroleum Industry

The integrated petroleum companies also required local representation with some personal investment and motivation. For historical and economic reasons they evolved a franchise system in which franchisees were much more closely tied to the franchisor than was the case with the automobile companies.[6]

Although the term franchising is not normally used by firms in the petroleum industry to describe their distribution system, the arrangement used is substantially equivalent to a franchise system. The differences come in the use of short-term building and equipment lease contracts by the oil companies to alter the relationship, if not the form, of their franchise agreement.

In the period prior to 1930, the retail outlets of almost all integrated petroleum companies were company-owned. Beginning around 1930, several integrated companies began to lease their stations to private operators, and by 1935 the practice had gained impetus and was spreading throughout the industry. In many cases, service stations were leased to those persons already serving in them as salaried managers.

The motivations under which the integrated oil companies withdrew from the direct operation of service stations originated in new legislation and in the beginning of the depression. These motivations differ from the largely economic ones noted in the discussion of the automobile industry. The process by which direct operation was abandoned is known as the "Iowa Plan." The terminology was adopted in 1935 when almost all refining companies and jobbers selling in Iowa responded to the enactment of chain store tax legislation by leasing out all company-owned stations in the state. However the dismembering of direct operations was more complex than an immediate response to chain store tax legislation would suggest. John McLean and Robert Haigh have suggested that the Plan might have existed even without the legislation. The Iowa Plan of operation actually preceeded the enactment of chain store tax legislation in some states and was adopted in states where there was no such legislation. A number of reasons have been advanced by McLean and Haigh for the changeover during the 1930–1936 period.

First, the average gallonage sold by service stations began to decline markedly after 1926, and company owned and operated service stations were hardest hit by gallonage losses because their selling prices were frequently not competitive with those of stations run by independent contractors. Also, it was difficult for company stations to make price adjustments quickly to meet changing conditions in local markets.

Second, as declining gallonages were exerting pressures to reduce costs as a means of maintaining profit margins, company-owned stations were faced with substantial new chain store and Social Security taxation. The chain store taxes were based both on the number of stores and on gross receipts of the chain as a whole, making it virtually impossible for a company to operate a chain of outlets on a profitable basis. The Social Security legislation required of company outlets a contribution of six percent of payroll charges. Independent contractor stations and discount marketers which did not meet criteria for minimum numbers of employees could avoid the expense completely.

Third, self-employed retailers were able to reduce their labor costs by working longer hours for the same wages, whereas company-owned stations were subject to the overtime provisions of the wage and hour laws. The advent of service station unions at about this time was followed by strikes in a number of major cities, and the wage increases granted in response to union demands placed company-operated stations at a competitive disadvantage with independent contractors, who were self-employed.

The leasing of company-owned service stations to independent dealers satisfactorily solved each of these problems which had placed company-owned outlets at a competitive disadvantage.

The resulting structure of the petroleum industry is one of a variety of integration bonds which differ from those in any other industry. The distinct types of arrangement identified by McLean and Haigh as existing between the supplier-franchisor and dealer-franchisee, in order of intensity of integration, are:

1. The supplier owns the land and building and operates the station;
2. The supplier leases the land, owns the building, and operates the station;
3. The supplier leases the land and building, and operates the station;
4. The supplier owns the land and building, and rents these to the station operator;
5. The supplier leases the land, owns the building, and rents to the station operator;
6. The supplier leases the land and building, and rents to the station operator;
7. The station operator owns or leases the station, leases to the supplier on a long-term basis, and the supplier leases or rents back to the station operator on a short-term basis;
8. The station operator owns or leases the station from a third party, the supplier furnishes pumps, signs, tanks and other equipment on a short-term lease arrangement, usually at a nominal charge;
9. The station operator owns or leases the station and all equipment, the supplier sells to him for branded resale;
10. The station operator owns or leases the station and all equipment, the supplier sells to him for unbranded resale.

The great range of degrees of integration represented here, and the lack of operating freedom for the station operator under at least arrangements four through seven,[a] underlie the question as to whether these arrangements truly represent a franchise system, and whether the station operator may be considered as an independent businessman in any meaningful sense.

---

[a] Under any one arrangement, the franchisee may have varying degrees of operating freedom depending on the nature of arrangements other than the leasing-ownership one.

Cooperative and Wholesaler-Sponsored Groups

Retail members of voluntary franchise groups, either cooperative or wholesaler-sponsored, typically operate their stores under a common trade name, use similar operating procedures and physical layout, contribute to a common advertising and promotional program, and purchase most or all of their inventory requirements from one source. This source is a retailer-owned warehouse in the case of a cooperative group, and a sponsoring wholesaler in the case of a wholesaler-originated group. Although examples from the drug and hardware fields date back to the turn of the century, voluntary groups were confined largely to the grocery field prior to the mid-1950s. The motivation for the creation of voluntary franchising groups came largely, as in the case of the petroleum industry, from the competitive pressures exerted by low cost vertically integrated competitors. However, it should be noted that a great deal of cooperative purchasing and warehousing took place long before the advent of chain stores, and sometimes under a group-name identification.

Food Retailing. In the grocery field, the cooperative chain movement had a slow and irregular development until 1925, with early cooperative efforts directed mainly toward group buying and warehousing in an attempt to save some of the cost of wholesaling. With the increasing importance of corporate grocery chains after 1925, independent retailers began to more actively seek the advantages arising from cooperative activities with other merchants. Voluntary chains in the grocery field employed many of the methods pioneered by the corporate chains: eliminating the wholesale function as a profit-making part of the business; seeking the special discounts and concessions given by manufacturers and processors to large-scale buyers; and introducing private or controlled brand merchandise.

Wholesaler-sponsored food chains were started under the premise that the retailer would agree to buy most or all of his goods from the sponsoring wholesaler. The wholesaler in turn could thus reduce his sales force and bring his expense ratio in line with that of the chain-store warehouse. In return, the retailer received lower prices; the right to use the common trade name; assistance in store layout, display, and promotion; and the right to sell the chain's privately branded goods. The share of the retail grocery market going to voluntary groups has grown markedly since World War II, rising from 32 percent in 1950 to 48 percent in 1968.[7]

It is interesting to note that some corporate food chains have developed a franchise operation involving independent food retailers. A number of food chains now operate such wholesaler-sponsored groups, with independently owned food stores carrying on business under a common name, and serviced on a franchise basis by the wholesale division of the food chain.

Drug Retailing. In the drug field, the biggest and oldest of the voluntary programs are those operated by Rexall and Walgreen through their wholesale divisions. Conventional drug wholesalers undertook a number of voluntary programs in the early 1960s, in part as devices for redistributing cooperative advertising allowances from vendors. By 1968, 12.5 percent of drug firms had wholesaler-sponsored retail chains, and most firms provided both private brand merchandise and supporting financial, merchandising, and promotional services. These outlets, combined with those in the Rexall and Walgreen systems, accounted for 56.5 percent of all drug stores operating during 1968.[8] Data on cooperative groups in the retail drug field are harder to come by, but it is reported that the member organizations of the National Drug Cooperative Association had 950 affiliated outlets in early 1968.

Hardware Retailing. Statistics are also less than perfect in the hardware field, but it is obvious that cooperative and wholesaler-sponsored groups are becoming increasingly important. One trade estimate is that 10,900 hardware stores, being 39.9 percent of the total, took part in wholesaler-sponsored programs in 1968.

Automotive Aftermarket. Franchise systems have also become common in the automobile aftermarket, which includes both automotive parts and the home and auto field. One trade estimate is that 25 percent of the wholesalers engaged in the distribution of automotive parts, accessories, and chemicals belong to wholesaler-sponsored voluntary programs. The home and auto field, a segment of retailing which has shown dramatic growth in recent years, is dominated by franchised outlets. Of the 67,000 home and auto stores operating during 1969, 34,200 held manufacturer-franchises from Firestone, Goodyear, or Goodrich, and 8,500 held wholesaler-franchises from Western-Auto, Gamble-Skogmo, or Coast-to-Coast Stores.

Motel and Hotel Referral Chains. There are three types of franchise programs common in the motel and hotel field, only one of which can properly be called a voluntary group. Conventional franchise programs such as those offered by Quality Courts Motels, Holiday Inn, and Congress Inns involve the usual arrangements covering architectural design, operating procedures, common advertising and promotion, and use of the common trade name or trademark. Coowner franchise programs such as those used by TraveLodge and Imperial 400 are similar to these, except that the franchisor may retain an equity interest in the franchised units.

The voluntary group, which includes Best Western and Emmons Walker, are the so-called referral motels. These systems do not use common architectural styles or operating practices, but do utilize the same trade name, common advertising and promotion, and a customer referral service which covers all members. At the end of 1969, 2700 motels were affiliated with conventional franchise programs, 750 in coowner programs, and 2,648 as members of referral groups. The three types in total accounted for almost 450,000 rooms.

Variety Store Retailing. The variety store field has traditionally been dominated by national and regional ownership-chains. The only significant franchise system in the market is the Ben Franklin program, which had 2,320 stores during 1969, with sales volume totaling more than $350 million.

Trademark Licensing Franchise Systems

The preceeding sections have discussed the use of franchising by well-known companies in areas of business long-recognized as being franchised. The recent phenomenal expansion of franchised business dates back only to about 1950, and has been concentrated in nontraditional areas. A large portion of the expansion has occurred in the area of trademark licensing franchise systems. In such systems, a trademark owner may or may not produce a product or operate a service, but does license franchisees to produce the product or operate the service in other geographic areas, and under the trade name of the franchisor. A major share of the following products and services is distributed through trademark licensing franchise systems:

1. automobile, truck and trailer rental (Hertz, Avis);
2. carpet and upholstery cleaning services (Duraclean, Wade-Wenger ServiceMaster);
3. coin-operated laundries and dry-cleaning services (Arnold Palmer Dry Cleaning Centers, Speed Queen);
4. part-time manpower and help agencies (Kelly Girl, Manpower);
5. specialty food and beverage dispensing (Tastee Freeze, Mister Donut, Chicken Delight, Howard Johnson's);
6. tool and equipment rental (Abbey Rents, United Rent-Alls).

In addition, a minor but rapidly growing segment of literally hundreds of categories of products and services is distributed through trademark licensing franchise systems. Representative among these are:

1. business aids and service (Fedder Data Centers, Muzak);
2. cosmetics (Carnaby U.S.A., Lily Daché);
3. dance studios (Arthur Murray, Inc., Fred Astaire Studios);
4. employment agencies (Tom McCall & Assoc., Snelling & Snelling);

5. sports and recreation (Revell Raceways, Winchester Trap and Skeet Shooting);
6. personal service and coin-operated laundry and dry-cleaning (Arnold Palmer).

A representative success story is that surrounding the establishment of the Mister Donut of America, Inc. chain of franchised roadside drive-in donut and coffee shops. In the 10 years following its founding in 1955, Mister Donut parlayed a $25,000 cash investment in one shop into a franchised chain of 210 outlets with annual sales volume of $20 million. The 1969 edition of *The Franchise Annual* lists 238 separate franchisors in the food operations category, with an estimated 90 of these having 1968 franchise system sales in excess of one million dollars, with several of them in excess of one hundred million.

Not to be overlooked is the so-called celebrity franchising phenomenon of recent years, which has included names like Eva Gabor in wig boutiques; Tony Bennett in spaghetti restaurants; Johnny Carson in "Here's Johnny's" restaurants; Jerry Lewis with movie theatres; Mahalia Jackson with "Glori-Fried Chicken"; Joe Namath with "Broadway Joe's" restaurants; and Rowan and Martin with "Laugh-In Restaurants." Celebrity franchising is concentrated in the fast-food and limited menu specialty food areas and seems to have found its greatest success there. Arthur Treacher's name was first applied to a household cleaning service franchise system, which was unsuccessful. Treacher has since moved on to a new fish-and-chips specialty food promotion, which has been somewhat better received.

Size of Franchised Business

The United States Census of Business does not distinguish franchised business from other types except in the case of automobile dealers. Estimates of the size of franchised business have been made from time to time, usually without any indication of the source of the compiler's statistics. The most quoted estimate of the size of franchised business is that prepared by the International Franchise Association in late 1963, and subsequently published in *Dun's Review* and several other publications.[9]

The IFA estimated the magnitude of 13 major segments of franchised business in the United States and arrived at an estimated annual dollar volume of $59.215 billion, just over 10 percent of the gross national product and a little over one-fourth of the country's total retail sales. Many of the subsequent estimates of the size of franchising appear to have been based on an application of these percentages to current figures for gross national product or total retail sales, — and thus work backward to derive a figure for franchised sales. My own research suggests that this IFA estimate was low by some $22 billion in 1963, primarily because it underestimated the size of the wholesaler-retailer segments of franchised business. Table 3–1 projects the 1969 total for franchised business at $124.4 billion, and for total franchised business excluding passenger car dealers, gasoline service stations, and bottlers of carbonated beverages, at $37.6 billion. It must be emphasized that these are conservative estimates; the latest *Franchise Annual,* or the Department of Commerce' listing of franchised business, records literally hundreds of businesses in dozens of categories that are not included here. My listing is undoubtedly incomplete in all the listed categories — and particularly so in

Table 3–1

Total Dollar Sales and Number of Franchisees by Representative Component Areas of Franchising for 1969

	Franchised Establishments (number)	Sales ($000s)	Percent of Total Retail Sales
I. Product and Service Franchise Systems			
1. Manufacturer-retailer systems			
passenger car dealers, franchised	36,200	56,610,000	15.6
gasoline service stations	287,600	27,200,000	7.5
hearing aids	3,800	98,000	
swimming pools	1,200	79,000	
water conditioning systems and services	2,400	310,000	
2. Manufacturer-wholesaler systems			
bottlers of carbonated beverages	4,000	3,000,000	
3. Wholesaler-retailer systems			
food retailing			
cooperative voluntary programs	16,000	7,800,000	
wholesaler sponsored voluntary programs		5,040,000	
drug retailing, total voluntary programs	14,900	4,750,000	
hardware retailing, total voluntary programs	12,600	1,600,000	
home and auto stores and automobile aftermarket, total voluntary programs	43,600	6,350,000	
variety store retailing, total voluntary programs	2,650	390,000	
II. Trademark Licensing Franchise Systems			
4. Trademark licensor-manufacturer systems			
fabricated textiles (B.V.D. garments, Fruit of the Loom, etc.)	N.A.	725,000	

Table 3–1 (continued)

	Franchised Establishments (number)	Sales ($000s)	Percent of Total Retail Sales
5. Trademark licensor association— association-member systems bread industry (Quality Bakers of America, Inc., Independent Bakers Cooperative, Inc., etc.)	280	936,000	
milk industry (Quality Chekd Dairy Products Association, All-Star Dairy Association, etc.)	301	712,600	
mattress industry (Spring Air, Sealy Restonic, Serta, etc.)	800	165,000	
6. Trademark licensor-retailer systems carpet and upholstery cleaning services	4,000	145,000	
moving companies	5,000	1,400,000	
roadside food, beverage, and soft ice-cream restaurants	32,500	2,538,000	
temporary help services	500	130,000	
franchised hotels and motels (regular, coowner, and referral)	6,098	1,138,500	
automobile, truck, and trailer rental services	17,000	2,080,000	
coin operated and regular laundry and dry-cleaning services	39,600	610,000	
tool and equipment rental	4,900	607,500	
Total, Representative Franchised Businesses	535,929	124,424,600	34.5
Total, Representative Franchised Businesses Exclusive of Passenger Car Dealers, Gasoline Service Stations and Bottlers of Carbonated Beverages	208,129	37,614,600	10.4

Sources: U.S. Census of Business, Retail Trade Summary Statistics; U.S. Census of Business, Wholesale Trade Summary Statistics; U.S. Census of Business, Selected Service Summary Statistics; Moody's Industrials; trade publications; private estimates by industry officials; government studies on specific industries.

the trademark licensor-retailer systems area. For example, incomplete or nonexistant information has caused me to disregard virtually all franchisor offerings in a whole range of new areas: travel agencies, art galleries, youth nightclubs, nursing homes, beauty salons, shoplifting controls, diet programs, and social introductions. I would estimate, however, that the figures given do represent in excess of 90 percent of the dollar volume of franchised business operating today.

The dearth of statistical data on some industry sales between census dates makes it difficult or impossible to arrive at total figures for years more recent than 1967–68. In projecting these figures to 1969, one might use the alternatives of assuming that each franchised sector of business has been growing no more quickly than the gross national product, or, that it has been growing no more quickly than total sales at retail, or, that some segments of franchised business have been without growth, while the remaining segments have been growing no more quickly than one or more of these widely used indicators. I have used the second alternative, of assuming that the sectors for which only 1967–68 data are available have grown at a rate equal to total sales at retail since then. Incidently, it must be pointed out that the comparison of franchised sales with total sales in the *retail* sector is misleading, as a substantial segment of franchised sales represent wholesale transactions.

The total dollar figure, rough though it obviously is, does indicate that franchised business is of a scale which justifies the interest that it attracts from federal regulatory agencies. In fact, the component areas of franchised business which I have included were chosen in part because their contractual arrangements were such that they were each affected in similar ways by legislative provisions aimed at franchising—notably in the area of tying arrangements, territorial and customer restrictions, exclusive dealing, and exclusive franchising.

It is sometimes argued that the old component of franchised business, consisting of passenger car dealers, gasoline service stations, and bottlers of carbonated beverages, has grown relatively more slowly than has franchised business as a whole. It is certainly true that these areas are of less interest than the dynamic, newer areas of the franchise boom. While there is no question that even the old component has grown markedly in an absolute sense, it is significant that the new component of franchised business has grown to account for a minimum of $37.6 billion of yearly sales, equivalent to 10.4 percent of projected total retail sales in the United States for 1969.

Table 3–2 gives an analysis of those franchise businesses listed in the 1969 edition of the *Franchise Annual* published by National Franchise Reports of Chicago. The *Franchise Annual* is an alphabetical guide to firms currently offering franchised business opportunities. The listings included are reflective of the new component of franchised business, in that they exclude passenger car dealers, gasoline service stations, and bottlers of carbonated beverages. The listing also excludes trademark licensor-manufacturer systems and trademark licensor association—association-member systems in their entirety. Each firm listed in the *Franchise Annual* master index was classified according to its standard industrial classification code so that the characteristics of small business franchises could be summarized.

The industry classification for the new component of franchised business was:

Table 3–2

Summary of Industry Classification of 908 Franchise Firms

General Description	Number of S.I.C. Classifications Listed	Number of Firms Assigned	Percent of Total Firms
Contract construction firms	5	8	.9
Manufacturing firms	7	9	1.0
Transportation, communication, electric, gas, and sanitary services	5	29	3.1
Wholesale and retail	69	268	29.5
Finance, insurance, and real estate	1	41	4.5
Services	49	553	61.0
Total	136	908	100.0

Source: Compiled from *The 1969 Franchise Annual,* Rogers Sherwood, publisher, Chicago, Illinois: National Franchise Reports (1969).

The disproportionate distribution of these firms is illustrated by a comparison with the distribution of all firms in the economy.

The largest concentration of franchise firms listed in the *Franchise Annual,* 61.0 percent, is in the services field, and this figure is far above that of 24.0 percent for the economy as a whole. The other differences are a lower involvement of franchisees in the construction and manufacturing areas and in the retail area, and in the considerably greater involve-

Table 3–3

Comparison of Distribution of Franchise Firms with All Nonfarm Firms in the Economy

	All Firms, U.S. 1969[1] Percent of Total	Franchise Firms Number	Franchise Firms 1969[2] Percent of Total
Total, all industries	100.0	908	100.0
Construction	9.4	8	.9
Manufacturing	6.1	9	1.0
Wholesale	6.7	102	11.2
Retail	41.0	166	18.3
Services	24.0	553	61.0
Other	12.8	70	8.9

[1] *Statistical Abstract of the United States,* 1969.

[2] Compiled from the *1969 Franchise Annual,* Rogers Sherwood, publisher, Chicago, Illinois: National Franchise Reports (1969).

ment of franchise firms in wholesaling, with 11.2 percent against a national figure of 6.7 percent. The conclusions most readily drawn from these figures are that a disproportionate number of franchised businesses are oriented to serving the public directly, and that franchised businesses are concentrated in those areas that require a relatively small amount of capital for entry.

This conclusion as to capital requirements for entry to franchised business is supported by an analysis of the capital requirements for obtaining a franchise. The sample used is the 175 franchisors who included a dollar figure in their listing in *The 1969 Franchise Annual*. As indicated in Table 3–4, half of the franchises can be obtained for an investment of less than $10,000, and more than three-quarters can be obtained for less than $25,000.

Table 3–4 Capital Required to Obtain Franchises

	Number of Firms	Percent	Cumulative Percent
$1000 or less	10	5.7	5.7
$1001–$2500	16	9.1	14.8
$2501–$5000	18	10.3	25.1
$5001–$7500	22	12.6	37.7
$7501–$10,000	22	12.6	50.3
$10,001–$15,000	20	11.4	61.7
$15,001–$25,000	32	18.3	80.0
$25,001 or more	35	20.0	100.0
	175		

Source: Compiled from *The 1969 Franchise Annual,* Rogers Sherwood, publisher, Chicago, Illinois: National Franchise Reports (1969).

Growth of Franchised Business

Since World War II, franchising has taken on a dramatic impetus, particularly in the nontraditional trademark franchising areas. The dynamism of this growth is exemplified by the soft ice-cream industry. Only one hundred outlets served this product at the conclusion of World War II. By 1969 there were more than 26,000 franchised soft ice-cream stands in operation. Another example in the food service area is the 30,100 franchised restaurants or roadside stands in operation at the end of 1969, compared with 3,500 in 1945.

The dramatic growth rate in franchised business has not gone unnoticed in the literature, although estimates of its magnitude have varied, and some wild claims have been made, and repeated uncritically in the popular press. My own limited investigations, based on a randomly drawn sample of franchisors listed in the 1964 and subsequent issues of the Department of Commerce' *Franchise Company Data for Equal Opportunity in Business,* plus some primary data, indicate that the nontraditional areas of franchising are expanding at an average rate of 7.5+ percent per year. If the growth rate from this sample is applied to the number of nontraditional franchisees listed earlier, one arrives at an estimate that a minimum of 13,100 new franchised outlets are being created, net, each year. The figure may be fairly accurate, because an analysis of 1967 data similar to that for 1969 shows that the number of new franchised outlets over that two year period was 24,700, or an average increase of 12,350 per year.

The number of franchisors has also shown dramatic growth over the past two decades. The *New York Times* estimated that in 1945 only 200 firms did business through franchise systems,[10] while a 1967 *Times* article claimed to have counted more than 750 substantial franchising operations.[11] The 1964 *Franchise Annual* listed 556 firms which offered franchise opportunities in 1963, while the 1969 *Annual* listed 908 firms which made offers in 1968.

There are several indicators of an increased public interest in franchising and in franchising opportunities. From January 1965 to January 1969, the Service Industries Division of the United States Department of Commerce received 92,000 requests for their publication, *Franchise Company Data For Equal Opportunity In Business,* and in mid-1969 were still receiving 400 requests per week. As a result of a single reference to the publication in the Kiplinger newsletter, the Department of Commerce received 2,800 enquiries requesting a list of franchisors, information about franchising, and information about government financial assistance to franchisors and franchisees.

Failure Rates in Franchised Business

There are indications that members of franchise systems have substantially lower failure rates than do comparable independent businessmen. *Printers Ink* has claimed an overall *small* business failure rate of 60 percent, compared to only 10 percent for franchisees.[12] Various studies show franchisor failure rates ranging from one percent to twenty-eight percent (of new franchisors) per year.[13]

A study undertaken by J. F. Atkinson of failure rates of members of franchise systems affiliated with the International Franchise Association indicated that the odds favoring success of franchised small business versus "all other retail" might be eight to one, or higher.[14] Atkinson defined a failure to include bankruptcies for any reason, any closings at a loss to the franchisee, and a 30 percent investment loss, even with "turnover" involved. Atkinson's sample was somewhat biased in that it included only franchisees of the more mature, established franchisors who characterize the membership of the IFA.

There is considerable evidence that most failure rates quoted for franchisors and franchisees are unreliable. Although many franchisors claim low failure rates for their locations, a distinction must be made between the failure of a location and the failure of a franchisee. If the franchisee fails, the franchisor may find a replacement, or take over the outlet as a company operation and claim correctly that the location has not failed. Franchisors with large, highly visible franchisee outlets will typically not permit a location failure in the short run after an outlet has opened. On the other hand, for public relations reasons some established franchisors will not permit franchisee failures, although they are willing to abandon an unsuccessful location and relocate the franchisee.

Figures on franchisee turnover are also often misleading. The most successful franchisees may be the ones most motivated to sell their operations in order to realize capital gains. Similarly, franchises requiring low investment and those utilizing mobile operations typically show higher turnover rates than do higher investment, fixed-location franchises — which does not imply, of course, that the former may not present the best investment to a franchisee with certain combinations of available capital and personal motivation.

The conclusion that franchise system failure rates *are* actually lower then those in nonfranchised systems is not an unreasonable one. The franchisee has the advantage of being required to use tested operating procedures and internal controls designed by qualified people — and thus mitigates the effects of inexperience or ineptitude. The strongest factor in the longevity of the franchisee over an independent businessman is probably the experience and expertise which are built into franchise system controls. In addition, the franchisee is provided with an established brand name, enforced quality maintenance through quality control, locational analysis on setting up operations, initial training, and continued field supervision. In some cases, the franchisor takes responsibility for advertising and merchandising, again minimizing the effects of franchisee inexperience or inability in these areas. By virtue of these advantages and of the other attributes of franchising, franchised dealers might reasonably be expected to show more stability and longer life than their independent counterparts.

Determinants of Growth in Franchised Business

The question may well be asked as to what factors have accounted for the dramatic growth rate of franchised business and its development into a sector of the economy that now accounts for a substantial portion of retail sales and of the gross national product of the United States.

Determinants of Franchisee Growth

The explanation for franchisee interest in franchising is apparent. A franchise system has great appeal for the person seeking a viable business opportunity because it reduces, and in some cases almost eliminates, the disadvantages normally encountered by small business in meeting chain competition. The franchisee also has the opportunity to enter business with a much smaller personal capital investment than might otherwise be the case. He sees that the economies and expertise available to the owner-ship chain in purchasing, in advertising, and in producing new and valuable management techniques are available to him, permitting him to match, partially or wholly, the distribution advantages of his large competitors.

In addition, there may also be psychological reasons why franchising succeeds in attracting as many as 13,000 new franchisees each year. Writing more than 50 years ago,[15] Professor Arthur S. Dewing observed that there was a strong psychological drive harbored by most men to accomplish something of significance during their lifetime. Professor Dewing also noted that a man tends to measure his own success first by the size, and second by the profitability of his business. The most power-ful motive leading a franchisor or franchisee to establish a business and to expand it may be the belief that the bigger the business, the more impor-tant the man.

Determinants of Franchisor Growth

The explanation for franchisor interest in franchising is neither as apparent nor as simple as that for franchisees. There are a number of operating characteristics of franchise systems that have special appeal for fran-chisors: advantages in financing, in personnel hiring and motivation, in personalized customer relationships, and in speed of establishing the distributive system.

Franchising permits producers and suppliers with limited financial re-sources to widen their distributive system with comparatively little capi-tal investment of their own. A major requirement of rapid system expan-sion is the availability of capital, which the franchisee or an intermediary can contribute to the organization. Capital shortages are especially critical in the early states of a large-scale distributive system because of early stage inefficiencies in advertising and distribution which occur before volume increases, and it is at this stage that franchising is most common.

It was in the past held that there was an availability of funds to a fran-chise system as a whole which were not available to individual members. In many geographic areas, banks considered the combined strength of a franchisor and a franchisee to be greater than the sum of the two parts, because they were willing to lend a franchisor-franchisee system more than they would as individuals. This has not been the case during the 1960s in the midwest and the far west, and probably is not in 1970 true anywhere in the United States, as banks are refusing to loan money to franchisees in cases where the franchise contract calls for the franchisor to have prior claim on franchisee receipts to satisfy its financial demands.

There is agreement among franchisors that it is difficult to obtain and motivate personnel to operate certain kinds of business operations unless they are also given an ownership interest. This is particularly true in those businesses requiring long hours of operation, a high standard of service at the point of sale, and relatively routine work. These conditions are common in gasoline service stations; roadside food, beverage, and soft ice-cream restaurants; automobile, truck, and trailer rental services; and a number of other areas where franchised business has become dominant. If manufacturers and suppliers who engage in franchise operations today had sufficient capital to expand distribution through company-owned outlets, it is very likely that many of them would still utilize franchising because of the shortage of competent managerial personnel in alternate arrangements.

Personal motivation is also felt to be higher under a franchise system. Robert L. Grover, President of Snap-On Tools Corporation, reflected the views of a large proportion of franchisors when he testified before a Subcommittee of the Committee on the Judiciary, United States Senate, that it was apparent to his company, in its method of direct-to-the-user distribution that they were

best represented by an independent businessman representing himself to the best of his ability, taking responsibility for adjusting customer problems on the spot, depending upon his own perserverance and ingenuity for his success or failure, and profiting to the maximum from extra effort.[16]

Franchising allows a wide geographical distribution of goods and services and permits the necessary distribution system to be built more quickly than might be true with a centrally owned system. The speed is a function of the reduced financial requirements of the franchisor, and also of the franchisor's ability to find, train, and motivate franchisees more quickly than he could build a sales force. In the Curry study, 25 percent of the franchisor-respondents replied that it was this potential speed in creating a distribution system that was their principal reason for utilizing a franchise system.[17]

Ingraham has noted that there may be some derivative benefits to be gained from the use of franchising.[18] Derivative benefits are defined as those that accrue as by-products of a successful franchise system. For example, the product/service diversification which may be inherent in franchise systems is illustrated by the finance subsidiaries, real estate investment departments, and container supply divisions which become feasible if their cost can be spread over a large number of users, and which are features of many successful franchise operations. These forward and backward diversification activities may add substantially to the profitability of the franchisor, particularly in those cases where the franchisee-buyer represents a captive market.

Qualitative Contributions of Franchising to the Economy

Perhaps the most important long-run contribution of the franchise form will be its role in broadening the distributive base of the economy through its encouragement of small business. In almost all cases (and even where closely controlled by the franchisor), the franchisee meets the practical tests for a small business. Most often he serves only a limited market, governed by the size of his capital and cash reserves, the number of his employees, his geographic access to customers, the structure of freight rates, and other business factors. That the economic base is broadened, and that in so doing franchising makes a contribution to the American economy was outlined by Judge Dawson in *Susser* v. *Carvel*.

The franchise method of operation has the advantage, from the standpoint of our American system of competitive economy, of enabling numerous groups of individuals with small capital to become entrepreneurs. . . . If our economy had not developed . . . [franchising], these individuals would have turned out to have been merely employees. The franchise system creates a class of independent businessmen; it provides the public with an opportunity to get a uniform product at numerous points of sale from small independent contractors, rather than employees of a vast chain. The franchise system of operation is therefore good for the economy.[19]

Not to be minimized are the social values which are implicit in the independent ownership of one's own business as opposed to being an employee of an integrated firm. The Federal Trade Commission has indicated that the social benefits involved may justify the existence of some of the controls involved in franchise systems:

Preservation of small business is judged by some, including Brandeis, to be a social goal which is more important than [even] the maintenance of competition. There is social benefit to the nation in having many independent self-employed people, and this benefit may or may not cost us something economically.[20]

Through franchising, the small businessman strikes what Philip Zeidman, former General Counsel of the Small Business Administration, calls "the classic bargain which a man makes with his society";[21] he sacrifices some of his own freedom in return for a measure of security.

One prominent legislator has gone so far as to label franchising the last frontier of the independent businessman at a time when economic concentration is increasing dramatically. His estimate is that, by 1975, 200 corporations will hold 75 percent of all manufacturing assets in the United States. Many independent businessmen, no matter how efficient their operations, will find it difficult to survive.[22] In 1963 the 200 largest firms, with only 3 percent of the business establishments in the United States, accounted for 41 percent of the value added by manufacture, 31 percent of total employees, 28 percent of total production workers, 42 percent of net shipments, and 46 percent of total new capital expenditures.[23]

It should not be assumed, however, that all franchised business remains small. In fact, a recent wave of acquisitions and mergers involving franchise systems considerably altered the size distribution of parent franchisor firms. In the 1964 to 1969 period alone, Consolidated Foods acquired Chicken Delight; Servomation Corporation bought Red Barn System; United Fruit took over J. Hungerford Smith (parent company of the A & W Root Beer chain and the Baskin Robbins ice-cream specialty stores); National Broadcasting Company, a subsidiary of Radio Corporation of America, bought Arnold Palmer Enterprises; Great Western United purchased Shakey's Pizza; General Foods purchased Burger Chef; Pillsbury purchased Burger King; and Household Finance purchased both the Ben Franklin system and the White Stores.

In merger and stock-exchange transactions, Radio Corporation of America merged with Hertz Corporation; Famous Artists Schools exchanged common stock for Evelyn Wood Reading Dynamics Institute; Pet, Inc. gained control of Stuckey's; and Union Tank Car took over the Lindsay chain. While all these transactions involved franchisors rather than franchisees, there is some support for a hypothesis that the larger and more financially sound the franchisor, the more probable the eventual conversion of the franchise system to an ownership-integrated one through purchase or nonrenewal of franchisee contracts. (This is certainly the personal observation of the writer, based on a number of interviews with executives in the franchise field and their legal counsel. It is supported by a confidential assertion made to the writer by an official of one large franchisor firm, who stated that a major purpose of the merging of their two companies was to provide the franchisor with sufficient financing to begin to buy back outstanding franchises.[24])

A final point worthy of consideration is the opportunity which franchising holds for members of minority groups seeking to establish themselves in business. Daniel P. Moynihan has pointed out that nonwhites have failed to maintain a proportionate status in the census category of "managers, officials, and proprietors." The figures as of March 1967, show that 14.2 percent of employed white males are "managers, officials, and proprietors," while only 3.5 percent of employed nonwhite males are in this category, and the nonwhite percentage actually dropped in the

1964–1967 period.[25] Less than 3 percent of the nearly five million businesses in the United States are owned by persons from the 30 million black, Spanish-surname and native Indian citizens who together make up almost 15 percent of the population. Approximately a quarter of those businesses are limited-income beauty parlors and barber shops.[26] As of January 1970, blacks held only 41 of the 36,000 franchised automobile dealerships, and operated 24 of the 13,822 commercial banks with 0.24 percent of the industry's assets. Of the 6,000 radio stations in the United States (of which 112 are beamed directly at the black community), only 11 are black-owned. The picture in the major population centers is similar. New York City, with a black population of about 1,100,000, has exactly twelve black-owned *or* managed enterprises employing 10 persons or more.

There is general agreement that inability to obtain proper financing and training are two of the most important reasons for the lack of nonwhites in the entrepreneurial class. The advantages of managerial assistance, lower financial requirements, and consumer acceptance of the trade-marked product or service have the potential to substantially reduce this imbalance. To date, this has most emphatically not happened. Of 138 franchise operations with 27,155 outlets surveyed by the Department of Commerce, only 354 were minority-owned. This is 1.3 percent, *less than half the national average* of minority businesses.[27] There are only eight nonwhite-controlled franchisors in the United States; among them All-Pro Chicken, Jet Foods, Rib Cage International, and Village Maid Services. The most substantial company in the group is All-Pro Chicken, which has seven area directorships, seven company-owned units in operation, and eight franchise units of which six are minority-owned.

Federal Reserve Board member Dr. Andrew Brimmer, is among those who would argue that minority-group capitalism is not a viable solution to nonwhite deprivation. Brimmer claims that the urban minority-group family, with its generally low income, high unemployment, large debts, and few assets, is one of the worst possible sources of business talent. Moreover, Brimmer maintains that self-employment offers a poor economic future for nonwhites; as a rule, they can make more money working for someone else.

In spite of the criticisms offered and the visible lack of success,[b] the United States Department of Commerce and the Small Business Administration have inaugurated a program to exploit the advantages of franchising by identifying franchisors which award franchises on a non-

---

[b]There are some success stories. In 1966 the first replacement of a nonblack by a black Oldsmobile franchisee took place in southside Chicago. The black business community responded to this black-owned dealership, sales and profits increased appreciably, and the success was followed by the transfer of additional automobile franchises to black ownership.[28]

discriminatory basis, and by circulating their names to minority-group citizens.[29] When and if funds are available, the SBA supplements these efforts with managerial and financial assistance (including loans under Title IV of the Economic Opportunity Act of 1964) to persons obtaining franchises under the program. In the period from March 1967, to December 1969, the SBA made a total of 2,611 franchise loans, involving 650 different franchise companies; 403 of these loans, or 15.4 percent, were to minority group persons. The franchise loans represented 6.9 percent of all SBA's loans during the period. The average dollar amount for all franchise loans was approximately $48,000; for minority franchise loans, approximately $25,000. The SBA and the Office of Minority Business Enterprise jointly sponsor a program named "25 × 2," which provides no funds but asks franchisors to provide 25 franchise opportunities to minority persons over a two-year period. As of July 1970, 95 franchisors had agreed to participate, including Arby's International, Lums, Mopar, Pizza Hut, Rayco, and Ziebert Process Corporation; none have as yet produced a profitable franchisee under the plan.

4

Market Organization and Vertical Channel Relations

Franchising and Market Organization

The market supplier (usually the manufacturer) must be concerned with the form of vertical market organization he will use. Some suppliers utilize vertical ownership integration through the levels of distribution, including retailing. The capital investment required has limited this degree of integration to only a few of the largest firms, notably the integrated petroleum companies. Even firms of this size have often chosen not to integrate completely, for reasons which range from the extensive management involvement required to labor union problems. Typically, there is separate ownership of the various stages of distribution, with arrangements between units in the channel that enable one dominant member to control or affect the marketing of the product.

In general, we find four forms of vertical organization within marketing channels: free and open bargaining, without restrictions; ownership integration; administered marketing channels; and contractual integration, including franchising. Conventional marketing systems of the free and open variety are being rapidly replaced by vertically organized marketing systems of the last three types, and this may be the most significant development in marketing organization in the past decade. Market competition increasingly involves rivalry between these types of systems, as well as between the units that comprise them. This has been most notable since 1960 when vertical systems began to penetrate the core markets of conventional channels, with the result that whole networks of individual firms were threatened.[1]

With ownership integration, one organization combines successive stages of production and distribution under a single ownership. Ownership integration maximizes the opportunity to achieve operating economies, usually through centralized coordination and control of activities. The growth rate for ownership integrated firms has been particularly rapid in recent years. It is claimed that firms operating 11 or more stores had a stable 20 percent of total retail sales between 1929 and 1958, and increased their share to 30 percent by 1968.[2]

With an administered system, a channel member influences or controls the behavior of vertically adjacent firms by exerting informal leadership within the channel. The objective is to achieve transportation, storage, and other economies, or to control the pricing and merchandising of the product at other levels of distribution. The greater the administrative

41

expertise of one channel member (or economic dependence by another member), the less the need for ownership or contractual integration and the greater the likelihood of reliance on an administered channel.[3] Manufacturing operations have historically relied on administrative expertise to coordinate reseller marketing efforts. There has been a recent expansion of such relationships through vendor-developed comprehensive programs for distribution through the entire channel. Davidson cites as examples the retail merchandising arrangements of O. M. Scott and Sons in lawn products, of Villager in women's apparel, of Magnavox in home entertainment, and of Kraftco Corporation in supermarkets.[4]

Finally, vertical coordination of marketing activities can be achieved through the use of contractual agreements. Such areas of contractual marketing as franchise systems are by no means the extent of such arrangements. Retailers who belong to programmed merchandising groups, stockless purchasing agreements, nonprofit shipping associations, or who take part in programs sponsored by resident buying officers account for a significant fraction of total retail volume. Negotiated contractual acquisition procedures in the governmental and military sectors account for more than 14 billion dollars a year in purchases, and contractual systems in the agribusiness sector are becoming more common. In total, contractual systems have expanded more rapidly in recent years than their corporate or administered counterparts, yet have received considerably less publicity.

It is important to note that each form of vertically organized marketing system features its own control mechanisms, and each system exhibits some intrachannel conflict behavior. Ownership integration shows the greatest control, which is exerted by corporate directives and enforced by status sanctions. Under stock ownership, control is exerted in two stages. The integrating firm votes the stock, and the directors thus elected issue instructions and apply sanctions. In an administered channel, the exercise of economic and political power (sometimes quite naked power) is relied upon to achieve systemic economies and channel leader control.

Under contractual integration, control is necessarily more indirect than under ownership integration, and may or may not be more subtle than under an administered system. However, every contractual arrangement by definition involves a restriction on one or both parties' freedom of action.[a] The traditional contract remedies of damages, rescission, and

---

[a] As early as the landmark *Chicago Board of Trade* case, the Supreme Court stated what must be obvious: "*Every* agreement concerning trade, *every* regulation of trade, restrains. To bind, to restrain, is of their very essence."[5]

A majority of the diverse economic arrangements arising under the heading of "contractual integration" utilize to some degree one or more of the principal franchise system controls of exclusive dealing, tying arrangements, and territorial and customer confinement. It must be emphasized that federal or state regulatory action *directed against the controls themselves* has an effect not only on franchise systems, but on a tremendous variety of contractual systems.[6]

specific performance are the overt sanctions available to both parties; the convert threat of nonrenewal is probably the most potent weapon for the franchisor. Whether a particular agreement with its control clauses will raise antitrust questions depends on the nature of the obligations involved, the size and share of market held by franchisor and franchisee, and other considerations.

The next section of this chapter discusses the extent of franchisor restrictions, both those imposed on the franchisee by contract and more informal, noncontractual restrictions. Chapter 5 provides an overview of the legislation and judicial interpretation applicable to these controls.

In considering whether control clauses are or are not restraining on competition—for example, whether a franchise system is entitled to the same controls as a nonfranchise, ownership-integrated system, remember that these systems are competing with those of free and open bargaining, and with administered marketing channels. The small businessmen who typically make up these latter two are also entitled to protection from preemptive activities on the part of their competitors and to the economic opportunity to exist on their own merits.

The Use of Contractual Restrictions in Franchise Agreements

The written contract between franchisor and franchisee is the central feature of the franchise relationship. The contract is the documentation of both guarantees and restrictions that pertain to each party. The formal franchise contract varies from those that do little more than restate verbal agreements to buy and resell a product to those that govern virtually every aspect of the franchisee's physical facilities and day-to-day operations.

There is considerable value in measuring the extent of franchisor restrictions, both those imposed on the franchisee by contract, and those informal restrictions arising from the day-to-day operations of the franchise system. The courts have recognized that the successful operation of a franchise system requires that the franchisor *must* control at least some activities of his franchisees. (By way of example, some degree of quality control is always necessary for trademark protection.) The need to evaluate those controls in the light of the managerial realities of franchising was mentioned in Chapter 1 and is widely recognized. This section provides an estimate of franchisor use of the most common franchise system controls.

The section discusses the use of contractual and noncontractual restrictions as investigated in three independent studies. All three were undertaken as research toward graduate degrees in schools of business administration. The three studies utilize data collected in the 1962–63,

44

1964–65, and 1965–66 periods, respectively.[b] Only one of the studies, by Curry, *et al.,* has appeared previously in published form.[8]

The Ingraham Study. The Ingraham study, entitled *Management Control Potentials and Practices of Franchise Systems,* is a doctoral dissertation prepared in 1962–63 and submitted to the University of California, Los Angeles, in August 1963.[9] Ingraham obtained case materials of franchisor and franchisee practices through personal interviews, correspondence, a study of franchise contracts, and a detailed questionnaire.

In evaluating the control mechanisms in franchise contracts, Ingraham used an Itemized Rating Scale[10] to assign numerical values to each of several dimensions of control in the franchise system. In this type of scale, the rater selects one of a number of categories that are ranked in terms of their position on the scale—that is, the respondent checks one of four or five alternative answers to a question. Ingraham measured the relative use of various control practices of the firms in her sample, assigned quantitative values to each dimension, and used the aggregated data as a basis for hypothesis testing.

The Gillespie Study. The Gillespie study, entitled *An Analysis of Control in Franchise Distribution Systems,* is a Master of Science in Marketing thesis prepared in 1965–66 and submitted to the Graduate College of the University of Illinois in 1966.[11] The data in this study were obtained from a self-administered questionnaire mailed to all firms listed in the 1964 and 1965 editions of *The Franchise Annual,* and to all member firms of the International Franchise Association. The present writer obtained and reprocessed Gillespie's mail questionnaire data cards to produce some of the results mentioned below.

The Curry Study. The Curry study, mentioned earlier, was prepared in early 1966 as a research report at the Harvard University Graduate School of Business Administration and later published by the Marketing Division of the American Management Association. The eight coauthors of the study obtained information on franchisor and franchisee practices through reviews of the existing literature, personal depth interviews with 15 franchisors and 35 franchisees, structured correspondence with 15 franchisor and franchisee consultants, and a questionnaire distributed to 560 franchisors listed in the *1965 Franchise Annual.* (Of the 560 mail

[b] A fourth study, entitled *The Franchise System of Distribution,* was prepared in mid-1963 under a grant from the Small Business Administration Management Research Program. About two-thirds of this study (which is neither theoretical nor quantitative, but deals with current operating concepts and problems) was devoted to "Franchisor Policies and Operating Methods," including a general discussion of contractual restrictions on franchisee purchases, territory and customer selection, pricing, physical appearance and business format, sales performance, and recordkeeping.[7]

questionnaires, 40 were returned with "moved, no forwarding address" stamped on the envelope. The total response was 94, for a rather low response rate of 18 percent.)

Nature and Extent of Franchisor Controls

Gillespie investigated the nature and extent of controls by examining three problem areas: scope of franchisor control, level of franchisor control, and communication (feedback) methods employed by the franchisor to evaluate franchisee performance.[12]

The scope of control was measured in terms of the number of franchising managerial activities which the franchisor controls through one or more mechanisms. The following twelve activities were used in Gillespie's analysis:

1. control over franchisee source of products for resale or for use as ingredients;
2. control over franchisee source of equipment;
3. control over franchisee product assortment;
4. control over franchisee resale pricing;
5. control over the quality of product or service offered by franchisees;
6. control over franchisee's facilitating services such as business hours, credit, and delivery;
7. control over quality and content of franchisee advertising;
8. establishment of franchisee sales quotas;
9. requirement for franchisee training programs;
10. requirement for standardized franchisee recordkeeping systems;
11. requirement for use of a registered trademark by franchisee; and
12. control over architectural design of franchisee's place of business.

The level of control is dependent upon the type of control mechanisms that the franchisor uses to govern these twelve franchisee activities. The following mechanisms, ranked in descending order with respect to their control potential, were measured in the Gillespie study:

1. *contract agreement.* Those activities of the franchisee which are regulated *in the franchise contract* are most effectively controlled, since the franchisee is legally bound by the contract;
2. *franchisor approval.* The franchisor may require the franchisee to obtain approval from him before initiating certain actions (such as handling new product lines);
3. *policy.* Franchisor policy on franchisee operations is included in an operating manual, or otherwise formally expressed to the franchisee;
4. *recommendation.* The franchisor recommends to the franchisee

how to perform an activity, the kind of activities to undertake, and/or the level of performance the franchisee should expect if the activity is performed in a certain way; and
5. *would like to know.* The franchisor requests that the franchisee keep him informed of what is being done so that, if future action is required, he will have knowledge of the situation.

The franchisor may use one of these control mechanisms, or a combination of them. The greatest degree of control exists when all franchisee activities are included in the formal franchise contract. The least degree of control exists when only one activity is included in the franchise contract, and all others are in the category of would like to know.

The third important element to an effective control system is the communication (feedback) mechanisms employed by the franchisor to evaluate franchisee performance. The effectiveness of such a communication system is a function of the number of franchisee activities within the scope of communication, the methods employed to monitor performance, and the frequency with which information is communicated. Gillespie found that franchisors employed one or more of the following communications mechanisms:

1. periodic reports (monthly, quarterly, or annually);
2. face-to-face periodic visits by
    (a) franchisor home office personnel to franchisee
    (b) franchisor field staff personnel to franchisee
    (c) franchisee to the home office or field office for consultation; and
3. Contractual control over the franchisee's source of supply for products and/or equipment, requiring purchases to be made only from the franchisor or from a list of approved suppliers provided by the franchisor.

Extent of Franchisor Control. For the franchisors included in the Gillespie sample, all 12 managerial activities measured were frequently within the franchisor's sphere of influence. The average over 12 activities was 91.5 percent—which means that 91.5 percent of franchisors included the average managerial activity in their sphere of influence. Virtually all respondents—98.0 percent—included the activities of resale price maintenance, advertising quality and content, sales quotas, training programs, recordkeeping systems, and trademark. The least mentioned activity, that of quality control, was mentioned by more than three-quarters of all franchisor respondents.

Level and Mechanisms of Franchisor Control. To what degree do franchisors use the franchise contract to govern the various managerial activities of the franchisee? Gillespie's analysis of responses indicated that 60.5 percent of total franchisors in the sample included all 12 previously mentioned managerial activities in the franchise contract. There are two distinct groups of activities involved here. The top six of these activities — source of products, source of equipment, product assortment, quality of product or service, training program, and use of a registered trademark — are included in the contract 78.2 percent of the time on the average, while the bottom six are included only 42.9 percent of the time on the average. When combined with the activity "control of resale pricing," these top six managerial activities seem to be those perceived by franchisors as determining the output, and perhaps the profit, of the franchisee at the point of sale.

The data indicated that, for all respondents in the sample, the most widely used method of control over those managerial activities not included in the contract was a combination of policy statements and recommendations given the franchisee. There are interesting differences in the use of policies and recommendations by large and small franchisors, and these are discussed later in this section.

The control mechanisms of approval and would like to know were used very little, as was the category of does nothing. The approval category is an inefficient mechanism, with only activities that arise very infrequently being so covered. The categories of would like to know, and does nothing, are very weak control mechanisms and probably are little used for this reason.

Franchisor Communication Mechanisms. Effective control is dependent upon the communication (feedback) system used by the franchisor to monitor his franchisee's activities. Two questions arise in regard to such communication: (1) For what activities do communications occur? (2) What mechanisms are used to provide the required information?[c]

The data indicated that communication mechanisms are used by franchisors for virtually all franchisee activities mentioned. The average franchisor had communication mechanisms controlling 89.0 percent of nine measured franchisee managerial activities. For individual activities, the average ranged from highs of 94.8 percent for source of product and 93.7 percent for source of equipment to a low of 79.5 percent for standardized recordkeeping systems.

Exclusive Distribution Agreements

Exclusive Franchising. One major aspect investigated by Ingraham was the extent to which franchisors granted exclusive franchise territories to their franchisees, and the conditions under which such territories could

---

[c] In approaching these questions, Gillespie dropped consideration of three of the original twelve franchisee activities — required training programs, use of registered trademark, and control over architectural design. Each was considered an activity which, once instituted, was unlikely to require much feedback or administration by the franchisor.

be altered. Fourteen of seventeen respondent companies did grant exclusive territories. Of the seventeen franchisors, six retained full control over territorial allocations, three retained partial control, two were undetermined, and six had no control at all.

Exclusive Dealing and Tying Arrangements. Because of the similarity between exclusive dealing and tying arrangements, the authors of the three studies discussed have treated them together.

Ingraham asked respondent franchisors three questions:

1. Is a franchisee required to purchase all, part, or none of his equipment from you?
2. Do you limit the type of product a franchisee can sell?
3. Do you limit the volume of his inventory that he can secure from other suppliers?

All but 2 of the 17 companies exercised some control over equipment purchases; 11 of 17 limited the type of product the franchisee could sell; only 3 limited the volume or percentage of inventory obtained from outside suppliers. Only one company did not exercise any control.

Gillespie's data, collected three years after Ingraham conducted her study, support these findings. Gillespie found that 86.6 percent of franchisors controlled their franchisee's source of products for resale or use as ingredients—compared to Ingraham's figure of 64.7 percent (11 out of 17). Gillespie's figure for control of source of equipment was 83.6 percent—compared to Ingraham's 88.3 percent (15 of 17).

The franchisor learns of his franchisee's purchases of products or of equipment in one of two ways: (1) by requiring that purchases be made only from the franchisor; or (2) by requiring that purchases be made only from a list of suppliers approved by the franchisor. Franchisors utilized the franchisor only category most commonly. The average for all firms was 41.9 percent of total respondents requiring purchase from franchisor, and 22.3 percent requiring purchase from a franchisor-approved list of suppliers.[d] The franchisor is thus the franchisee's prime source of products for resale or for use as ingredients, and/or of the equipment which produces the product or provides the service.

The Curry study, prepared about a year after Gillespie's study and utilizing a sample which overlapped Gillespie's, found that 58 percent of respondents admitted to having a *contractual* restriction on the fran-

---

[d]There was a 35.9 percent no response figure which cannot be evaluated (although we cannot assume that nonrespondents do not use these communication devices). Thus, the percentages stated above must be treated as minimum estimates, rather than as approximations of the true proportions for the franchisor population.

chisee's purchasing behavior, while 39 percent did not have such a restriction, and 3 percent did not respond.

Territorial and Customer Restrictions

Neither Ingraham nor Gillespie considered the question of territorial and customer restrictions in their respective studies. The Curry study considered it in only a very secondary way. When asked if there were any *contractual* restrictions on their franchisee's choice of sales territory, 82 percent of the 94 respondents to the Curry questionnaire replied "yes," 15 percent "no," and 3 percent "no response."[13]

This indication of the widespread use of territorial and customer restrictions is supported by Edwin H. Lewis, who concluded in his own study of franchisor policies that:

[most of] the better franchises give protection for segments of cities, entire cities, or metropolitan areas. In some cases, additional counties which can best be served by the franchisee in the metropolitan area are added. Franchisees who are given protection over a large area may be permitted to operate additional units within the area, if they so desire.[14]

Similarly, a reading of *Hearings* before the Subcommittee on Antitrust and Monopoly of the United States Senate dealing with franchised business gives the impression that the *major* contractual restriction found in franchise contracts relates to territorial and customer protections given the franchisee by his franchisor.[15] Nevertheless, almost all studies of franchising have chosen to disregard the issue, and the only estimate of the incidence of these restrictions known to this writer are those in the Curry study as quoted above.

Resale Price Maintenance

The legal status of resale price maintenance would suggest that this restriction would not be widely used by franchisors. This conclusion is neither supported nor refuted by the data available. Gillespie found that 97.0 percent of franchisors controlled (or suggested) their franchisees setting of resale price. However, only 41 percent of respondents included control of resale price in the franchise contract, while 59 percent of respondents did not. This is supported by Curry, who found that only 24 percent of the respondents in the sample included control of resale price in the franchise contract itself.[16] Both Gillespie and Curry concluded that the relatively low percentage for pricing restrictions resulted from the Antitrust Division's scrutiny of price clauses for indications of conspiracy to restrain competition.

Other Restrictions

There are a number of less significant restrictions which commonly appear in franchise agreements. Gillespie found that franchisors sought to impose restrictions on franchisee recordkeeping systems in 99.3 percent of the cases represented in his sample; on the quality and content of franchise advertising and promotion in 95.5 percent of the cases; on facilitating services such as business hours, credit, and delivery in 90.3 percent; and on the architectural design of the franchised business in 85.1 percent.

These high figures are substantiated in the study by Ingraham. For example, respondents were asked questions concerning the control they exercised over the advertising activities and advertising expenditures of their franchisees. Sixteen of the seventeen franchisors attempted some control over the content of advertising. However, only moderate control existed over the media in which advertising was placed, and very little control was placed on the franchisee's choice of advertising agency. There was little follow-up activity by franchisors in policing franchisee advertising.

Noncontractual Distribution Restrictions

While the most obvious control devices are those specified in the formal franchise agreement, there are many informal methods of control which may be equally important. Thus, operating manuals and standard operating procedures which are continually updated are one means to achieve continuing control. One of Curry's franchisee respondents (whose franchise agreement required adherence to a set of standard operating procedures that was subject to arbitrary change) felt that his franchisor used this clause intentionally to restrict franchisee freedom through the introduction of new controls and procedures.

Requirements concerning warranty procedures can also be used as an informal control device. Nationwide Safti-Brake requires that its franchisee's customers mail their warranty applications directly to the franchisor to activate their warranty. The franchisor can then analyze the cards returned to determine what product lines the franchisee is merchandising, his total sales volume, and—through a provision for customer comments—whether the purchaser is satisfied with the service provided by the franchisee.

The franchisor can also influence the behavior of the franchisee through training procedures and routines. Curry quoted franchisors as claiming that proper training in the prescribed operating methods and in allegiance to the franchise system as a whole is habit forming and strongly influences the franchisee's future behavior.

A franchisor might influence franchisee purchases in other noncontractual ways: by financing a portion of the inventory purchased directly from the franchisor, by extending lines of credit, and by granting cumulative quantity discounts to franchisees. In practice, this does not appear to happen. An analysis of trade credit practices for the franchisees in the Ingraham sample showed that most inventory purchases were on a cash-and-carry basis. It was typically the franchisee who was required to finance the production and inventory of the franchisor, rather than the reverse. This is consistent with the trade credit practices of automobile and petroleum franchisors and with the motivations for franchisors establishing franchise systems as discussed earlier.

**Control Exercised by Large Franchisors
versus Control Exercised by
Small Franchisors**

Both Ingraham and Gillespie were concerned with testing the hypothesis that larger companies exercise more control over the operating activities of their franchisees than do smaller companies. The results of the two investigations are not consistent. Ingraham reached the tentative conclusion that a greater degree of control over franchisees is exercised by larger than by smaller franchisors. Gillespie concluded that the small franchisor exercised as much contractual and noncontractual control as the larger franchisor. (Gillespie divided franchise firms into large, medium, and small systems. The differences found between sizes of firm, whether measured in dollar retail volume, number of franchises, or number of states in which franchisor has franchisees, was not statistically significant at the .05 level.) It should be pointed out that Ingraham made no effort to weigh the various areas or dimensions of control which she rated. It is unrealistic to assume that these are of equal importance in comparing large versus small franchise companies, or that the results are unrelated to the type of business or the nature of the product involved. For these reasons, Ingraham's assertion to have confirmed the hypothesis that larger franchisors exercise more control should be accepted with caution.

Gillespie assumed (as Ingraham claimed to have shown), that large franchisors would acquire greater overall *contractual* control than would small, since a large franchise system would appear to be more difficult to manage through informal control techniques. Gillespie's results did not support this assumption. The small franchisor generally exercised as much contractual control as the large franchisor.

It might also be assumed that large franchisors would make greater use of tying clauses than would small franchisees, since a large franchisor is more likely to have an established tradename or a recognized product that could be used as the tying good. This assumption was also not supported by Gillespie's questionnaire results. The small franchisor exercised as much contractual control as the large, both for source of products and source of equipment.

Control Exercised in Franchise Systems
versus Control in Corporate or
Administered Systems

An objective of the Gillespie study was to compare the extent of control exercised under franchise systems with the control possible under corporate or administered systems of channel control. Gillespie found that franchisors were well aware of the potential control available to them through the franchise contract, and that they made considerable use of it. They did not approach total control through the franchise contract itself, since the average for all managerial activities thus controlled was only 60.6 percent.

Gillespie concluded that franchisors, in exercising control over the franchise system, approximated more closely the degree of control associated with a corporate as opposed to an administered distribution system.

One of the conclusions of the Curry study was that, among franchisors, there is an overall trend towards less restrictive franchise contracts, and to an increased use of less formal controls. Here too, the available data are not conclusive. While only 20 percent of franchisor respondents to the Curry questionnaire stated that they sometimes had been hindered by the antitrust laws (with none replying often, and the remaining 80 percent replying never),[17] the antitrust question has become by far the chief topic of discussion at meetings of the International Franchise Association, Boston College Center for the Study of Franchise Distribution, and similar groups. Furthermore, there continues to be constant change in the requirements set out in franchise contracts. In the Curry study, 62 percent of respondents stated that they had revised their franchise contracts 2 to 5 times, 10 percent had revised between 5 and 10 times, and 2 percent had made more than 10 revisions.

Conflict and Cooperation in the Franchise
Marketing Channel

Between member firms in each type of franchise system (and indeed, in every vertical marketing system), there exists a dynamic field of conflicting and cooperating objectives. Despite the conflict situations and forced cooperation which occur, franchise system members usually have more harmonious interests than conflicting ones. All members of the system have a mutual interest in the promotion of the franchised good. Only in the division of total franchise system profits (and sometimes, in the location of system/channel leadership) are they really in conflict. Nevertheless, an emphasis on the cooperating rather than the conflicting objectives of franchise system members has led some writers to a concept of the system as just an extension of the franchisor's own internal organization. Some conflict in a franchise system must, however, be expected, just as it must be expected within an ownership organization.

Unfortunately for simple generalization, the degree of conflict or cooperation in the franchise marketing channel varies with the stages in the evolution of the arrangements. Initially, most franchisees are fairly anxious to cooperate with the franchisor, particularly when they recognize the value of his services and the franchise package. As the franchisee grows and matures, this may change, particularly if the services provided by the franchisor are intangible. For example, if the franchisee obtains only an initial expertise accompanied by the use of a nationally known trademark, he may begrudge the franchisor his continuing financial returns and may distrust franchisor attempts to exercise control. The situation is most common in trademark licensor-retailer systems. (In one study, 38 percent of the franchisor respondents to a questionnaire indicated that they had been involved in legal disputes with their franchisees. The proportion of disagreements which exist below the level of formal litigation must be much higher.)[18]

A franchisor with a new product or untested idea may find it necessary to offer franchisees highly protective arrangements as to territories, customers, and conditions of sale. In a mature franchise system, the reverse may occur. The sales and profit interests of the franchisor may require fewer restrictions on franchise activities, but in the meantime franchisees may have become organized and may insist upon the maintenance of restrictive and exclusionary arrangements. The older members of the franchise system frequently have a number of reasons for maintaining the system/channel status-quo against internal or external innovators. Where traditional members can band together in some formal or informal manner—where there is strong franchisee solidarity—a bargaining relationship, and ultimately a collective bargaining relationship, may arise. Witness, for example, the behavior of automobile franchisees and petroleum franchisees in relation to their franchisors. Much of this bargaining is within the marketing channel, and hence outside the normal boundaries of economic analysis and antitrust.

How does a franchisor dominate the franchisee members of the system? The new franchisee, because of his limited financial resources and organizational status, finds himself in a very subordinate position vis-à-vis the established, knowledgeable franchisor. The franchisor tries to control the franchise channel through the building of product acceptance with advertising, sales promotion, and packaging of his trademarked goods. When the franchisor has developed a high degree of consumer loyalty, the other channel members must accede to his leadership. Many franchisors concentrate on the covert threat of refusing to sell or to deal with uncooperative franchisees to achieve dominance. Reliance on legal-contractual threats has been common in the past, but is probably of declining importance today. Several recent legal decisions have indicated that the franchisor's exercise of his dominant bargaining power to impose unwritten restrictions upon his franchisees, where those restrictions are proscribed in his written contracts, violates one or more of the laws on trade regulation. That is, a franchisor may not exercise his bargaining position to impose unwritten terms on his franchisees that he could not legally impose in his contractual relationship.

A vertical system can adjust to its conflicting-cooperating environment in three different ways. It may have a franchisor who forces franchisees to cooperate in an autocratic relationship. It may have a franchisor who helps franchisees to cooperate in a democratic relationship. Or, it may have a franchisor who offers no strong leadership, with a resulting anarchistic relationship.[19] Where anarchy exists, as in the case of some of the newer, relatively unorganized trademark licensor-retailer systems, it may be postulated that there is a good chance that the conflicting dynamics will destroy the marketing channel/franchise system. If autocracy exists, as is the case in most of the older, established manufacturer-retailer systems, there is much less probability of this happening.

5 Legislation and the Regulation of Franchise Systems: an Overview

One of the most important current problems facing the franchise industry is its legal status under the antitrust laws. Increased interest in the antitrust aspects of franchise agreements is shown in the sharp rise in activity by the Justice Department, the Federal Trade Commission, and by private parties. In 1949 the Justice Department advised American automobile manufacturers that their territorial and other resale restrictions might be in violation of the antitrust statutes. By 1952, all territorial restrictions had been removed from automobile retailing in litigated cases such as *Snap-On Tools Corp.*[1] and *Sandura*.[2] Recent treble damage actions in which the plaintiff's action was sustained include *Simpson* v. *Union Oil*,[3] a case involving resale price maintenance under a consignment arrangement, and *Osborn* v. *Sinclair Refining Co.*,[4] where a tying agreement supported by refusal to deal was held to be illegal.

This chapter will discuss antitrust legislation and judicial or administrative agency interpretation relating to the principal marketing restrictions found in franchise contracts. The restrictions discussed relate to: (a) exclusive distribution (including exclusive franchising, exclusive dealing, and tying); (b) the franchisee's freedom in choosing a territory or customers to be served; (c) resale maintenance; and (d) some relatively minor restrictions on issues such as maintenance of product quality, and the format of franchisee advertising and promotion. Although there is little case law on these issues and no definite answers to the validity or nonvalidity of restrictions in all contexts, a discussion of the present status of case law will clarify some of the points which a market supplier must consider when choosing a franchise system of distribution, and the constraints on his decisionmaking freedom which exist once the franchise system is operational.

It should be pointed out that, although the various controls can be separated for academic consideration, they are rarely found singly in practice. Thus, exclusive franchising and exclusive dealing often appear as the consideration for each other.[5] Territorial restrictions are frequently coupled with customer restrictions.[6] Quality control provisions often include a limited tying arrangement.[7] As one result of this intermingling of controls, few of the franchising antitrust cases to reach the courts have been limited to a single restriction. Sometimes consideration of the restrictions is clouded by other issues in the case, in particular the question of the relative dominance of the franchisor in various markets.

Exclusive Distribution Agreements

Exclusive Franchising

It is necessary to define the term exclusive franchising with some care, because there are few concepts connected with franchising which have been so widely misunderstood and misused. Exclusive franchising is an agreement, by a market supplier or franchisor with a franchisee, that he will not sell his product to any other franchisee within the first franchisee's territory, and (usually) that he will not sell there directly himself. In essence, exclusive franchising implies *only* a system of highly selective distribution. It does not require the existence of a reciprocal exclusive dealing arrangement (although this is often found); nor does it require the granting of exclusive territorial rights to the franchisee; nor does it require a use of tying arrangements in conjunction with the franchised product or service.

There are a number of business advantages said to accrue to a market supplier who adopts an exclusive franchise system. By restricting the number of franchisees, the franchisor can lower his selling costs and credit and bad debt problems; can attain economies in order filling, in packaging, and in shipment; and can better estimate future franchisee demand for purposes of production scheduling.

It may be necessary for the franchisor to grant exclusive franchises where the product or service requires substantial franchisee investment (in showroom or servicing facilities, inventory, personnel training), or a commitment to substantial advertising or sales promotion activities. This is particularly true where the franchisee is required to erect a building according to detailed blueprints furnished by the franchisor, and where the possibility of selling the building or converting it economically to other uses is low.

Virtually all the reasons advanced by the franchisor as motivation for undertaking exclusive franchising also appear as reasons advanced by the franchisee for needing it. In addition, it is sometimes suggested by franchisees that there is a prestige and advertising value inherent in having geographic exclusivity for a nationally known product or service.[8] Finally, there is no question that a prime attraction of exclusivity, to the franchisee, is the assurance that substantially all demand for the franchisor's product or service occuring within the territory will accrue to the exclusive dealership.

The legal status of exclusive franchising under the antitrust laws is determined under Sections 1 and 2 of the Sherman Act, and Section 5 of the Federal Trade Commission Act, the text of which is found in Appendix A. There is no question that exclusivity has some anticompetitive effect on the economy. If other outlets are unable to sell the product economically in the territory under exclusive franchise (because of shipping or travel costs), then intrabrand competition is effectively foreclosed. Nevertheless, the courts have held in general that exclusive franchises are *per se* legal, and that a franchisor may grant rights to use his trade name to whom he wishes, given only that he does not engage in an unfair act or an unreasonable restraint of trade, or seek to monopolize the relevant market.[9]

Lacking unfair, unreasonable, or monopolistic conduct, a franchisor is permitted to deal with some franchisees and to refuse to deal with other potential franchisees in the same areas;[10] to assure those franchisees selected of their exclusive status;[11] and, subject to requirements of good faith in dealing, to drop those franchisees whose performance is deemed unsatisfactory.[12] Even the Auto Dealer's Day In Court legislation, discussed in Appendix B, has not been found to destroy these rights of the franchisor.[13]

The franchisor cannot deliberately choose as sources of supply or channels of distribution the suppliers[14] or the customers[15] of competing franchisors with the intent of driving those franchisors out of business. Nor can he make his selection of franchisees as part of an unlawful conspiracy[16] or boycott.[17]

Refusal to Deal. There is one significant question related to the franchisor's right to select and drop franchisees which has not yet been answered by the courts. This relates to his right to refuse to deal with franchisees as a method of controlling their purchases, customers, or resale prices. Prior to 1945, virtually all cases acknowledged a supplier's right to refuse to deal with anyone in the absence of monopolization. The Court stated in *United States* v. *Klearflax Linen Looms, Inc.,* 63 F. Supp. 32 (D. Minn. 1945): "A refusal to sell, while it may be lawful *per se,* cannot be used in order to achieve an illegal result . . . one may not use a refusal to deal if the purpose is the creation or maintenance of monopoly." Cases since 1945 have had differing interpretations.[18] For almost thirty years, the law was based on the so-called Colgate Doctrine, which said:

In the absence of any purpose to create or maintain a monopoly, the act does not restrict the long-recognized right of trader or manufacturer, engaged in an entirely private business, freely to exercise his own independent discretion as to parties with whom he will deal. And, of course, he may announce in advance the circumstances under which he will refuse to sell.[19]

What the franchisor may do beyond merely announcing the circumstances under which he will refuse to sell was, in part, indicated by the Supreme Court in the *Parke, Davis* case.

If a manufacturer is unwilling to rely on individual self-interest to bring about general voluntary acquiescence which has the collateral effect of eliminating price competition and has taken affirmative action to achieve uniform adherence . . . the customer's acquiescence is not then a matter of individual free choice prompted alone by the desirability of the product.

The full effect of *Parke, Davis* in limiting the Colgate Doctrine application was evident in the *Warner* v. *Black & Decker* case.

Considering the course of Supreme Court antitrust decisions . . . since Colgate, it seems . . . that, although that doctrine may not be wholly dead . . . it has been reduced to almost imperceptible proportions . . . almost anything more than a bare refusal to sell . . . will constitute illegal [activity].[21]

The *Warner* case was concerned with a franchisee who bid against his supplier for a government contract and won, and was then terminated as a franchisee. The Supreme Court indicated that, when the supplier's actions

go beyond mere announcement of his policy and the simple refusal to deal, and he employs other means which effect adherence to his resale prices, then he has put together a combination in violation of the Sherman Act.[22]

The law today seems to be that a franchisor may advise his franchisees with respect to any competitive activity, but that he may not automatically terminate them for failure to conform to his advice. A large franchisor is probably *per se* forbidden to use his right of refusal to deal to control the purchases or competitive decisions of his franchisees. In particular, termination of a franchise for refusal to implement resale price maintenance in non fair-trade states is forbidden not only as an unfair act, but as an activity pursuant to implied contracts in restraint of trade.[23] Where a franchisor threatens to refuse to deal with a franchisee who has not followed the franchisor's resale price policy, the court may find that there exist tacit agreements between the franchisor and his other franchisees pursuant to which they have sold at maintained prices.[24] The issue in question is then no longer whether the franchisor has the right to refuse unilaterally to deal with franchisees, but whether he and his franchisees may combine to restrain competition through resale price agreements.

Exclusive Dealing and Requirements Contracts

Exclusive dealing (which is normally found reciprocally with exclusive franchising) is the agreement by the franchisee to purchase, sell, or otherwise deal only in products supplied or approved by the franchisor. For the purposes of this study, exclusive dealing problems can be broken down into two distinct types.[25] The first type involves a franchisor prohibiting his franchisees from selling products which, although not competitive with those trademarked products sold, involve issues of quality maintenance and dilution of franchisee sales efforts.[a] The second type involves a franchisor who requires his franchisees not to sell trademarked products which are competitive with those involved in the franchise system. Essentially all of the case law involving exclusive dealing has been concerned with this latter type.

From the franchisee's point of view, one reason for accepting exclusive dealing is that it may be possible to obtain an exclusive franchise from the market supplier in return for the promise to deal exclusively. An exclusive dealing arrangement also makes the source of supply more certain, a situation of considerable importance during times of shortage. Dealing in only one supplier's products eliminates the need to carry inventories as large as those necessary where several different brands are stocked. Finally, the market power of the franchisor may be so great that he can force exclusive dealing arrangements on his franchisees.[26]

Regardless of the validity of the business purpose underlying exclusive dealing, such arrangements may still cause anticompetitive effects in the marketplace. Once a large or dominant supplier in a market obtains for his exclusive use a correspondingly large share of available outlets on a lower level of distribution, he has probably imposed prohibitive cost disadvantages on existing or potential rivals, since they are likely to have to create new outlets in order to participate in the market. The same is true where a group of suppliers collectively (if not collusively) obtain exclusive obligations from dealers, — and thus produce an aggregate foreclosure. It is also argued that the consumer is forced to pay higher prices because of the absence of interbrand competition within each outlet.

Nevertheless, exclusive dealing requirements have traditionally not been considered to be *per se* illegal except when accompanied by an attempt to monopolize or fix prices. The relevant statutes are Sections 1 and 2 of the Sherman Act, Section 3 of the Clayton Act, and Section 5 of the Federal Trade Commission Act, the texts of which are found in Appendix A. However, if an exclusive dealing arrangement does not fall within the aegis of Section 3 of the Clayton Act, it is probably not forbidden by Section 1 or 2 of the Sherman Act.[27] For this reason, the relevant cases have been concerned chiefly with Section 3.

The uncertain legal status of exclusive dealing arrangements at present arise from Supreme Court decisions in the *Standard Stations* and *Tampa*

---

[a] This is illustrated in *Susser* v. *Carvel Corp.* (see note 7). Another example is the service station franchisee who wishes to take on an automobile trailer rental franchise to be operated from the service station. Usually the oil company franchisor does not like to have the station cluttered up with trailers from stock and may forbid the taking on of the second franchise on the grounds of potential damage to the first.

cases.[28] At issue in *Standard Stations* were contracts obligating service stations to take full gasoline requirements, and in some cases accessories, from Standard. The Court refused to consider economic justifications for exclusive dealing and held that the quantitative substantiality of trade flowing through exclusive marketing channels, by itself, constituted the substantial lessening of competition which Section 3 sought to prevent. The Court construed the statute to prescribe the following test. Even if the supplier's market dominance did not imply adverse market effects, exclusive dealing arrangements nevertheless violated Section 3 whenever they "foreclosed competition in a substantial share of the line of commerce affected," since this foreclosure created the likelihood of economic harm. Until 1961, virtually all district and circuit courts followed the quantitative substantiality test thus laid down by the Supreme Court.

In 1961 the Court again considered the legality of exclusive dealing in the *Tampa* case, and this time indicated that it *would* consider economic justifications for exclusive dealing. Many have felt that the severity of the mechanical market foreclosure rule was lessened by *Tampa,* but this has not been established in the courts.[29] However, the *Tampa* case may be unique in that the requirements contract involved covered less than one percent of the coal produced and sold on the Eastern seaboard.

In general, it may be said that the Court will inquire into the economic circumstances surrounding the imposition of exclusive dealing requirements and their economic effect on competitors. If there is a valid business reason for the exclusive requirement, and if competitors are not foreclosed from a source of supply, then the restrictions are probably legal.

The latest Supreme Court case involving the *Brown Shoe Company*[30] has raised, but not answered, some further questions. In its decision, the Court described the central policy of Section 3 of the Clayton Act and Section 1 of the Sherman Act to be an absolute freedom of purchasers to buy in an open market, and not merely as curbing only unreasonable restrictions, or restrictions which may lessen competition. All the implications of the *Brown* decision will probably not be resolved until later cases show whether the Court will apply a different rule where the facts are different, and in particular where the restriction does not involve a significant number of stores.

Tying Arrangements and Full-Line Forcing

Another method by which a franchisor may restrict the source of products purchased by his franchisee is through the use of tying arrangements. A tying arrangement may be defined as an agreement:

by a party to sell one [tying] product but only on the condition that the buyer also purchases a different [tied] product, or at least agrees that he will not purchase that product from any other supplier.[31]

Where leverage power resides in the tying product, it can be used to facilitate sales of another product. Where the power is used by a seller to force the buyer to purchase his whole line of goods, the arrangement is known as full-line forcing. Although the concepts of tying and exclusive dealing are distinct, classification of actual agreements as one or the other is often difficult. A tying arrangement, as well as exclusive dealing agreements, may include a requirements contract for the tied product.

The relationship of tied and tying products takes one of several forms.[32] First, the goods may be complementary, used in fixed proportions as the cases of nuts and bolts, or shoes and shoelaces. Such goods, although physically separable, are usually considered as one product, and the arrangement is not a tie-in under the antitrust laws.[33] Second, the goods may be complementary, with variable quantities of one product used with a fixed number of another as in the case of razor and blades, or a pen and ink. Third, the goods may be complementary, with completely varying proportions as in the case of bread and butter. In the fourth case, the goods are independent of one another or are substitutes, as in the case of an automobile and a television set, or a refrigerator and a radio. The final three relationships may have antitrust consequences; the first is excluded because the products must be separate marketable entities for the law to apply.

In cases where the franchisee is licensed to use a trademark or trade name, a related issue is whether the trademark can be the tying "product." The courts and regulatory agencies have answered this question in different ways. In *Susser* v. *Carvel,* a private antitrust action, the franchise agreement between Carvel and its franchisees required the latter to purchase from Carvel, or from approved sources, all ingredients which formed part of the final ice cream product. The court ruled that the agreement constituted a tying arrangement, with the Carvel trademark the tying product.[34] The Federal Trade Commission, in a proceeding brought under Section 5 of the F.T.C. Act against Carvel on the same franchise agreement clause, indicated that a trademark alone was not a tying product.[35]

The statutes relevant to a market supplier's use of tying agreements are Section 1 of the Sherman Act, Section 3 of the Clayton Act, and Section 5 of the Federal Trade Commission Act. Before these statutes are applied, several issues must be considered to determine whether a given franchise agreement does constitute tying. The first issue is that of separability, because in order for an agreement to constitute tying there must be at least two separate products which are the subjects of the agreement.[36]

This involves tests such as whether other manufacturers sell the products separately, and whether the price for the system as a whole is markedly less then the sum of prices for the separate components.

Once separability is established, there is a further question as to whether the tied product *must* come from the franchisor. If the answer is no, then illegality has generally not been found. In the *Denison Mattress* case,[37] the franchise agreement specified a source other than the franchisor for materials used in the production of mattresses. The court could find no tying agreement, because there was no tied product sold by the franchisor. However several more recent cases, notably *Atlantic Refining* and *Goodyear Tire,*[38] suggest that this criterion may no longer hold.

A variation of tying is found in the case of a franchisor who offers inducements in the form of special services and loans of money and equipment as consideration for a franchisee's agreement to concentrate on his lines. In one recent case[39] – the Brown Shoe Company, the second largest shoe manufacturer in the country by dollar volume, had for years entered into franchise agreements with a number of independent shoe retailers. In exchange for such benefits as free signs, business forms, and low-interest loans, each franchisee agreed to concentrate purchases of shoes in the grades and price lines manufactured by Brown, and to refrain from stocking or selling competitive shoes of equal grades and prices. Retailers who did not comply were denied these benefits.

The Federal Trade Commission charged, under Section 5 of the F.T.C. Act, that Brown's franchise plan constituted an illegal tying arrangement, with special benefits offered by Brown to franchised dealers as the tying product. It was found that the leverage of these special benefits was used to secure exclusive patronage for Brown to the detriment of competition in the shoe manufacturing industry. While Brown was not a trademark licensing case, it does suggest that the entire package of rights which a franchisor makes available to his franchisees may be viewed as separate from the franchisor's product and may serve as a tying device.

A matter of further interest in *Brown Shoe* relates to the amount of competitive foreclosure necessary to invalidate an exclusionary program. Brown had tied up only one percent of total retail shoe outlets, and approximately four percent of the choice outlets for which the program was designed. The F.T.C. argued successfully that this degree of foreclosure, in the context of the shoe industry, was sufficient indication of probable competitive injury to warrant the issuance of an order against the company.

There may be more justifiable reasons for full-line forcing agreements (total requirements contracts) than is true for normal tying arrangements. For example, a small franchisor may be able to prove that requirements contracts are necessary for him to engage in business,[40] or to introduce a new product or service.[41] A large franchisor cannot foreclose a substantial section of the market for too long a period of time,[42] nor can he foreclose franchised outlets for all products for all time irrespective of the size of market affected. The antitrust laws permit partial or full requirements contracts involving substantial purchases over a substantial period of time only if a small share of the market is involved, if the purpose of the agreement is to ensure the customer a sufficient supply of an important commodity or to ensure to the supplier a market for his output, and if there is no resulting trend to concentration in the industry.

Territorial and Customer Restrictions

Territorial Restrictions[43]

In General. Territorial restrictions exist where a market supplier places certain geographic restrictions on resale, by the franchisee, of the franchised goods or services. Two general methods are commonly used in limiting the geographic area in which a franchisee may sell. In an exclusive territorial division, the franchisee agrees to concentrate his business solicitation within the territory and not to make sales outside the territory. He may normally sell to anyone who comes into his territory. In the closed territorial division, the franchisee is completely forbidden to sell to anyone who does not maintain a place of business (or residence, if the product is sold to individuals) in his territory. There are variations of the two types, but the majority of territorial restrictions are of these kinds. In both cases, there exist at least tacit understandings that all franchisees in the system are similarly bound and that territories will not overlap. In practice it is not easy to separate exclusive franchising from territorial restrictions, because one of the franchisor's main purposes in imposing territorial restrictions is usually to protect the exclusive franchises he has granted.

Territorial restrictions are enforced in a variety of different ways. The most extreme sanction is the termination of any franchisee who sells outside his closed territory, but this is seldom invoked. Typically, the franchisor employs a system of after-the-fact sanctions which is flexible enough to provide varying degrees of deterrence. Enforcement is usually through the device of a profit pass-over which requires the cross-selling dealer to pay all or some portion of his net profit on the sale to the franchisee in the invaded territory. The percentage pass-over depends upon the degree to which the franchisor wishes to discourage cross-selling, and his desire to preserve good will by avoiding refusals to sell. The passover system is itself backed with the threat to terminate the franchise of any dealer who refuses to make the required payment.

Given the sanction of termination, territorial restrictions have the effect of restricting or eliminating intrabrand competition in the areas affected. With a lesser sanction than termination, the barrier to intrabrand competition is no greater than the required pass-over payment. To the extent that the pass-over reimburses a servicing expense incurred by the invaded franchisee but included in the purchase price of the selling franchisee, it merely prevents unjustified profit-taking and has no effect in deterring intrabrand competition.

Vertically imposed territorial restrictions were not seriously challenged by the Justice Department until 1950. During this period, on the basis of the ancillary restraint doctrine in the *Addyston Pipe* case, the Supreme Court upheld the validity of some closed territorial arrangements.[44] After 1950, the Justice Department filed a number of complaints alleging that vertically imposed territorial restrictions were *per se* illegal. More than 20 of these were settled by consent decree until *White Motor* in 1963, which was litigated and went to the Supreme Court. *White Motor* reaffirmed two principles: that territorial restrictions, horizontal or vertical, which are incidental to price fixing arrangements are illegal *per se*; and, that horizontally imposed restrictions, with or without the participation of the franchisor, are naked restraints of trade and also illegal *per se*.

White Motor was followed immediately by two more cases, *Snap-On Tools* and *Sandura,* in which the Courts of Appeal considered the business justification offered and upheld vertical territorial restrictions, given the circumstances presented. In *Sandura,* the Sixth Circuit held that, for a small franchisor in an industry dominated by giants, the interbrand competition which existed made territorial restraints reasonable in spite of the restriction on intrabrand competition.

The next cases of interest to be decided by the Court were *Sealy* and *Schwinn,*[45] handed down on the same day in June 1967. In *Sealy,* the Court reserved opinion on the legality of a territorial allocation among small concerns which was incidental to the use of a joint trade name and advertising plan and which did *not* include price fixing. In *Schwinn,* the Court upheld a District Court finding that "where a manufacturer sells products to its distributor subject to territorial restrictions upon resale, a *per se* violation of the Sherman Act results." The same *per se* illegality was applied "to restrictions of outlets with which distributors may deal and to restraints upon retailers to whom the goods are sold." The Court did not find all vertical territorial restrictions to be *per se* illegal. In the case of agency or consignment sales, where title and risk of loss remain with the franchisor, there is no *per se* illegality if there is no price fixing, and if there are sufficient alternative products available to nonfranchised retailers. The franchisor can continue to restrict territories and customers if he retains title and risk, and if the effect of the restriction is not unduly harmful to competition.

Closed Territorial Agreements. As indicated above, the closed territorial agreement is a method of distribution whereby the market supplier-franchisor forbids the franchisee to sell to anyone who does not maintain a place of business or residence in his territory. Usually, the closed territorial agreement specifies in detail the geographic boundaries of the franchisee's territory. There are variations, for example where franchisees are given nonadjacent closed territories with the areas in between open to all competing franchisees.

The closed territory is almost always found in conjunction with exclusive franchising. While closed territories are of principal benefit to the franchisee, there are a number of advantages which are said to accrue to the market supplier. Where service or installation of a product is necessary, customers usually desire a distributor who has some physical proximity to their place of business or dwelling. A franchisee who did not sell the product will likely not service or install it as carefully as did the selling franchisee who received most of the profit on the transaction. To the degree that territorial security reduces the incidence of improper servicing, it may prevent injury to the market supplier's good will and, hence, to his present and future sales.

The recent Supreme Court decision in *Schwinn* seems to hold that closed territorial arrangements will be judged on a *per se* basis rather than on a rule of reason basis where the goods are sold. In the agency or consignment case, and perhaps where a newcomer or other special situation exists, the rule of reason will be the appropriate test. There are no specific criteria which bring a case within the realm of reasonableness, the most cited ones being those set out in the Attorney General's Report on the Antitrust Laws:

it seems relevant to focus . . . on (1) the percentage of business controlled, (2) the strength of the remaining competition, and (3) whether the action springs from business requirements or purposes to monopolize.[46]

The final criterion, the purpose of the restriction, is the critical one. Without a proper business purpose, there is an implied intent to monopolize. The closed territory is then illegal *per se,* and other criteria are of no relevance.

The first criterion—that of the percent of the market controlled by the franchisor in relation to competition—was clearly of significance in *Carvel,* and is critical to a determination of whether a restraint on intrabrand competition is significant. The strength of remaining competition is of importance for the same reason, and this was a key factor in the *Snap-On Tools* case.

Area of Prime Responsibility Agreements. The area of prime responsibility agreement is a method of distribution whereby the market supplier-franchisor requires the franchisee to adequately represent and promote the sale of the franchised product or service in a designated geographic area. The arrangement assures the market supplier that the franchisee will concentrate on interbrand competition and on the development of one market. At the same time, aggressive franchisees are not discouraged from invading the territory of less aggressive ones, and the latter are thus motivated to improve their performance. Use of an area of prime responsibility clause is normally accompanied by the determination of a sales quota for each relevant geographic area. Failure to meet this quota, plus evidence of cross-selling activity, may be grounds for termination or nonrenewal of the franchise contract.

With an area of prime responsibility contract, the public policy objection to decreased intrabrand competition is lessened, since franchisees are allowed to solicit business in any area so long as they also develop their own area of prime responsibility adequately. The Justice Department and the Federal Trade Commission have not attacked area of responsibility clauses to date.

Zone of Influence Agreements. A zone of influence agreement, which is almost always found in conjunction with an area of responsibility clause, forbids a franchisee to establish an outlet outside his zone, and in some cases prohibits him from changing the location of his outlet within that zone without the permission of the franchisor. The zone clause does not restrict to whom, or where, or what the franchisee may sell; but only *from* where.

To the franchisor, the zone agreement has the advantage of ensuring an even placement of franchisee outlets – and thus maximizes the exposure of his products or services to the consuming public. It is argued that, if location selection were left solely to the discretion of the franchisee, the distribution of locations would be uneven and uneconomic from the point of view of the total franchise system.

The legality of the zone has been upheld in the few cases in which it has come under question. In *Boro Hall*, General Motors successfully defended a treble damage suit under the Sherman Act, brought by a dealer who was not allowed to establish a used car lot outside his zone.[47] In a more recent zone case, the arrangement under challenge was a provision of the General Motors franchise contract limiting the franchisee to a single business location and forbidding him to operate from a branch sales office unless the appropriate division of G.M. gave its written permission. Partly in response to information supplied and pressure exerted by three Chevrolet dealer associations, G.M. invoked its one place of business requirement to prevent certain of its franchisees in Southern California from selling to or through discount houses. The Government charged that the zone contract provision and the way it was enforced both constituted unlawful restraints of trade in violation of Section I of the Sherman Act.

The Supreme Court decided in favor of the Government, but only on the narrow basis of a finding that there existed a classic conspiracy in restraint of trade between G.M. and its franchisees.[48] (While many would find amazing an argument that a few dealers could compel General Motors to adopt a policy, the fact remains that the argument was considered and accepted by the Supreme Court.) This is an application of the doctrine found in *Parke, Davis* that a control, to qualify as truly vertical, must be free of any trace of horizontal origin, purpose, or enforcement. The relevance of the G.M. case is that it suggests a franchisor, in enforcing a zone agreement, can only be sure of avoiding an antitrust action for illegal conspiracy by making his own periodic surveys of franchise location practices, and neither looking to his franchisees for assistance nor accepting any should it appear.

Customer Restrictions

In General. Market division is also accomplished when a franchisor restricts the type of customer to whom the franchisee may sell. There are two possibilities. The right to sell to preferred customers, such as federal and state governmental units and national corporations, may be reserved either to the franchisor himself or to a favored class of franchisees.

The franchisor's motivation in reserving the right to sell to preferred customers is not always clear, because the restriction is usually accompanied by the argument that franchisees could not effectively compete for the reserved account in any case. The franchisor may have some advantage over his franchisees because of cost economies achieved in selling through one level rather than two. It is also argued that, if an individual franchisee is allowed to bid for such business, he may provide inadequate delivery and servicing for which the customer will blame the product and not the franchisee. Where the franchisee tries and fails to make the sale, he may alienate the customer through his unfamiliarity with the techniques and requirements of centralized purchasing. Finally, it is argued that for a franchisor to refrain from bidding on national accounts would result in a diminution of interbrand competition, since other producers, selling directly, could probably underbid the individual franchisee.[b]

Given the sanction of franchisee termination, customer restrictions have the same effect as territorial restrictions of hindering or eliminating intrabrand competition for the customers affected. With a lesser sanction than termination, the barrier to intrabrand competition is no greater than the required pass-over payment or other financial penalty imposed by

---

[b] The White Motor Company defended its restriction on franchisee bidding for government business on the basis that it could not fairly bid against its own distributors and dealers, and its distributors and dealers could not compete on an equal basis with manufacturers of other trucks. The customer restriction thus increases . . . competition by enabling the White Motor Company to compete for . . . business on equal terms with, and under as favorable circumstances as, competing manufacturers of trucks.[49]

the franchisor. Most courts have treated customer restrictions as not being *per se* illegal, approving them when they are found to result from a reasonable business justification.

Restriction on Sale to an Identified Account. This restriction is the situation where the market supplier-franchisor reserves to himself or to other franchisees the right of sale to certain identified accounts, usually federal and state governments and other large volume accounts. Inclusion of the restriction in the franchise agreement serves the purpose of unequivocally informing the franchisee that identified accounts are off limits. Then, when the franchisor or other franchisees deal with these accounts, the invaded franchisee will not resent it or expect a commission rebate.

In the absence of a customer restriction, vertical intrabrand competition does take place. In *Klearflax Linen Looms, Inc.* the franchisor, the only manufacturer of linen rugs in the United States, was historically the sole bidder on federal government contracts to purchase such rugs. For two consecutive years, however, it was successfully underbid by one of its own franchised dealers. Klearflax then refused to fill the franchisee's order for delivery to the government, an action that was held by a district court to be an attempt to monopolize trade in these rugs and thus a violation of the Sherman Act.

The *White Motor* case examined a restriction on sale to a government account. The Supreme Court held that the restriction was not *per se* illegal, but should be decided on the reasonableness of its business justification. In a concurring opinion, Justice Brennan noted that the problem of obtaining adequate distributor servicing could have been overcome by "less drastic measures as, for example, improved supervision and training, or perhaps a special form of . . . warranty to . . . governmental and fleet purchasers to protect against unsatisfactory . . . servicing."

Restriction on Sale to One Classification of Customer. A market supplier-franchisor with a clearly segmented final market may require his franchisees to limit their sales solicitations to single segments of that final market. Such a division of customers may be justified where the segments of customers have different needs for service or require different selling techniques. The restriction is normally accompanied by the granting of an exclusive franchise to service that customer group to which the franchisee is confined.

It is also common that franchisees with differing duties obtain the product at differing rates of discount. The difference in discount might raise problems under the Robinson-Patman Act where two franchisees compete for the same accounts, as the differential discount might not be justified by differential selling costs.

In the *Roux Distributing Company* case, distributors of cosmetics were classified according to the type of wholesaling they carried out and were confined to selling to that classification of customer.[50] (One group of jobbers sold only to drug wholesalers and beauty supply dealers. These in turn sold to retail outlets and beauty salons or beauty schools, respectively.) The restriction on customer class was strictly enforced through threat of termination of the selling agreement. The F.T.C. adopted a rule of reason approach to the case, finding that the restriction did not lessen competition because the three groups were not in potential competition with one another.

Restriction on Use After Sale. Where a market supplier-franchisor sells part of his output through franchisees, and another part directly to quantity purchasers for consumption or processing, he may restrict the latter from reselling the product at all. This is known as a for use provision, and it is used to prevent quantity purchasers, who often buy at a favorable price, from competing with franchisees by periodically dumping excess supplies on the market. Such sales could undermine the franchisor's whole channel of distribution, and might allow goods to reach the hands of unauthorized outlets.[c] It could also subject the market supplier to the sort of Robinson-Patman Act violation discussed in the previous section.

There have been very few cases concerning this type of restriction; those that have occurred have been settled on a rule of reason basis. In *Chicago Sugar Co.* v. *American Sugar Refining Co.*,[52] the Seventh Circuit Court upheld a contract clause requiring the purchaser of sugar not to resell on the grounds that such a resale would unreasonably disturb the existing market supply and price structure. *The Hands Off Period.* Where considerable presale expense is involved, a market supplier-franchisor may require his franchisees to refrain from selling or soliciting a customer for a specific period after another franchisee has incurred such an expense. This hands off period typically runs for 60 or 90 days, allowing the customer a chance to think over the purchase and to close the sale. The restriction is in common use in the sale of complex machinery. Sanctions range from pass-over of the entire profit on the sale, to termination of the franchise relationship.

There has been no litigation to date on this restriction; it would appear reasonable so long as the length of the hands off period is not so great as to unreasonably restrict intrabrand competition within the market.

---

[c]Travers and Wright point out that the restriction may also be used by a manufacturer of complex equipment who desires to keep parts out of the hands of unauthorized dealers who may misuse or misrepresent them, or by a manufacturer of a scarce commodity who wishes to allocate supply and prevent profiteering.[51]

Other Restrictions

There are a number of less significant restraints and controls which commonly appear in franchise agreements. The franchisor may, for example, seek to impose on his franchisees restrictions on

(1) quality standards to be maintained;
(2) quantity, quality, and format of advertising and promotion;
(3) management practices used in running the franchised business;
(4) facilitating services offered (especially credit, delivery, and business hours);
(5) employee training programs;
(6) required use of standardized recordkeeping and accounting systems;
(7) standardized architecture and site landscaping; and
(8) usage of trademarks.

While these controls hardly seem to be anticompetitive in the usual sense, franchisors using them are not free from antitrust problems. Each control does represent a restraint on trade; the legitimacy of each has been judged on a rule of reason standard based on whether the control is intended to serve a legitimate business purpose. The standard used may be summarized as follows:

The cases are not numerous which have held covenants in partial restraint of trade lawful, but the cases do point out that courts are prone to look at the primary purpose of a contract to determine its validity. If the primary purpose, however, disguised, is to stifle competitors and create a monopoly, then the agreement or contract is struck down. However, the cases seem to follow the principle that if the primary purpose of the contract is lawful, e.g., to protect one in the fruits of his labor, and if the arrangement was actuated by or could be explained on the basis of legitimate[d] business justification as opposed to the desire to increase market control through economic leverage, then the court will generally hold any incidental restraint of trade, not harmful to competition or the public, to be lawful.[53]

In practice, each of the eight restrictions mentioned above has fared well under the scrutiny of the courts when it has been defined as serving legitimate business purpose, and where competition has not been substantially lessened. For this reason, it is sufficient to discuss the legal position and precendents of the first two of these restrictions.

Quality Standards To Be Maintained. There are several cases that have upheld the right of a franchisor to insist upon quality standards which

---

[d] Some stress should be placed on the word "legitimate"; one business purpose, in many specified instances, is to limit competition.

are necessary to ensure the integrity of the product, and which do not unduly restrict competition. In the *Denison Mattress Factory* case, one of the restrictions upheld was the franchisor's provision that:

to assure uniformity of the nature and quality of Spring Air products manufactured and sold by Manufacturer and other related companies licensed under Spring Air trademarks, Licensor may designate a supplier or suppliers for any or all materials specified in the specifications for Spring Air products, and Manufacturer shall purchase all materials so specified by Licensor.[54]

The court ruled that the requirement was reasonable and served a legitimate business purpose, and that Denison was bound to follow Spring Air's judgment in the matter.

Format of Advertising and Promotion. Contractual restrictions designed to control the quality, quantity, or format of franchisee advertising and promotion have been upheld by the courts where the restrictions have a basis in good business practice as opposed to an intent to increase vertical market control through economic leverage. In *Susser* v. *Carvel,* the Second Circuit upheld a requirement on Carvel's franchisees that they:

Operate their stores in accordance with a Standard Operating Procedure Manual . . . [which] describes the advertising which they may use, the color they must paint their store, . . . the colors of their employees' uniforms, and many other details.[55]

State Antitrust Law

Although seldom enforced with any vigor or consistency, there has been antitrust or similar legislation on state statute books for more than 80 years. This legislation has been most significant to franchising as the basis of the unlawful or unenforceable contract defense. In *Jackson Brewing Co.* v. *Clarke,*[56] the Texas Court of Civil Appeals held that resale price maintenance, exclusive dealing, and territorial confinement were all violations of Texas antitrust laws. Based on that finding, the court upheld a lower court decision that a franchisee was not liable for certain monies owning to his franchisor. Under the Texas antitrust law, debts incurred pursuant to an illegal agreement are not collectible. Thus, state antitrust laws, of which Texas' are a prime example, may be more restrictive than are corresponding federal statutes.[e]

---

[e] The same is true of franchise regulatory bills in nonantitrust areas. As of October, 1970, prospects for U.S. Senate action on Senator Harrison Williams' bill to make franchisors disclose pertinent information about their companies to prospective franchisees were vitually nil; earlier in 1970, an almost identical bill was introduced by State Senator Clark Bradley in the California State Senate, and passed unanimously.

It is not likely that franchise agreements will be protected from questioning under state antitrust laws on grounds that they involve interstate commerce, or because federal antitrust action is pending against the franchisor. The critical question in recent state antitrust cases has been whether or not the restrictions under challenge have a substantial effect on local commerce. Where such effect exists, courts have upheld the jurisdiction of the state. Further, most state antitrust laws provide for multiple damages — and thus encourage private antitrust litigation.

6

Tying Arrangements in Franchise Systems

The Supreme Court, in its most important ruling on vertically imposed marketing restrictions, has suggested that it may not be sufficient to demonstrate sound business reason and intent on the part of a franchisor who would impose controls. Assuming nonpredatory motives and good business purposes, it may be necessary to demonstrate that the impact of the control in the marketplace is procompetitive.[1] This is an interpretation of the decision held by a number of economists, and one with which the writer concurs. The interpretation comes in part from a literal reading of the wording of the decision, and in part from a reading in relation to earlier decisions.

This chapter discusses the Court's analysis of tying arrangements and the commonly cited business justifications for the use of tying, and presents an economic analysis of the several possible functions served by tying. A final section attempts to show that several legitimate functions of tying arrangements satisfy the Court's requirement for sound business purpose, and also have a procompetitive impact in the sense of encouraging the development of new business enterprises. Several criteria for antitrust enforcement are recommended which are analogous to the criminal law principle of least necessary force, and it is shown that procompetitive results may stem from their adoption.

The Scope and Status of Tying

Common Tying Situations

In the previous chapter, tying was defined as in the *Northern Pacific* case: "an agreement by a party to sell one product but only on the condition that the buyer also purchases a different [tied] product. . . ." Although this formal language may not seem to cover situations common to the everyday experience of the reader, there are in fact a number of customary practices which involve tie-ins. A book club may offer copyrighted books at low price (or without charge) on the condition that a member obligate himself to purchase an additional number of books per annum. An encyclopedia usually has a separate copyright on each volume, yet the publisher will sell the individual volumes as a set only. A box at a baseball game is ordinarily offered for sale only on a seasonal basis, and not for individual games.

There are a number of other arrangements sometimes thought of as being tie-ins, which in fact are not. Thus, pairs such as retail drugs and television tubes, and gasoline and glassware do not represent tie-ins, because while there may exist price inducements to purchase the goods together, there is no requirement of buying one to obtain the other, and each may be purchased by itself.

From a businessman's point of view, tying may take a number of forms. The seller, in threatening to withhold the tying product, may coerce the buyer not only into buying other products, which is the traditional case, but into buying noncommodities such as credit in the *G.M.A.C.* case; transportation, as in *Northern Pacific*;[2] engineering, advisory, or delivery service, and so on. Coercion or inducement may also be imposed by the buyer. In a common situation, a buyer may refuse to buy from the seller unless the seller buys from him, the case of reciprocal buying. While it is not common to think of reciprocity as a tying arrangement, the analogy is apparent if one thinks of the process of exchange (and its reward, the purchase price) as the withheld or tied product.

By threatening to withhold services, which may be outside the Clayton Act, a seller induces the buyer to take products which he might obtain elsewhere. (The Clayton Act does not cover noncommodities. In the services cases to date, induce is a better description of what has happened than coerce.) Such a threat was the situation in *Brown Shoe,* which was discussed in Chapter 5.[3] The F.T.C. charged, under Section 5 of the Federal Trade Commission Act, that Brown's franchise plan constituted an illegal tying arrangement with the special benefits offered by Brown to franchised dealers the tying product. The Court held that the leverage of these special benefits was used to secure exclusive patronage for Brown to the detriment of competition in the shoe manufacturing industry.

The Trademark as a Tying Good

An arrangement of particular interest to franchisors occurs where the franchised trademark is the tying item. In *Susser* v. *Carvel*,[4] a basic issue was whether a *per se* rule should be applied to a tie-in utilizing a trademark, rather than a patent, as the tying item. A tying arrangement wherein the tying item is patented is a *per se* violation of the patent laws under the doctrine of patent misuse.[5] Often when discussing the rule of tie-in illegality courts have included copyright examples with patents, but have never mentioned trademark examples. On the other hand, Mr. Justice Goldberg stated in *Loew's Inc.,* that:

Even absent a showing of market dominance, the crucial economic power may be inferred from the tying product's desirability to consumers or from uniqueness in its attributes.[6]

This language would support an argument that because they are the principal criterion by which a buyer measures the desirability of the franchised good, sufficient economic power is inherent in a trademark to consider a trademark tie-in on the same basis as one concerning a product, if not on the same basis as a patent or copyright.

Is Tying 'Per Se'?

Four market practices are commonly considered in the literature as being *per se* violations of the antitrust laws: price fixing, group boycotts, tying arrangements, and division of markets. However, the standards of proof associated with each of these violations are quite different. In fact, there are a significant number of cases in which tying arrangements and division of markets are *not per se* prohibited.

The Supreme Court has demonstrated some inconsistency in its requirement of necessary business justification for tying arrangements. In the 1958 *Northern Pacific* case, the Court ruled that restrictions having a pernicious effect on competition were illegal without inquiry into "the business excuse for their use."

The Court retreated from its firm stand on business excuse in the 1961 *Jerrold Electronics* case,[7] where it recognized that under some circumstances tying is essential to maintaining a viable business. Jerrold had negotiated tying agreements with buyers of its television booster device. The purchasers were required to have the system installed and serviced by Jerrold, and to buy a full community television antenna system in order to obtain the boosting device. The Court said that, although all the necessary requirements for a *per se* violation were present, because of unique circumstances the tie-in involving the service requirement was neither unreasonable nor illegal. A number of unique circumstances were cited by the Court. The tying equipment used by Jerrold was sensitive, and past experience with less technically complex systems had indicated a need for servicing with high quality equipment. Payment by the franchisee-operators to Jerrold was contingent upon successful operation of the system, and most of the operators had no technical skill or experience using similar systems. The Court felt that it was likely there would have been a high incidence of nonservicing without a compulsory servicing contract, since servicing was expensive and many operators were close to financial insolvency. Finally, Jerrold had only limited service facilities, and this might have caused more impatient franchisees to attempt to install the equipment themselves. Seeing in the combination of these factors the possibility of a series of failures which could have ruined

Jerrold, the Court found the tying arrangement to be reasonable. The Court stated that, "any judicially, as opposed to legislatively, declared *per se* rule is not conclusively binding on this court as to any set of facts not basically the same as those in the cases in which the rule was applied." The opinion further noted that a blind application of the *per se* doctrine to a tying arrangement which has sufficient redeeming virtue would result in a gross injustice.

In two cases following *Jerrold*, this approach was maintained. In the 1962 *Brown Shoe*, The Court said that a tying agreement used by a small company to break into a market might not constitute a violation of the antitrust laws.[8] In the 1963 *White Motor*, the Court noted that tying arrangements did not necessarily fall within the category of trade practices which were illegal *per se*. Such statements opened the door for evidence of business justification to be admissible in a number of lower court cases on tying.

A more recent statement by the Court on tying arrangements may indicate a trend away from the rule of reason approach. In the 1965 *Atlantic Refining* case, the central competitive characteristic of the arrangement involved was held to be the same as that in a tying agreement: "the utilization of economic power in one market to curtail competition in another." Atlantic had contracted with the Goodyear Tire & Rubber Company to sponsor the sale of Goodyear products to Atlantic's wholesale and retail outlets. Although Goodyear carried the prime sales responsibility, Atlantic was responsible for promoting the sale of Goodyear's products and received a commission on all such Goodyear sales. The F.T.C. found the sales-commission plan inherently illegal as "a classic example of the use of economic power in one market . . . to destroy competition in another . . . ," the Court of Appeals agreed, and the Supreme Court affirmed the decision. The Court refrained from calling the arrangement *per se*, but stated:

Upon considering the destructive effect on commerce that would result from widespread use of these contracts by major oil companies and suppliers, we conclude that the Commission was clearly justified in refusing the participants an opportunity to offset these evils by a showing of economic benefit to themselves.[9]

It can be argued that the facts of the *Atlantic* case were hardly ideal for arguing the merits of tying arrangements. No new industry was involved, no small businessmen were attempting to enter a market, and no enforceable specifications were required. The only apparent justification for the Atlantic system seems to be that of economic advantage.

Given this history of judicial interpretation of the legality of tying arrangements, it is possible to make an informed guess as to the current status of tying, both where the franchisor is a supplier selling a product and where he is a licensor establishing a retail business. The distinction is significant.

Where the franchisor is a supplier *selling a product*, where he is shown to exert economic power in the market for the tying good, and where substantial commerce in the tied good is involved, there is a presumption of a violation of the antitrust laws. However, possible illegality cannot be ascertained without a rule of reason examination of a number of market factors, for example dominance, substantial commerce, and extent of market. The Court will consider the kind of redeeming virtue to tying which it found in *Jerrold* and will not find illegality in a tie-in which has such redeeming virtue. Thus, a substantial proportion of tying arrangements involving a supplier selling a product will be considered on a rule of reason, rather than a *per se* basis.

Rufus E. Wilson, former Chief of the General Trade Restraints Division, Federal Trade Commission, has pointed out that where the franchisor is a licensor establishing a business embracing an overall format or design of operation (which includes all the trademark franchising systems), the criteria of illegality are quite different. Wilson suggests that such business licensing franchisors can engage in tying arrangements so long as (1) the agreement has a lawful main purpose (not one which is established solely for the purpose of gaining a group of captive dealers); (2) there is a showing of business necessity for the restriction (and the necessity cannot be achieved by some other means than tying); and (3) competition is not substantially affected by the imposition of the tying restrictions.[10]

The Court's Theories of Tying

The Leverage Theory

Virtually all the Supreme Court's analysis and condemnation of tying arrangements has been based on the so-called leverage theory. Briefly stated, this says that the purpose of a tying arrangement is monopolistic exploitation. This exploitation is achieved by "artificially extending the market for the 'tied' product beyond the consumer acceptance it would rate if competing independently on its merits and on equal terms."[11]

The term monopolistic leverage itself is ambiguous. A distinction should be made between leverage as a revenue-maximizing device, and leverage as a monopoly-creating device. The first involves the use of existing power, the second the addition of new monopoly power.[12] Different conclusions can be reached about the propriety of tying if the result is only a means of utilizing a power already possessed, of if the tie-in creates a second monopoly beyond the scope of the first. In general, the Court's use of leverage has referred to the establishment of a second monopoly.

The view that tying allows the wielding of monopolistic leverage is still widely accepted, and until quite recently the Court (and most econo-mists) have accepted the leverage theory quite uncritically. An economic analysis of the implications of the leverage theory is presented later in this chapter.

The Coercion Theory

Situations like the tying of independent or substitute goods, which are difficult or impossible to analyze by use of the leverage theory have led the Court to adopt a second theory of tying, the so-called coercion theory. The coercion theory focuses on the comparative bargaining power of the two parties. "By conditioning his sale of one commodity on the purchase of another, a seller coerces the abdication of buyer's inde-pendent judgment as to the 'tied' product's merits . . ."[13] In coercion cases the tying item may be a trademark or trade name, or a service or other nonproduct.

In the *Atlantic* case, the Supreme Court sustained the F.T.C.'s attack on the agreement between Atlantic and Goodyear in which Atlantic used its economic power over franchised gasoline service stations to coerce these buyers to carry Goodyear's tires, batteries, and accessories (TBA). The Court was concerned with the relative bargaining position of the small Atlantic franchisees. Since the lease of a service station required the franchisee to make a substantial investment, it was unwise for him to risk his whole business by not complying with a tie-in demanded by his franchisor.

The coercion theory was also applied in the Supreme Court analysis of the *Loew's, Inc.* case in 1962. The offense here was the block booking practices of large motion picture distributors under which small inde-pendent television stations were coerced into accepting inferior pictures along with feature films.[a]

If we consider that there are reasons other than leverage (and to a lesser extent, coercion) for the use of tying arrangements, and that these serve purposes other than the simple suppression of competition, it is useful to look at the managerial justifications offered by franchisors for the use of tie-ins, and at the insights provided by formal economic analysis as to the rational and impact of these justifications.

Business Justification for the Use of Tying

In the majority of cases, the quality of business justification put before the courts has been superficial and its tone self-seeking. In the *Inter-national Salt* case, a manufacturer argues that his goods will not function

---

[a] Hale and Hale comment that: ". . . the notion of 'coercion' would logically require the reduction of all disparity in economic resources. Otherwise, no regularly employed adult could buy a paper from a newsboy without the hazard of rescission of the sale."[14]

properly unless used in conjunction with other of his products. In *Standard Oil*, a trademark owner protests that the inherent value of his mark will decline unless only his own high-quality products are sold with it. In each case, the franchisor or manufacturer attempts to protect the goodwill of his business through use of a tie-in.

In arguments not related to goodwill, the *Times Picayune* demanded that buyers sign tying agreements as a competitive reaction to another supplier who was engaged in tying. In *Crawford Transportation*, it was argued that the tie-in offset a competitor who was achieving the same results through procedures not available to the seller.[15] (In very few cases are the motives of the buyer considered. In *Northern Pacific*, the buyer needed the tying product and had no alternative but to sign. In *International Salt*, the buyer was assured a competitive price and was indifferent about whether to sign. In *Standard Oil*, he received a *quid pro quo* in the form of an assured supply.)

In very few franchise cases has any effort been made to demonstrate that the restraint is one which in fact promotes competition; where the attempt has been made, it has generally been inadequate. The consequence has been that, in the absence of a showing of the sort required by the rule of reason, the skepticism shown by enforcement agencies has increased.

In general, the business justifications put before the courts can be grouped under two headings: the goodwill or integrity of the product defense, and the counting defense.

The Goodwill or Integrity of the Product Defense

The goodwill or integrity of the product defense to tying is based upon the contention that the tying and tied products must be used together if the tying product is to function properly. The argument continues that, if the products can be purchased separately, the buyer might use an inferior product with which the tying product might malfunction. The argument is reinforced by showing that the malfunctioning of the tied product of the combined system would not be easily traceable to the inferior quality of the substitute for the tied product, and, therefore, blame for the failure would be likely to fall on the tying product.[16]

The Supreme Court has never expressly accepted the goodwill defense in a tying case, although it has recognized that the defense could be valid in some circumstances. In the *International Business Machines* case,[17] where IBM tied the purchase of tabulating cards to the leasing of its machines, the Court rejected the goodwill defense because there was evidence that other manufacturer's cards conformed to a reasonable standard of quality. IBM argued that cards which fit imperfectly or were inadequate nonconductors caused their accounting machines to function incorrectly. There seems to have been little to the contention, since the federal government had successfully used cards of its own cut in IBM machines.

In a similar case, the International Salt Company argued that its own rock salt for use in its brine producing machines averaged 98.2 percent pure sodium chloride, but that the salt from other producers was often as low as 95 percent. The Court observed that no evidence had been presented "that the machine is allergic to salt of equal quality produced by anyone except International."

The Counting Defense

The counting defense was first set out in the *Heaton-Peninsular Button-Fastener Company* case in 1896.[18] Heaton argued that its sale of un-patented staples had been tied to its sale of fastening machines because "the fasteners are thus made the counter by which the royalty propor-tioned to the actual use of the machine is determined." Similarly, the number of replacement blades used in a sawmill planing machine has been argued to measure the use of the machine,[19] the amount of ink used in a mimeograph to meter the use of the mimeograph,[20] and the amount of salt processed by a salt dispenser to meter the use of the dispenser.[21] In virtually all cases, the Court has found these counting defenses to be without merit.

Economic Explanations for the Use of Tying

In this section, it will be argued that the Supreme Court's analysis of tying arrangements has been incomplete, particularly insofar as its acceptance of the leverage theory is concerned. There are a number of economically valid explanations for tie-ins other than the suppression of competition in the market for the tied good, and the profitability of tying does *not* depend on the extension of monopoly from the tying to the tied market. Tying arrangements can be used to achieve a number of nonpricing and pricing functions, several of which are highly defensible on rule of reason and procompetitive grounds, others less so.

The Economics of Leverage

In the past decade, the leverage theory has been subjected to more system-atic theoretical investigation, and it has been noted that there are a number of purposes for which tying arrangements may be instituted which bear no relationship to leverage. The following analysis of the various possible relationships between the tying and tied products draws on the work of Bowman, Hilton, and of Baldwin and McFarland.[22] In each of the three cases presented, it is important to note that any monopoly position in the tying product is felt to be socially justifiable. The only issue is the unjustified extension of this monopoly power, through leverage, to the tied product.

Complementary Goods Used in Fixed Proportions. Consider the relationship between tied and tying products where the goods are complements used in fixed proportions, as in the case of nuts and bolts. Although physically separable, such goods are normally considered as one product, and the arrangement is not a tie-in under the antitrust laws. Even if it were, leverage would be unprofitable compared to the return available from use of a profit maximizing price for the tying, or monopolized product. If the price of the tying product is set at a profit maximizing level, the tied product can be sold at a competitive price, or at cost. Any increase in the price of the tied good is equivalent to an increase in the price of the tying good, and would affect total revenue similarly. Thus, the nonmonopolized good might as well not be tied from the standpoint of total revenue, and perhaps of profitability.

Complementary Goods Used in Variable Proportions. Consider the relationship where the goods are complements, with variable quantities of one product used with a fixed quantity of another—as in the case of ink with a duplicating machine. A manufacturer with a monopoly in the production of duplicating machines could, through a tying arrangement covering the ink, increase his total profit over what he might earn from the profit maximizing price for the machine.[b] The monopolistic profit in ink sales is then a function of the usage of the duplicating machine. Even if the ink were sold at a competitive market price, the manufacturer could have achieved the same total profit situation by basing his duplicating machine price (or rental, or royalty payment) on the estimated use of the machine rather than on calendar time. Any increase in the price of his ink would then reduce the rental or royalty payment which he could demand. Conversely, he could reduce the price of ink below competition, or even below cost, and raise his rental or royalty charges on the duplicating machine proportionately. The tied product thus becomes a meter, measuring the use of the tying product. Such an arrangement may be used in place of a simple price discrimination scheme.

Consider also the relationship where the goods are complements, but

---

[b] The relationship is exactly that found in *Henry* v. *A.B. Dick Co.*, (see note 20). If the meaning of leverage is confined to extension of monopoly power to the ink market, there is no real leverage in this case unless there are no uses for ink other than with duplicating machines.

with completely varying proportions as in the case of grass seed and fertilizer. Assume that a seller with a monopoly on grass seed tied sales of seed to sales of lawn fertilizer, where fertilizer was formerly sold in a competitive market. Here we have a distinct possibility of leverage occuring. If there is no use for fertilizer except as a nutrient for lawns, the tie-in will lead to a monopoly in the fertilizer market. If there are alternative uses for fertilizer, the seed monopolist will achieve some monopoly power in the fertilizer market proportional to the importance of fertilizer as a lawn nutrient vis-à-vis other uses. As the monopolist raises the price of fertilizer, the amount of seed he can sell at what was previously his profit maximizing price will fall. The amount of leverage that can be exerted is thus a function of the elasticity of the demand curve for fertilizer, and the magnitude of shifts in the demand curve for grass seed caused by increases in the price of fertilizer. If the demand for fertilizer is highly inelastic in the range of competitive prices, the leverage will result in increased profits because of the existence of the tying arrangement. If the demand for fertilizer is very elastic in the competitive range, the demand curve for grass seed might shift substantially, no effective leverage could exist, and the value of the tying arrangement would approach zero.[23]

There is one further case, the situation of full-line forcing, which is worthy of mention. Here, the goods are usually complementary, and are sold in fixed proportions (although the combination of tying and tied goods is not normally considered as one product, as in the case of nuts and bolts). With full-line forcing, the use of leverage becomes a certainty. In the early *A. & B. Gratz* case,[24] Gratz tied cotton baling material in the fixed proportion of six square yards of burlap bagging to six steel ties. This meters the use neither of the burlap nor the ties and does permit the extension of a monopolistic position from the tying to the tied item.

The three cases of complements used in various proportions blend into one another. The distinction is conceptually important, because leverage does not exist in one case, may exist in the second, and will always exist in the third. Moreover, the existence of leverage in the completely varying proportions case depends on the responsiveness of sales of the tying good to price changes in the tied good, whereas the other cases are not dependent on the shape or elasticity of the relevant demand curves.

Noncomplementary Goods. Baldwin and McFarland have suggested a final case in which the goods are independent of one another, or are substitutes. In this case, it is not clear how leverage in the sense of extension of monopoly can operate.

If a customer is told that in order to acquire a copyrighted phonograph record he must also purchase a case of canned soup, he will certainly, in weighing the offer, simply add as much of the price of the soup as lies above what it is worth to him by itself to the price of the record.[25]

At best, the profits available from such an arrangement will be only equal to those available from simple price discrimination without a tying arrangement.

Nonpricing Functions of Tying

To Prevent Use of Inferior Substitutes for the Tied Good. Franchisees may attempt to use inferior substitutes for a tied good either because of ignorance, or because their interests conflict with those of the franchisor. In the ignorance case, both the franchisor and franchisee suffer a loss of patronage. An example is a franchised new-car dealer who installs foreign-made accessories that inhibit the performance of the automobile.

In the conflicting interests case, a franchisee may make a conscious choice of selling a component which will increase his own profit, but simultaneously decrease the profit of the franchisor and/or of the franchise system as a whole. Consider the case of a franchised Howard Johnson roadside restaurant, where the tying item is the franchised trade name, and the tied item the chicken which is served in the restaurant.

In many freeway locations, these "Ho-Jo's" obtain as much as 95 percent of their patronage from nonrepeat customers, primarily interstate travellers and intrastate travellers living more than 25 miles from the franchised location. These customers base their patronage on Howard Johnson's reputation of serving a certain quality-price combination of food from a standardized menu. In this situation, the local franchisee finds it profitable to reduce the quantity and/or quality of the portions served – for example, of chicken, the most popular dinner meal. In so doing, the franchisee lowers his cost structure without significantly reducing sales to nonrepeat buyers.[c] While the local franchisee is not concerned with the effect of his reduced offerings – the effect is external to him – sales and profits of the other members of the franchise system will decline if dissatisfied buyers decide not to patronize its restaurants in other freeway locations. Thus, the purchase and use of a complementary product that increases the return to a local franchisee may reduce the profitability of the total franchise system, for the system loss is external to the decision process of the individual franchisee.[d] For Howard Johnson to prevent this situation, it must require its franchisees to sell complements of standardized quality. Where

[c] Although less likely, the franchisee might also choose to increase his price structure over that charged by other members of the system for identical food items. An equivalent argument holds for the franchisee who finds it more profitable to sell a superior chicken at higher prices to a nonrepeat buyer who would prefer a lower quality-price combination.

[d] The mathematically trained reader will recognize this as a decomposition problem, where constraints must be placed on the decision processes of subunits so that, in maximizing their profits, the subunit decisionmakers will also maximize profits of the system as a whole.

it is difficult to specify such characteristics as the flavor of a chicken, a tie-in of chicken supply to use of the trade name may be the most efficient way of implementing the requirement.

To Exploit Technological Complementarity. Professor Hilton has suggested the explanation that there may be some technological complementarity in the production of the tied items.

In rural areas, firms offer to paint farmer's barns in return for painting an advertisement on one side of it. They make this tying arrangement instead of an offer of money to the farmer because of the technological complementarity of the painting operations.[26]

Hilton points out that, in the *Times-Picayune* case, the newspaper may have incurred complementarity savings on the dual insertion of copy in both a morning and afternoon paper. While the Court did not find any significant savings arising from reuse of type already set, as a minimum the paper might achieve some economies on the expense of receiving an advertisement by telephone and composing it. This is an unsatisfactory explanation, however, for this and other technological economies can be reflected by a discount in the price of the complementary good. In the 18 years prior to the *Times-Picayune* case, the paper did in fact offer a one cent-per-line discount to retail advertisers who inserted an identical advertisement in each of the two papers.

To Reduce Franchise Fees Payable by Franchisee. Richard Markovits has postulated an interesting, although probably hypothetical situation in which a franchisee (in a trademark licensor to manufacturer system) might introduce a tie-in to reduce the franchise fees which he must pay.[27] Assume that a manufacturer-franchisee for Forstmann fabricated textiles sells both Forstmann trademarked goods, designated F, and a second nonfranchised product line, designated P. The latter is produced on a unique machine under royalty. Where the royalty rate per sales dollar of P is less than the franchisee fee paid per sales dollar of F, the franchisee can minimize his total franchise plus royalty payments by selling F at less than his profit maximizing price, but incorporating a tie-in whereby his customers must purchase a specified amount of P at a proportionately higher-than-competitive price. By reducing the proportion of franchise good sales to total sales, such a tie-in lowers the average franchise fee/royalty percentage applied to total sales.

An equivalent result can be had with the simpler expedient of a normal price reduction on F, combined with a hidden cash or services rebate from buyer to seller. The only apparent advantage of instituting a tying arrangement to accomplish the same end would be to lessen the probability of the franchisee's mispractice being detected.

Pricing Functions of Tying

To Increase the Profitability of Nonmarginal Cost Pricing. One price-related objective of a tying arrangement is to increase the profitability, for the franchisor, of nonmarginal cost pricing,[e] while simultaneously making it easier for franchisees with limited capital to enter the franchise system.[28] A more formal economic argument supporting this hypothesis is presented in Appendix C, and the reader should consult that Appendix in conjunction with this section.

Begin with the assumption that, because of its use of a recognized trademark and the resulting differentiated product, virtually all franchise systems face a negatively (downward) sloped demand curve for the product or service which they sell to ultimate users. For similar reasons, the franchisor faces a negatively sloped demand curve for those goods or services which he sells to franchisees.

A seller who faces such a negatively sloped demand can maximize profits by restricting output and increasing price above marginal cost, hence the idea of nonmarginal cost pricing. Such a seller sacrifices some (opportunity) profit on lost unit sales, but earns a higher profit on each sale made at the higher price. The higher the ratio of additional profits to sacrificed profits, the greater the probability that the seller will practice nonmarginal cost pricing. A seller can further improve this ratio by entering into tying arrangements for substantial quantities of goods.[f] For example, if the elasticity of demand for the tied product is less than that of the tying product for a comparable increase in price, such a tie-in enables the seller to use nonmarginal cost pricing to increase his ratio of additional profits to sacrificed profits.

Because of the downward sloping demand curve there arises a transaction surplus, defined as the difference between the marginal cost of a given quantity of a product and the amount that buyers are willing to pay for that quantity. This transaction surplus is normally shared between sellers and buyers. Seller (franchisor) surplus is the difference between total revenue received by the seller from sales of a given quantity of product and the total marginal cost he has incurred to produce and distribute that quantity.[g] Buyer (franchisee) surplus is the difference between the

---

[e] Use of the term nonmarginal cost may be misleading to the reader who is not familiar with the terminology of economics. It always refers to pricing above marginal cost—a seller (in a one-product firm) who sold *below* long-run marginal cost would incur losses which would drive him out of business.[28]

[f] Both Burstein and Markovits have argued that the increased profitability will only be possible if full-line forcing is used, and thus if leverage is introduced. A full requirements tie-in is not necessary. All that is required is that the volume of tied goods is more than sufficient to cover the pricing and enforcement (or nonenforcement) costs of operating the tie-in.

[g] Seller surplus and seller profits are not equivalent. In arriving at accounting profits, sellers must deduct from surplus the total of fixed costs, variable pricing, and promotional costs. Where pricing and/or promotional costs are positive, maximization of seller surplus may not be equivalent to maximization of profit.

total cost of a given quantity of product to its buyers and the greatest dollar value they would have paid rather than forego this purchase entirely. Put another way, buyer surplus is the gross utility to the buyer of purchasing that good rather than its closest substitute.

If the seller were vertically integrated through the distribution level, he would not be concerned about how the transaction surplus were divided between seller and buyer—he would simply price his goods at his own marginal cost, and the total transaction surplus would accrue to the same organization. However, since the nonintegrated firm will not benefit from the surplus realized by its buyers, it will always price above marginal cost so long as it faces a negatively sloped demand curve.

For the seller who practices single pricing (charging his customers no basic fee, and charging the same price for each unit of product purchased), nonmarginal cost pricing will reduce the total transaction surplus available, but will increase the absolute size of seller surplus. The impact of the lost surplus falls entirely on the buyer and is external to the seller's decision. Without a vertically integrated organization, the price set will always exceed the price which would jointly maximize the transaction surplus to the seller-buyer system. (The actual price chosen will be that which equalizes marginal revenue and marginal cost, this being the point that maximizes seller surplus *given* a system of single pricing.)

Since the seller surplus available from single pricing profit maximization will always be less than the total transaction surplus available, the seller will always find it profitable to implement lump-sum pricing if he can. Under lump-sum pricing, he charges his customers a lump-sum fee (a franchise fee) for the right to purchase and/or resell the product. This fee is in addition to the per-unit price. If demand were certain, a seller who combined lump-sum and marginal cost pricing could increase his seller surplus to equal the total transaction surplus available.

However, a seller who practices lump-sum and marginal cost pricing will almost always be able to increase his returns even further if he can get away from marginal cost pricing. Ideally, he will reduce (but not eliminate) his lump-sum franchise fee, and through a tying relationship, charge each customer more than marginal cost for each incremental purchase of the tied good. In so doing, the franchisor is both following the good business practice of maximizing returns, *and* is serving the procompetitive purpose of easing entry into the franchise system for potential franchisees with limited financial resources and limited ability to pay a high initial franchise fee.

The reason why returns can be increased by lowering the lump-sum fee is found in part in the unrealistic assumption of a certain demand. In reality, the franchisor and franchisee do not know the location and shape of the demand curve for the franchised good. However, we do not require the assumption of a certain demand for our analysis, and the introduction of a realistic assumption of imperfect information about demand actually increases the profitability of nonmarginal cost pricing. (The existence of imperfect knowledge is demonstrated in the fact that a franchisor's lump-sum franchise fee normally remains fixed over a considerable period of time.)

Under conditions of uncertainty or risk, franchisees do not know how successful a franchise system might prove to be in a future period. They will thus be unwilling to pay the franchisor a fee equal to the expected value of the right to purchase his product at his marginal cost. The greater the uncertainty, the greater should be the difference between the true expected value of the franchise right, and the fee that franchisees are willing to pay for it. (The less certain the situation, the greater the risk aversion behavior of franchisees, particularly those with limited resources. The franchisor is less averse to risk taking than the weighted average of his franchisees, and is usually better financed. As a result, he will charge less than the sum of the expected value of the losses which he absorbs.) By engaging in nonmarginal cost pricing, the franchisor can transfer part of the risk of an uncertain demand curve to himself through charging a smaller lump-sum fee and receiving a higher per-unit price on his tied sales.

Similarly, where the franchisor has difficulty in estimating his own future sales to franchisees, and thus finds it difficult to plan his own requirements for production facilities, advertising and promotion, and so on, he can increase his expected returns by reducing his franchise fee and increasing the price of his tied product through nonmarginal cost pricing. Again, there exists a procompetitive result of lowering the initial franchise fee and lowering barriers of entry to the system.

One other rationale deserves mention. Where buyers are not separated by the cost of transferring the seller's product, there is a possibility of buyer arbitrage, whereby one buyer resells to another nonfranchised buyer (frequently a discount house or other price cutter), at a price below lump-sum plus unit cost, but above unit cost. Given recent Supreme Court rulings, it is not clear that a franchisor can legally move to dissuade this practice, even though buyer arbitrage reduces the seller's return by depriving him of the lump-sum fee which new franchisees pay, and by lessening the value of new franchise sales.

The franchisor can reduce or eliminate this buyer arbitrage quite legally, by reducing his franchise fee and increasing his unit price above his marginal cost until the difference between average and unit price is less than the cost of cross-selling the product.

The choice of a product to tie can also be explained on the basis of maximizing returns from nonmarginal cost pricing. In searching for a good to tie-in, the most profitable choice in terms of maximizing seller surplus will be one with a steeply negatively sloped demand curve to the left of the relevant output, a steeply positive slope of the corresponding marginal cost curve to the left of this point, and a large dollar volume of output. A combination of these conditions will maximize the seller surplus that can be realized by elimination any given amount of transaction surplus through nonmarginal cost pricing.

To Increase the Profitability of Price Discrimination. A second price-related objective of a franchisor tying arrangement is to increase the profitability of price discrimination, while simultaneously making it easier for franchisees with comparatively flat demand curves to remain in the franchise system. A graphical argument supporting this hypothesis is presented in Appendix D, which the reader should consult in conjunction with this section.

Whenever demand elasticities for different franchisees are not equal at the franchisor's single profit maximizing price, the franchisor can increase his gross profit through the practice of price discrimination — that is, by charging different franchisees different per-unit prices for the product or good.[h] The practice of price discrimination may or may not be illegal under relevant antitrust statutes.[i]

---

[h] What happens to the total level of output if a monopolist is permitted to discriminate in price between buyers? The question has been considered by a number of economists over the past half century, usually in conjunction with studies of utility rate structures, but the answer is not conclusive. Edgeworth argued that the introduction of discrimination into a technological monopoly would produce an increase in welfare. (It should be noted that output and welfare are not quite synonomous, as the introduction of discrimination violates one of the conditions for Pareto optimality.) Pigou believed that whether an increase or decrease in output resulted would depend on the shape of the several demand curves, and so the situation was indeterminate. Mrs. Robinson also claimed that the answer depended on the relative convexity or concavity of the demand curves, and she concluded that the most common case was one in which price discrimination would yield an increase in output.[29]

[i] The question of legality is far from clear cut. While a franchisor who practices price discrimination risks antitrust action under the Robinson Patman Act, the practice is not illegal *per se*. Section 2(a) of the Act, applying to goods of "like grade and quality," makes price discrimination unlawful only "where the effect of such discrimination may be substantially to lessen competition or tend to create a monopoly in any line of commerce, or to injure, destroy, or prevent competition with any person. . . ." Section 2(f) makes it unlawful to knowingly receive or to induce a discrimination in price. Indirect means of price discrimination are also banned. However, it is not clear that a franchisor selling to franchisees *not in competition with one another* (perhaps because of geographic separation) either lessens direct competition, or that the effect is substantial.

Even lacking direct competition, the practices discussed are nominally illegal under Section 3 of the Act, which makes it unlawful to sell at prices lower in one part of the country than another. However, Section 3 is a criminal statute outside the jurisdiction of the Federal Trade Commission and cannot be invoked as the basis for private treble-damage actions. As a result, Section 3 is rarely if ever used.

Price discrimination is also mentioned in legislation in every state of the union, sometimes as the subject of special legislation covering specific industries such as insurance, sometimes included with statutes prohibiting monopolies and restraint of trade. Again, the prohibition is against price discriminations which have the purpose or effect of destroying or substantially lessening competition, or tending to create a monopoly.

Even where it is legal, however, price discrimination may be unprofitable to implement. To properly discriminate among franchisees, the franchisor must learn the position and shape of the relevant franchisee demand curves, must prevent franchisees from learning of the lower prices being paid by others, and must prevent buyer arbitrage. It can be shown that a properly designed buying arrangement can assist the franchisor in overcoming each of these problems, and thus can increase the profitability of price discrimination.[j]

To implement price discrimination, there are two alternative tying arrangements which a franchisor might adopt. Instead of charging geographically separated franchisees different prices, he may charge each the highest prevailing price and offer to sell to each, at less than its prevailing market price, some quantity of another product which they also use. The quantities supplied will vary, by franchisee, inversely with the prices that would be charged under a discriminatory scheme. Or, the franchisor may charge each franchisee the lowest prevailing price, but condition some of his sales on a promise to purchase varying amounts of a second product for more than its prevailing market price. In either case, there is a secondary, and procompetitive result of making it easier for franchisees with comparatively flat demand curves to buy for less—and thus to enter and/or remain in the franchise system.

Under either plan, the franchisor can successfully hide his discriminatory pricing from those franchisees being discriminated against. The first arrangement has the added advantage that it may decrease the ability of franchisees to engage in buyer arbitrage, by forcing each to purchase more of the underpriced product than he can use if he buys the original product to cross-sell. Assuming the underpriced product is nontransferable (for example trademarked supplies) and the franchisee cannot resell the overpriced product except at a loss, this tying arrangement will greatly reduce the overall incentive for franchisees to engage in buyer arbitrage. Under the second arrangement, the cross-selling franchisee does not have to purchase more of the overpriced product than is re-

---

[j]For the argument to hold, the producer of the tying goods must not already be selling the tied good to others at a price above marginal cost (and equal to the going market price for that good). With nonmarginal cost pricing for the tied good, the franchisor cannot extract all his potential profit from the sale of the tying good. The franchisor can sell the tied good at marginal cost price—but only if he is not currently selling it to nonfranchisees at above marginal cost prices. If he is, then in order to increase his profits from tying he will have either to absorb a loss of profits from his general sales of good, or else attempt to discriminate between buyers. If the tied good is sold by a small number of producers under oligopolistic conditions, it would be politically difficult for only one seller to suddenly start to price at marginal cost levels. As Burstein has pointed out, the latter situation describes the circumstances of the *American Can* case, *United States* v. *American Can Co.,* 87 F. Supp. 18 (N.D. Cal. 1949).[30]

quired in order to buy the underpriced one for resale, hence this system will not reduce buyer arbitrage.

Whenever a franchisor produces a tied product which is *complementary* to the tying product, and which is sold in a competitive market using nonmarginal cost pricing, the franchisor may increase his gross profit by using a tying arrangement rather than an overt price concession to prevent the losses that otherwise would result from the tied product's nonmarginal cost price. The situation is not trivial, as it is far from uncommon for a tie-in to be imposed using a tied product produced in a nonperfectly competitive market.[31]

To Implement A System of Meter Pricing. A third price-related objective of a franchisor tying arrangement is to implement a system of meter pricing. This is a subcase of the price discrimination explanation, with many of the arguments being analogous, but because it is frequently mentioned in the literature (as the 'counting' defense, described earlier), it will be treated separately here.

The business justification and procompetitive aspects of a system of meter pricing were set out as early as 1911 in the *A.B. Dick Co.* case Purchasers of A.B. Dick duplicating machines were informed, through the sales contract and by a metal plate attached to each machine, that a condition of sale was that owners use in the machines only the ink supplied by Dick. In defending its practice, Dick stated that:

. . . the machines were sold at cost. They were therefore purchased by many who, had a manufacturing profit been added, would have been unable to enjoy the patented inventions. The patentee's profits on the supplies represented royalty; this accrued only in proportion to the licensee's use of his machine. An accounting on any other basis would have been vexatious to both parties.[32]

Thus, tying was defended as being a form of meter pricing by which payment is geared to the use being made of the tying product. The pro-competitive aspect is that the competitive position of small users vis-à-vis larger users in the same industry is enhanced when patented machines are made available at a low initial cost.

If we substitute the Chicken Delight franchised trade name for the patented Dick machine, and the tying of paper containers for the tying of ink, we have an analogous situation where the lump-sum franchise fee can be set at cost—and thus enhance entry to the franchise system and the use of paper containers as a meter for the sale of chicken and shrimp under the trade name.

It is now apparent why the metering case is simply a subcase of the price discrimination explanation. Clearly, Chicken Delight's trade name is worth more to intensive users—to those franchisees with the largest sales potential. However, for Chicken Delight to determine in advance how intensively each franchisee will use the tradename would be most difficult. Also, to prevent those franchisees who purchased use of the tradename at a low price from reselling to those who would have to pay a high price might prove impossible.

A tying arrangement resolves all these problems. The trade name (plus the training provided by the franchisor, the architectural design, site selection, and other services) can be sold at cost, with sale of related supplies tied to it. Through the sale of supplies, the franchisor has a method of measuring the intensity with which his franchisees use the trademark. By charging a higher than competitive price for supplies,[k] the franchisor receives the equivalent of a royalty from use of his trademark and can maximize his gross profit.[l]

The analogy of meter pricing with pure lump-sum pricing is apparent if one considers the outright sale of Dick's duplicating machine as the sale of the right to use the machine at the supplier's marginal cost, which is zero. The analogy with nonmarginal cost pricing is apparent if one considers meter pricing as the sale of a service (for example, the intended use of a duplicating machine with marginal cost of zero). Thus, meter pricing can perform the same function for franchisors of durable goods that lump-sum and nonmarginal cost pricing can for franchisors of nondurable goods.

Meter pricing may even be profitable where the demand curves for each franchisee are essentially equal. By making franchisee payments a function of their use of the durable good, meter pricing can reduce the amount of seller surplus lost by the franchisor because of his own ignorance, or because of franchisee uncertainty, risk aversion, or ability to engage in buyer arbitrage by using the tying good to yield benefits to other potential buyers.

The Criteria of Least Necessary Restraint

The previous analysis has established a theoretical economic basis for frequently observed behavior, that of tying arrangements being included in both franchise and nonfranchise relationships. The purpose of the discussion is not to claim that a given situation would, in the real world,

[k] In a 1970 San Francisco lower court case, it was alleged that Chicken Delight did in fact charge above a competitive price for tied supplies, notably dip mix, spice mix, and paper packaging goods. The franchisees felt that the overpricing by the company was excessive, stopped using the franchisor's distinctive packaging items, and began using plain paper plates and containers. Trial judge George B. Harris ruled that the packaging tie-in was improper, because company supply of the tied item was not necessary to preserve the goodwill in the trademark. Chicken Delight has indicated that it will appeal the decision.

[l] The same result could be achieved in the *Dick* case by giving the machine away for nothing, and charging a higher price for ink. But infrequent users would then demand an oversupply of machines (in fact, all users might then demand an oversupply). A lump-sum payment combined with a nonmarginal cost royalty overcomes this problem.

uniquely produce a tying situation. The situations postulated simply provide a rationale for a number of observed tying arrangements.

Whether the reader disagrees with one or more of the individual explanations for the use of tying is somewhat irrelevant. The significant thing is that, in some cases, tying can be shown to have a good business justification which is unrelated to any intent to extend a monopoly from one market to another, and it can be shown to have some procompetitive effects and not to be substantially anticompetitive (at least in its initial impact). If we start from a position that tying arrangements are suspect, but should *not* be *per se* illegal, the next task is to consider under what conditions tying might be permitted and whether there are defenses which might be *per se* acceptable for tying situations.

The Concept

The concept of least necessary force is found in criminal law, where a law enforcement officer (or a citizen defending his home) is required to carry out his duties using the least possible force necessary to attain his lawful objectives. If an analogy were carried to an antitrust law setting, the question might be asked: "Is a given restraint in a franchise agreement more restrictive than is necessary to achieve the reasonable business purpose which it is claimed to serve?"

The question has not been asked very frequently over a considerable number of years,[33] although the practice of invalidating contract restraints that are more restrictive than necessary was one of the major developments in early common law, and was the heart of the doctrine of reasonably ancillary restraints.[m]

Are there methods of least necessary restraint whereby the business objectives associated with tying arrangements in franchise systems might be accomplished? It is clear that in some cases legitimate aims served by tie-ins can be attained by less restrictive means.

Consider the obvious case of *Times-Picayune*. While there are economies in running the same advertisement in both a morning and afternoon newspaper, any cost saving could as easily be reflected in a lower joint advertising rate. Is there any justification for making the joint rate

---

[m]To repeat what was stated in Chapter 1, the rule of reasonably ancillary restraints may be stated as follows: Where challenged conduct is subservient or ancillary to a transaction which is itself legitimate, the decision is not determined by a *per se* rule. The doctrine of ancillary restraints is to be applied. It permits, as reasonable, a restraint which (1) is reasonably necessary to the legitimate primary purpose of the arrangement, and of no broader scope than reasonably necessary; (2) does not unreasonably affect competition in the marketplace; and (3) is not imposed by a party or parties with monopoly power. It permits . . . business arrangements of benefit to the parties, and perhaps to the public, which have no injurious effect in the sense of antitrust policy."[34]

compulsory through a tie-in? Probably not. It is highly unlikely that this tie-in was formulated with any but anticompetitive intent.

All situations are not as clear cut as *Times-Picayune*. Consider the use of tying to support meter pricing. Any antitrust proponent can guess that in some situations meter pricing systems can be implemented simply by attaching a meter to the differentiated machine involved—with no tying arrangement necessary. But the procedure is far from universally satisfactory. In a great many situations meters can be tampered with, and for a product like a riveting machine meters would be somewhat unsuitable.

Where conventional meters are unsatisfactory, the alternative remains of obtaining variable rentals by charging franchisees a royalty on their output of endproducts. This alternative might be suitable, but only where the tying product's contribution to franchisee sales is predictable, and where the franchisor can be assured that franchisees are reporting their sales accurately. Unless all these conditions are met, endproduct royalties will not be a satisfactory method of measuring how intensively franchisees are using the tying product. Thus in many (but certainly not all) situations, we are left with tie-ins as the most efficient metering device available to the franchisor, and perhaps the only available way of exploiting the profitability of meter pricing.

The Quality Control/Goodwill Case

The alternatives most often offered for the quality control or goodwill defense for tying are as follows: a contract clause requiring use of the tying product with other products which conform to stated specifications; a performance warranty applicable only if the equipment is used in conjunction with the seller's other equipment or service; or a cost-justified price-difference service or repair contract permitting the seller to charge a higher price for servicing equipment when used with equipment other than the sellers'. These alternatives are undoubtedly less restrictive than tying, in that they do not foreclose competition in the market for the tied product. But their use is less effective than tying in protecting the franchisor's quality control and goodwill in a number of circumstances.

Jerrold Electronics is a good example of a tying arrangement which was no more restrictive than necessary to facilitate a reasonable goal— that of promoting the entry of a complicated new product in the face of dealer shortcomings and consumer ignorance. After examining the alternatives open to Jerrold, the Court concluded that "the limited knowledge and instability made specification an impractical, if not impossible alternative."[35] (Specification refers to the use of quality specifications imposed on equipment to be used in conjunction with the Jerrold equipment.) The possibility of using performance warranties or cost-difference servicing contracts was not considered by the Court as open to Jerrold until the industry was well established.

As an example of a case where the quality control defense was mis-used, consider *Dehydrating Process* v. *A. O. Smith Corp.*[36] Here, the court allowed the defendant to tie-in its patented unloader to its patented silo. Eighteen of thirty-six buyers who had bought a total of eighty un-loaders over a six-year period prior to 1957 had complained about mal-functioning. The court felt that customers had blamed the unloaders rather than the silos. The Court also refused to consider other less restrictive alternatives because the suit was private, and the plaintiff did not claim that other satisfactory equipment was available. No evi-dence was given that the defendant could not have specified minimum standards for silos to be used with its unloaders, or have specified a list of acceptable silo manufacturers in a manner similar to *Denison Mattress*. It can also be argued that, if Smith's goodwill were endangered by only eighteen claims and six refunds over a six-year period, the company was probably not deserving of special protection.

To illustrate the situation of a franchisor providing specifications to his franchisees, consider the case of the franchised Howard Johnson restaurant which was discussed earlier. To assure the quality and quantity of chicken served, the franchisor could simply send each franchisee detailed specifications for the chicken and its "fixin's." This approach is neither completely effective nor costless. As in most other food in-dustry cases (Carvel as one example), the consumer's expectation is for a uniform taste and quality which cannot be easily specified to alternative suppliers. Also, franchisees will always be tempted to ignore quality standards where they are offered a good buy on a complement whose deviations from the standard appear to be minor. Whenever the interests of franchisor and franchisee thus diverge, the need to police adherence to quality control standards increases. In this situation, a tie-in will minimize inspection costs, and may be the only effective method for preventing the use of inferior components.

Time Restrictions. Even where a tying restriction is valid for quality control or goodwill purposes, and where there are not less restrictive means available whereby the relevant business objectives involved might be accomplished, the validity of a *per se* legal status for a tying arrange-ment is limited in time. Restrictions that are justified when a franchisor is struggling to become established may not be justifiable later on, when a market position has been achieved, and when franchisees have had an opportunity to learn what is in their own best interest—something which is *not* always obvious on entering a franchise system. (Businessmen refer to this as being penalized for business success, but all businesses are subject in some way to it. Virtually no corporate giant had in its early years the range of antitrust problems which confront it today.) A time-limited tying arrangement is not unknown in franchising. After his first year in business, a franchised Mister Donut outlet is no longer required to buy his raw materials from the franchisor, but he does have to purchase ingredients of comparable quality. The franchisor feels that one year is a necessary minimum for the franchisee to learn the importance of close quality control to the success of his operation. As a practical matter, most franchisees do buy from the company or from recommended suppliers, where they can be sure of getting the correct mix.

The Newcomer/Infant Industry Case

A market newcomer, as used here, is any company selling its product in a market which is novel for that company. An infant industry is one which is new to a particular geographic area or set of customers, although not necessarily new *in toto* in the economy. Thus, the case may refer to an existing franchisor marketing a product new (in an informational sense) to that market, as well as to a new entrant to an established industry.

Underlying the newcomer/infant industry case is the assumption that it is procompetitive to stimulate new businesses and product or service innovations by keeping entry barriers at low levels. (The Supreme Court has never heard a case where an antitrust defendant based a defense upon his status as a newcomer to the market or as a member of an infant industry. However, it can be predicted from comments in several cases that such a defense might have considerable weight.)[37] In establishing and building a market for a new product, a franchisor may encounter problems that threaten his own and/or the new industry's survival. These problems often are related solely to product newness and consumer ignorance, rather than to any economic inefficiency on the part of the franchisor. Similarly, a new entrant into an established industry may encounter substantial barriers to entry requiring the use of marketing techniques whose anticompetitive aspects might otherwise be suspect. A strict enforcement of antitrust laws against a newcomer in either the new entrant or new market situations serves only to make existing barriers to entry more rigid, to help consolidate the market positions of established sellers, and to discourage the growth of competition.

The essence of the newcomer/infant industry case is that market newcomers should be permitted to cite this status as a defense to antitrust actions against marketing activities, such as tying, which would be invalid if used by an established company. For example, most of the rationale behind the Court rejecting alternatives to Jerrold's tie-ins was related to the television antenna systems industry being new. If the industry had been well established, adequate alternate equipment and servicing would undoubtedly have been available, and Jerrold could have protected its goodwill by specifications or performance warranties. The antenna system operators would have been neither technologically naive, nor financially shaky, and Jerrold's arguments would have been weak indeed. The Court also mentioned that Jerrold, unlike RCA and Philco, who were in the same market, did not have a diversified business to absorb losses from the antenna business. One implication is that a large diversified company entering a new industry should not be allowed to tie, while a smaller, nondiversified company can legally do so. This would be consistent with least necessary restraint insofar as protection of goodwill to encourage public trust in the trade name is concerned.

The validity of the newcomer/infant industry case is also limited in time. At the time of the *Jerrold* decision in 1960, the Court found the defendant's policies no longer justified because the less restrictive alternatives which had not been available during the early years of the industry (1950–1954) were present by the late 1950s. It takes good legal antennae to desist from a marketing practice that was innocent in its inception but has become illegal merely because of the franchisor's growth. The most feasible alternative might be the establishment of an arbitrary time period—Donald Turner, former Assistant Attorney General in charge of the Antitrust Division, has suggested three to five years—beyond which any assumption of *per se* legality for a practice by a market newcomer or a seller in an infant industry would no longer be valid.

The Lowered Barriers to Entry Case

In 1923, one of the first cases brought under the Clayton Act introduced the issue of barriers to entry as a consideration in judging tying arrangements. In *F.T.C.* v. *Sinclair Refining Co.*,[38] the Court upheld the practice of Sinclair and 30 other refiners of leasing underground tanks to retail service stations at a minimal rental, often one dollar a year, with the tying proviso that the equipment could be used only for storage of gasoline supplied by the franchisor. The Court was impressed with the lowering of financial barriers to entry at the franchisee level, but did not take into consideration that the same leasing practice tended to raise barriers to entry at the franchisor (gasoline distributor) level.

Such a raising of barriers to market entry has been viewed by writers such as Kaysen and Turner as the principal evil of tying arrangements.

A tie-in always operates to raise the barriers to entry in the market of the tied good to the level of those in the market for the tying good; the seller who would supply the one, can do so only if he can also supply the other, since he must be able to displace the whole package which the tying seller offers. Developing a substitute for the tying product may be very difficult, if not impossible. . . . few firms are prepared to supply machines like those of IBM, whereas many may be prepared to supply punch cards.[39]

Kaysen and Turner are mistaken in claiming that no procompetitive lowering of barriers to entry can come from a tie-in. Where barriers at the franchisee level are lowered, even at the cost of temporarily raising barriers at the franchisor level, we may have one of the exceptions to any proscription against tying. As described earlier, this includes objectives such as increasing the profitability of nonmarginal cost pricing, while simultaneously lowering franchise fees; using tying arrangements to implement price discrimination (where legal); and implementing a meter pricing system as a form of price discrimination. In each case, the test of least necessary restraint must be applied: "Is the tie-in a more restrictive device than is necessary to achieve the business purpose which it is claimed to serve?" Application of the test will mean that many, if not most tying arrangements which are defensible under lowered barriers to entry, will have their validity limited in time as competitive alternatives arise.

The Effect on Competing Sellers

Donald F. Turner has raised one serious objection to the line of reasoning implicit in the least necessary restraint argument.[40] Turner questions whether economists have placed too much emphasis on the effects of tie-ins on buyers—and not enough on the effects on competing sellers. In the absence of leverage, and given good business justification and a procompetitive effect of lowering the barriers to new entry, the usual effect of a tying arrangement is to foreclose a portion of the market to competing sellers of the tied product. Turner points out that the courts have been as concerned with the interests of competing sellers as with the effects on buyers.

The effects of tying arrangements on competing sellers are indeed important, both on the grounds of equity and on the economic grounds of long-run social benefits derived from the competitive and innovative influences associated with freedom of market entry. Under the least necessary restraint argument, most barriers to entry to the tied market would be nonpermanent in that they would be limited in duration. Also, the barriers would be insurmountable only in the case where the tying good is patented, and the tied product has no use other than with the tying product. In such a case, the tied product normally would not have been produced prior to the introduction of the tying good. No existing competitors would be foreclosed, even though new entry is restricted. Nevertheless, Turner's point is valid, and a sufficiently high amount of competitive foreclosure would be enough to invalidate a tying arrangement by overcoming any procompetitive effect that might exist. According to *Carvel*, anticompetitive effect in a trademark licensing case is determined by standards of a Section 3 requirement case as shown in *Tampa Electric Co.* v. *Nashville Coal Co.*

The effect on competing sellers proviso, which is analogous to the existing quantitative substantiality rule, is not of great importance as a limited factor in our discussion. It would never arise under the new-comer/infant industry case, and seldom under the quality control/good-will case, although it could arise under the barriers to entry case. Even in the latter, the time limitation on the justification for the tie-in would weaken the possible impact on competing sellers.

With the introduction of this proviso, we have satisfied Rufus Wilson's three factors for weighing the legality of a restrictive purchasing arrangement in the field of franchising. We have also satisfied all but one of the requirements of the doctrine of ancillary restraints. Ancillarity requires that the party imposing the restriction have no monopoly power. The franchisor does have some monopoly power where the trademark is the tying good, but we have assumed that such power, arising as it does from trademark law, is not detrimental to the public good.

Extension of the Criteria

It is possible that there is hardly an area of antitrust law where analysis and understanding would not be improved by asking the question: "Is a given contractual clause more restrictive than is necessary to achieve the (reasonable) business purpose which it is claimed to serve?" In the next two chapters, the least possible restraint criteria will be applied to territorial and customer restrictions, and to exclusive dealing and exclusive franchising. A further concept, the failing company case, will be introduced to go along with the quality control/goodwill, newcomer/infant industry, and lowered barriers to entry cases mentioned above.

7 Territorial and Customer Arrangements in Franchise Systems

The issues of legal and economic doctrine raised by the imposition of territorial and customer arrangements and similar vertical restrictions have been extraordinarily troublesome. The legal conundrum is that a set of separate agreements between a franchisor and his franchisees, imposing territorial or customer restrictions, appears to result in a market division and a refusal to deal. Under established antitrust doctrine, such a result is illegal if agreed to amongst the franchisees.[a] Further, doctrine regards resale price fixing agreements as being generally *per se* illegal; the avoidance of all competition between franchisees through vertically imposed territorial arrangements is even more restrictive of competition than the avoidance of price competition alone.

The economic issues have centered around the much-repeated proposition that vertical restrictions on *intrabrand* competition may enhance *interbrand* competition by fostering competition between territorially limited franchisees and other manufacturers or franchise systems.[b] A case can be made that antitrust scholars have not properly weighed the relative values to the economy and to the society of intrabrand and interbrand competition to determine which (if either) should enjoy a preference in the development and enforcement of antitrust statutes. It can be argued that interbrand is generally far more significant than intrabrand competition in an economy where vertical ownership integration is both endemic and largely beyond the reach of antitrust controls.

On the other hand, when a franchised good is differentiated in the minds of consumers from apparent substitute products, the freedom from competition by others selling identical products can give the franchisee considerable market power in that he is enabled to charge higher prices

---

[a] A division of markets among competitors has been a *per se* violation of the Sherman Act from the beginning. In fact, the impetus for the whole *per se* violation doctrine came from the opinion of Judge Taft in *United States* v. *Addyston Pipe and Steel Co.,* 175 U.S. 211 (1899), a price-fixing and market division case. In *Addyston Pipe,* the Supreme Court held that the Sherman Act was violated by an agreement among competitors to divide the market, because it eliminated competition even more completely than did price fixing.

[b] Intrabrand competition arises because of differences in the cost and demand conditions facing franchisees, and their differing responses to a given market environment. Where a good is distributed through an ownership-integrated marketing channel we would not expect intrabrand competition to develop. Where a good is distributed through independent multi-product outlets, the phenomenon which E. T. Grether has called enterprise competition makes the price and nonprice attributes of the good important considerations in competitive strategy, and intrabrand competition results.

than would otherwise be possible. Although Chevrolet dealers must compete with Ford and Plymouth dealers, a Chevrolet dealer could raise his prices significantly to buyers who have a preference for Chevrolets if there is no intrabrand competition from nearby Chevrolet franchisees.

There are two criteria, product differentiation and market share, which command attention. If there were no product differentiation, then the elimination of intrabrand competition would have only minimal anticompetitive effect. Conversely, a high degree of product differentiation with accompanying inelastic demand might make intrabrand restrictions intolerable from a public policy point of view. As a measure of the extent of product differentiation, Bain suggests the sensitivity of the market share of the individual franchisee to price variations, which can be estimated by comparing the franchisee's market share before and after a price change.[1] The market share is also relevant, because as the market share of a franchisor becomes larger the importance to consumers of having a choice among sellers of the same good increases.

The Court's Analysis of Territorial and Customer Arrangements

Following the *White Motor* case in 1963,[2] franchisors won lower federal court victories in *Sandura, Snap-On-Tools, Denison Mattress, Schwinn,* and *Sealy.*[3] The government chose to appeal only two, *Schwinn* and *Sealy,* to the Supreme Court. The Court decisions in these two were awaited by franchisors with the hope that they would produce guidelines of legality for restrictions vertically imposed by franchisors on their franchisees. The hope was not realized. In *Schwinn,* the Court sustained the validity of marketing practices used by Schwinn for all but about 15 percent of its sales, but invalidated a number of practices in language difficult to use as a guideline for the future. In *Sealy,* the Court characterized the franchise system as horizontal in effect, and ruled that territorial restrictions on Sealy franchisees were one element of the aggregation of trade restraints of which price fixing was the primary evil. Therefore, the package of restraints were *per se* illegal.

The Schwinn Case[4]

Arnold, Schwinn & Company is a family-owned business manufacturing bicycles and a limited number of parts and accessories. Over the years, Schwinn's distribution system has included every possible way of getting a bicycle to the consumer, including private brand sales through Montgomery Ward and Sears, Roebuck, and direct sales to the street corner bicycle servicing dealer.[5]

The company developed the Schwinn Plan method of marketing during the mid-1930s. Under the plan a jobber or distributor serving a geographic area extended to the retailer the option of buying bicycles directly from the factory. The jobber then forwarded the order, as a sales representative, to the factory. Schwinn shipped directly to the retailer, and performed the billing, credit, and collection functions. It then paid a commission on the sale to the jobber, equal to the difference between the jobber's cost and the Schwinn Plan price of the bicycle. Over 75 percent of all Schwinn bicycles were sold under this plan.

The salesman could also represent the jobber and sell directly from the jobber's warehouse, but at prices higher than Schwinn Plan prices since one more handling of the product was required. Most bicycle dealers purchased their basic inventory from Schwinn under the plan, and their fill-in needs from the jobber's warehouse stock, or occasionally from other dealers.

Also in the 1930s, Schwinn began to consign bicycles to some under-capitalized jobbers to enable them to carry a broader inventory. Schwinn shipped the bicycles to the jobber's warehouse, financed them, and insured them. When the jobber shipped the goods to the dealer, he remitted the jobber price of the bicycles to Schwinn. Title did not pass until Schwinn was paid. Under a variation of consignment used with three jobbers, Schwinn established the jobbers as agents. Under this arrangement, the jobber shipped the goods to the dealer, and billed the dealer on a Schwinn invoice, at Schwinn's warehouse price.

After World War II, Schwinn began a study of alternative means of bicycle distribution. In 1951, Schwinn learned that 94 percent of its sales were coming from only 27 percent of its retail dealers, while the remaining 73 percent of dealers were selling only 6 percent of its bicycles. In addition, as many as 84 percent of the 15,000 dealers on Schwinn's direct mailing list had been inactive during the previous year. Thus, more than three-quarters of the money Schwinn spent on direct advertising and promotion was being misdirected, and a large number of sales that might have been made if that money were spent on retail accounts with large sales potentials was being lost.

The findings led to the first Schwinn retail franchise program in 1952. Schwinn offered to establish franchises with substantial market potentials, and to use a selective franchise system rather than selling to all dealers on an indiscriminate basis as had been done in the past. Each franchisee agreed in turn to maintain a minimum average monthly sales volume of Schwinn bicycles, to identify their outlet with a standardized Schwinn sign and dealer decals, and "to display on the dealer's floor at all times (with position equal to and as prominent as that of any competitive bicycles) not less than six new models of Schwinn bicycles." This clause had significance in the Supreme Court decision, as it indicated that Schwinn was not insisting upon exclusive representation.

In operating its franchise system, Schwinn alone determined whether a franchise should be granted in the first instance, and whether it should be renewed or revoked. During the trial Schwinn presented proof of good business reason for 7,018 franchise cancellations and 2,202 franchise refusals. Both the District Court and the Supreme Court accepted this justification by refusing to find that Schwinn had used franchise refusals or terminations as a means of price fixing.

In an informal type of franchising program, Schwinn also began to reduce the large number of jobbers to whom it sold bicycles, with the intention of concentrating on distributors who specialized in bicycles. From 1952 to 1964, Schwinn reduced its number of distributors from 200 heterogenous types to 22 single-purpose bicycle distributors.

The results of Schwinn's selective retail distribution and franchising program were dramatic. In 1951, Schwinn had 8,669 active dealers who sold 144,000 bicycles. In 1962, it had 5,540 franchised dealers who sold 469,000 bicycles. Thus, a 36 percent reduction in the number of retail dealers coincided with a 225 percent increase in Schwinn sales. There was an accompanying increase both in the number of large dealers (selling over 50 Schwinn bicycles a year), and in the average number of Schwinn bicycles sold per franchised dealer, indicating that franchisees had more incentive to stock, promote, and advertise the Schwinn line. Further, this success was accomplished during a period in which the share of market held by extemely low-priced imported bicycles increased from 8.5 percent to 29.7 percent, the number of domestic producers fell from approximately 40 to 12, and all domestic manufacturers except Schwinn were reduced to selling primarily under private labels to nationwide chains and mass merchandisers with integrated wholesale and retail distribution.[6] Even so, while in 1951 Schwinn had the largest share of the United States bicycle market with 22.5 percent, by 1961 it had fallen to second with a market share of 12.8 percent. The decline resulted both from the increase in imports, and the growing market share taken by the Murray Ohio Company, the largest of the private label manufacturers.

The government, after a grand jury investigation, filed a civil suit against Schwinn in 1958, alleging that everything Schwinn did was illegal *per se* under one of three headings: price fixing, through the manipulation of franchise cancellations; boycott, through the reasoning that Schwinn and its distributors, in selling only to franchised dealers, thereby boycotted nonfranchised dealers; and territorial allocation, where Schwinn's restriction of its bicycle distributors to confine their sales to stated areas was viewed as a horizontal division of markets. Judge Perry found no illegal price fixing and no boycott, and confined his market allocation finding to a narrow territory change in Illinois and Indiana, from which decision Schwinn did not appeal. The government appealed, conceding in oral argument that it was no longer presenting a *per se* theory. (Schwinn provides an extreme example of the time lag and expense involved in a modern antitrust defense. The investigation, trial, and appeals extended over a decade, sent a 22,000-page record to the Supreme Court, and cost the family-owned company an estimated $1 million.)

On all factual issues, Schwinn's version of the case was accepted by the Court; the decision was not based on any disputed question of fact. In addition, the Court emphasized the following points:

1. The Schwinn franchise program was motivated by competition, and went no further than required by competitive pressures. However, the Court rejected a defense argument that Schwinn had adopted the challenged practices to enable it and its independent franchisees to compete more effectively with giants like Montgomery Ward and Sears, Roebuck;
2. Schwinn acted independently and not in agreement with competitors, jobbers, or franchisees. All Justices agreed that the Schwinn territorial arrangements were vertical and not horizontal in nature;
3. There was no evidence of price fixing, and the product market was not monopolized, since competitive brands interchangeable with Schwinn were freely available both to distributors and to retailers. Further, Schwinn jobbers and franchisees were free to carry other makes of bicycles and to special order unstocked makes for customers;
4. The company itself was not the largest domestic bicycle manufacturer, and its market share had been falling over a ten-year period. It was also pointed out that Schwinn was neither a failing company, nor a newcomer seeking to break into or remain in the bicycle business.

In spite of these facts, the Court upheld the District Court finding that "where a manufacturer sells products to its distributors subject to territorial restrictions upon resale, a *per se* violation of the Sherman Act results." The same *per se* illegality was found to apply "to restrictions of outlets with which distributors may deal and to restraints upon retailers to whom the goods are sold."

The Court did not find all vertical territorial restrictions to be *per se* illegal. In the case of agency or consignment sales, where title and risk of loss remain with the franchisor, the validity of these restrictions is subject to test under the rule of reason—and Schwinn's restrictions were found to be eminently reasonable. The test requires that the program be clearly vertical and not horizontal, that there be nonpredatory motives and sound business purposes underlying the program, that there be adequate interbrand competition, that dealers be free to handle competing products, and that there be no element of price fixing involved.[7]

Schwinn seemed to say that separate standards would be applied in judging the legality of sales on the one hand, and of alternative methods of distribution on the other. A franchisor cannot limit either the territory or the customers of his franchisees for those products which the franchisee *purchases.* The franchisor can restrict territories and customers if he retains title and risk, and if the effect is not unreasonably restrictive of competition.

Thus the Court overruled, at least in part, two recent decisions. First, *White Motor,* where it said that it did not know enough "of the business stuff out of which these [vertical] arrangements emerge," and second, in emphasizing the form of the transaction, it ignored its 1964 ruling in *Simpson* v. *Union Oil,* where it pointed out that antitrust considerations depended on the substance and not the form of the transaction.[8]

The interpretation of the Court's decision is far from universal. Betty Bock, Manager of the Antitrust Department of the National Industrial Conference Board, interprets the approach to mean that:

... the Court held squarely that intrabrand competition is not necessarily required under the Sherman Act and that where the imperatives of active interbrand competition conflict with abstract sentiment in favor of intrabrand competition, the former can prevail.[9]

Some antitrust specialists have suggested that if the Court really intended to declare vertical territorial and customer restrictions *per se* illegal where title to the product passes, in the sense that no inquiry into their competitive impact is permitted, its opinion would not have suggested exceptions such as failing companies and new entrants, or stressed the elements justifying the restrictions permitted with respect to consignment sales. Thus, it can be argued that what the Court has done is enunciated a modified *per se* (or modified rule of reason) doctrine which signifies only that the franchisor's burden of justification for restrictions will be greater in the future.

Whatever the interpretation of the *per se* status enunciated in *Schwinn,* the Court did leave unanswered some important questions. Having held that restrictions on the outlets with which franchisees may deal are illegal when the goods are sold, what did the Court mean when it mentioned "... the unusual method which may be permissible in an appropriate and impelling competitive setting . . ."? What is left of the newcomer or failing company defenses established in *White Motor*? What is the status of area of prime responsibility clauses, profit passovers, location clauses, and similar devices that do not expressly bar interterritorial sales or prevent sales to specified classes of customers? What comfort can a franchisor take from the government's assurance that "A decision holding illegal Schwinn's restriction on the resale of its products will have no effect on most forms of 'franchising' "?

In referring to the rule of reason evaluation in Schwinn the Court stressed that, in order for restrictions to be justified by a consignment arrangement, the dealers' functions were to be indistinguishable from those of an agent or salesman of the manufacturer. This suggests that a switching of labels or of the place of passage of title will not suffice to invoke rule of reason treatment. Will a franchisor-franchisee relationship where the latter makes decisions on the sale of products which reflect goals different from those of the franchisor allow a consignment to remain legitimate? Or, must the consignee's function be close to that of a mere salesman for the law to tolerate producer-imposed territorial restrictions? The former situation would require little change in existing franchising; the latter would drastically change existing relationships.

The Sealy Case[10]

Sealy, Inc., is the owner of trademarks for Sealy-branded bedding. For 40 years Sealy and its predecessors have been engaged in licensing and franchising manufacturers of mattresses and bedding products to make and sell such products under the Sealy tradename and trademark. Sealy also provides technical and managerial services to its franchisees, conducts advertising and other promotional programs, and engages in technical research and quality control activities.[11] The *Sealy* case is significant because the company's operation is representative of the whole trademark licensor association — association member systems type of franchising. A ruling on the legality of Sealy's operation would appear to apply equally to all franchise systems in the mattress, bread, milk, and perhaps other industries.

In its franchise contract, Sealy promised each franchisee not to license any other person to manufacture or sell in the designated area, and the franchisee agreed not to manufacture or sell Sealy products outside the area. The manufacturer-franchisee could, however, make and sell his private label bedding products anywhere he might choose.

In an ownership sense, Sealy and similar firms in the bedding industry are joint ventures of competitors. There are about 30 Sealy franchisees, and they own (disproportionately) most of its stock. Each member of the Sealy Board of Directors is a franchisee-stockholder or a franchisee-stockholder's nominee. Between board meetings, the company is run by an executive committee composed of Sealy's president and five franchisees. Control is thus exercised by the franchisee-stockholders in the day-to-day business of the company, including the grant, assignment, reassignment, and termination of exclusive territorial franchises.

The Justice Department initiated its attack on the Sealy type of franchise system in May 1960, filing complaints against Spring-Air Company, Restonic Corp., Serta Associates, Inc., and Sealy.[12] The complaints alleged price fixing and territorial allocation in violation of Section

1 of the Sherman Act. Spring-Air and Restonic signed consent judgements which disallowed resale price controls and territorial allocations. The *Serta* case was postponed pending a decision in *Sealy*.

The Court's decision was that because the franchisees controlled Sealy, the restrictions imposed were really horizontal and not vertical in nature and thus the company was in violation of Section 1.[c] The existence of price fixing nullified Sealy's arguments for the need to protect its trademark, and led the Court to refuse to consider arguments on the business or economic justification, or on the reasonableness of the controls involved.

The Court thus extended the *per se* rule in the area of territorial restraints. Prior *per se* cases had involved arrangements far more obviously horizontal in origin and far more anticompetitive in effect than were Sealy's. In showing no sympathy for the problems involved in a trademark franchising system, and in focusing its attention on the ownership of Sealy, the Court may have greatly weakened the trademark franchise as a means of distributing trademarked products. Uncertainty about the full meaning of the decision exists because the Court did not answer the question of what would have happened had market division not been part of an aggregation of trade restraints which included price fixing. The Court thus seems to have reserved opinion on the legality of use by small businessmen of a territorial allocation which is not vertical in nature, which is incidental to use of a joint trade name and common advertising plan, and which does not include price fixing.

Business Justification for the Use of
Territorial and Customer
Arrangements

As was true with tying, the quality of business justification of territorial and customer arrangements put before the courts has been superficial. There are three principal improvements in the efficacy of marketing which are claimed to arise from these arrangements.

First, the protection of profit margins from the incursions of intrabrand competition is claimed to be necessary to attract new franchisees, or to enable them to promote and distinguish a new product. Second, the limitations are said to assure the depth exploitation of a franchisee's territory by preventing his skimming the cream of another franchisee's low-cost

---

[c]To the argument that the restrictions were horizontal rather than vertical, Sealy asserted that "the stockholders and directors wore a 'Sealy hat' when they were acting on behalf of [the franchisor] Sealy." The Court replied: "We seek the central substance of the situation, not its periphery; and in this pursuit, we are moved by the identity of the persons who act, rather than the label of their hats."

sales. Third, the limitations are said to allow orderly marketing, and to prevent several specific cases of what is referred to as disorderly marketing. It will be shown that only one of these, the new franchisees case, merits much attention.

The 'Attracting New Franchisees' Defense

It is asserted that, without the promise of protection from intrabrand competition, some new or competitively weak franchisors would be unable to induce franchisees to make any appreciable investment in order to handle their products. The franchisee may be required to make heavy initial promotional expenditures to persuade consumers to try the product, and he will not make these expenditures unless he has some prospect of recovery through subsequent sales. He could not recoup his initial expenditures if new members of the franchise system, without the burden of start-up costs, were free to come in at correspondingly lower prices as soon as a demand had been created. Also, investments in a new franchise are associated with relatively high degrees of risk, and it is reasonable to think that territorial or customer restrictions may be necessary in some cases to mitigate this risk.

The justification for such territorial or customer restrictions could exist for only a limited period of time. Economic analysis recognizes no advantage to competition in shielding a weak firm from competitive pressures over the long run. While the numbers of firms and the industry structure are considered as indicative of probable competitive behavior in the market, it would be reversing the analysis to allow weak firms to restrict intrabrand competition to keep their dealers—and thus weaken competition—simply to increase the number of firms in the market.

Related to the new franchisees defense is the contention that a franchisor should be permitted to restrict intrabrand competition with the expectation that the higher prices his franchisees can obtain will be used by them for promotional expenditures—and thus will increase interbrand competition.[d] If valid at all, this justification also is subject to a time constraint. Economists are in general agreement that the resulting product

---

[d] Stone comments: "The increased prices which closed territories would thus seem to effect are not even apt to be offset by competitively desirable increases in output . . . in holding out closed territories as an inducement for distributors to handle his brand, a manufacturer is, in effect, attracting their efforts away, if not from the disposal of a more competitively distributed brand of the same product, from some other sector of the economy. In fact, the very reason for which the promise of closed territories facilitates the entries of some firms may make them retard entry, tying up the allegiances of available outlets so as to bar still other potential entrants unless they, too, are prepared to respond with closed territories . . . If a product (or an industry) is such that distribution capital cannot be retained without allowing a division of territories . . . the same investment could be better employed elsewhere, where current prices are high enough to signal entry on a more competitive basis."[13]

108

differentiation creates the most significant barrier to entry of new competitors, since the long-term promotion of established brands can be overcome by a newcomer only at great expense.

The 'Market Skimming' Defense

Franchisees often argue that they should be protected from the threat of another franchisee skimming the cream off their market. The cream refers to those customers who buy in substantial quantity, entail little selling cost, and/or are loyal and consistent in their purchasing behavior. These accounts are said to be of crucial importance to the local franchisee, enabling him to make enough profit to promote the franchised good to more difficult or less profitable accounts. The franchisee wants territorial protection to guarantee these easy, high profit sales. The franchisor may want to remove the incentive for an invading franchisee to skim the cream off contiguous territories rather than cultivating the less profitable accounts in his own area.

On first exposure, the idea of skimming the cream sounds unfair, but from the standpoint of economic analysis it is without substance. A franchisee can skim the cream from an adjoining market only if the dealer there is charging a higher-than-competitive price. High margins on sales to the cream accounts may simply reflect lower selling costs. In a competitive environment, the price to these accounts would be lower. Increased intrabrand competition would have the effect of reducing the price on cream sales. Each franchisee would still enjoy some locational advantage in selling to those customers in close geographical proximity to him. If he is still undersold by neighboring franchisees, and if he cannot survive on the remaining business, little competitive or economic interest is served by allowing him to remain in the market.

The 'Orderly Marketing' Defense

In recent years a number of specific cases of so-called disorderly marketing, which are allegedly correctable by territorial restrictions, have been put forth. Perhaps the best known case is that which I shall call the Coca-Cola problem.

The Coca-Cola problem arises with national manufacturers of beverage syrups such as Coca-Cola, Pepsi-Cola, and Seven-Up—and to a lesser extent with beer distributors. A typical six and one-half or seven ounce soft drink returnable bottle costs the franchised bottler about nine cents to buy, but is normally put in circulation for a deposit of two or three cents. The arrangement is economically viable because the bottle makes from 16 to 30 round trips before it is lost, broken, or destroyed. Soft drink franchisors argue that if their franchised bottlers were not restricted to well-defined sales territories, bottle raiding might take place; one franchisee might arrive at the store of a regular customer and find that a competitor had made the sale and had taken away his empty bottles. Such a system is disorderly, and it might lead to the failure of those franchisees who consistently lose bottles.

The solution, however, is much simpler than the closing of sales territories; simply raise the bottle deposit to the value of the bottle. This change may decrease sales to ultimate consumers who do not want to tie up more money in bottle deposits, but it may also reduce the absolute price maintenance that now exists in the carbonated beverage industry in the absence of intrabrand competition. (More likely, it may increase the sale of soft drinks in disposable, nondeposit containers as opposed to sales in returnable, deposit containers.)

Another situation of disorderly marketing arises in the drug industry, where manufacturers have cited their need for territorial restrictions to facilitate the tracing of defective goods that might lead to civil or criminal liability on the part of the drug manufacturer. The manufacturer may discover that a batch of drugs already shipped to distributors has lost its potency or contains impurities. The manufacturer knows which wholesaler received the batch, but the wholesaler does not keep records of which retailers might have received the defective goods. It is argued that if the wholesaler were restricted to distribution in a given territory, the list of retailers to be checked would be shortened, and the chances of speedy recovery of the goods would be improved.

Again, there exists a solution much less restrictive than the imposition of closed territories; simply require wholesalers handling drugs which are potentially dangerous to keep a record of the batch numbers of goods shipped to each retailer. This recording process may add a small increment to the cost of the affected goods, but the result is much less injurious than the potential for overpricing which exists where intrabrand competition is eliminated.

Another situation arises where a franchisor has a marketing plan which requires, as did Schwinn, that franchisees sell only to approved retailers and/or to ultimate consumers. Such restrictions are designed to keep the franchised product out of the hands of outlets which are deemed undesirable because of certain selling practices, in particular their propensity to cut price. In spite of the fact that they maximize sales volume in the short run, price cutters are said to harm the prestige and goodwill of the franchisor. Franchisors claim that discounters by reducing the resale profit margin may cause other outlets to abandon sale of the good, allowing the discount houses to raise their prices. Franchisors also point out that discount houses are not always equipped to provide servicing to more complex goods, and that if traditional outlets are driven out by discounters, the franchisor would have to establish vertically integrated servicing centers. However, the possibility always exists for a franchisor to include the cost of servicing in the initial price of the franchised good, and to rebate the servicing allowance to those franchisees (or others) who actually carry out the activity.

Economic Explanations for the Use of Territorial and Customer Arrangements

The economic literature dealing with the impact of territorial and customer restrictions in spatial markets is quite extensive,[14] but virtually all the models presented are dependent upon highly restrictive sets of assumptions. The relaxation of these to approximate the real world typically renders the analysis either trivial, or so complex as to be unmanageable.

Lee E. Preston has presented one model which is useful for purposes of illustration. He has produced an abstract model of a spatial market and examined the impact of restrictive practices on this market under specified conditions.[15]

Preston shows that, under one set of assumptions, territorial and customer arrangements can have the procompetitive effect of extending market access by assisting franchisors to find new franchisees, and can increase exposure of the franchised product by limiting each franchisee to a minimum feasible size and increasing the number of franchised outlets. The restrictions may also have implications in motivating franchisees to increase their depth coverage of narrowly defined markets rather than skimming customers over a wider geographic area.

As the framework of his model, Preston has a single franchisor and single-product franchisees marketing to potential customers under the following assumptions:

1. A set of potential market locations is evenly distributed along a line in space. Potential customers with varying sales likelihoods are located evenly along this line. The size distribution of customers is the same at each location.[e]
2. To establish a franchise requires a given amount of capital investment. The criterion used by franchisees in making this investment is whether they can attain a required net rate of return on invested capital.

---

[e] Preston's analysis treats only the territorial case. To interpret the model in the customer case (for example, restricting the franchisee to sales in one industry), consider each location as a different class of customer, with physical proximity of locations analogous to the similarity of product requirements and distribution channels between customer classes.

The spatial market is made linear rather than circular to simplify the argument, and to illustrate the concept of market depth using only two-dimensional space. The limits of the market may be interpreted as a vertical cross-section of a three-dimensional cone.

3. Franchisees encounter three types of variable cost: (a) the cost of merchandise for resale, which is constant per unit of product; (b) the cost of customer contact, which is constant per unit of distance between franchisee and customer; and (c) the cost of finalizing a transaction, which is constant per customer.

Given this cost structure, the profitability of franchisee sales to a customer in one location is directly proportional to customer size. The franchisee will contact potential customers at that location beginning with the largest and continuing down the size categories until he reaches that customer for whom the difference between revenue and merchandise cost is just equal to transaction cost.

The profitability of franchisee sales to customers of a given size is inversely proportional to the distance between franchisee and customer. The franchisee will extend his market coverage spatially to customers at other locations until (rising) contact costs equal revenue, less merchandise cost, less transaction cost. These two criteria define the intensive and extensive boundaries of the franchisee's market, and this market contains all potential customers for whom the difference between revenue and merchandise cost equals or exceeds the sum of transaction and contact costs. A graphic representation of such a spatial market is shown in Figure 7–1. For a franchisee at location *m*, the gross margin, contact costs, and transaction cost determine the spatial limits of the market at *i* and *q*, where only customers of size 100 will be served, and the depth of the market in terms of potential customer size, for example size 25 at *m*.

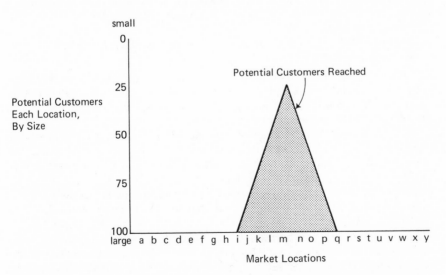

Figure 7–1. The Extent of a Franchisee Market by Spatial Span and Customer Depth.

If the return on capital attainable by the franchisee from one optimal size market is greater than that attainable from an alternative investment, then with unrestricted entry further franchisees will appear. So long as part of the spatial market remains uncovered, each will select a location such that his span does not overlap an existing franchisee. The resulting pattern of market coverage is shown in Figure 7–2. Even with unrestricted entry, it can be seen that a large number of potential customers will still not be reached by any franchisee.

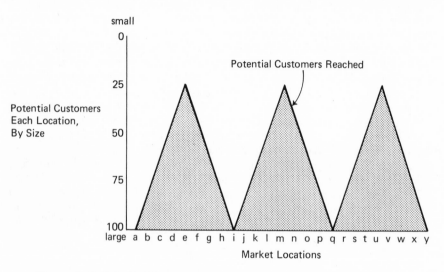

Figure 7–2. Market Coverage by Noncompetitive Franchisees.

If franchisees are still earning a greater return on capital than is attainable from an alternative investment, additional franchisees will attempt to enter the market. The franchisor will encourage new entry if he feels the result will be increased market coverage.

However, new franchisees will now include in their markets customers already served by existing optimal size franchisees. This results in a beginning of intrabrand competition, and a reduction in the size and profitability of individual franchisees. Competition for customers may take the form of price reductions or increased promotion, but either will reduce the level of franchisee profits below that level attainable without intrabrand competition. If price reductions are market-wide, the depth coverage of the market will be reduced because of lower net profits available from sales to smaller size customers. Even in the case of selective price reductions or selective selling cost increases, the profitability of any given volume of franchisee sales will be reduced, and the result will be the same. The final spatial span-number of franchisees balance will depend on the level of required investment and the shape of the relevant cost curves.

For the franchisor, this means that with intrabrand competition, the number of franchisees may stabilize to produce a lower level of market coverage than could be attained through the use of territorial or customer restrictions. The franchisor may increase his total sales through the use of such restrictions as compared with permitting intrabrand competition between franchisees. In a market corresponding to Preston's model, a franchisor might restrict the territory or customers served by his franchisees such that they would earn a normal return on investment while attaining levels of market coverage and a sales volume that serve the good business purpose of maximizing the franchisor's profits. The resulting pattern of franchisee market coverage is shown in Figure 7–3.

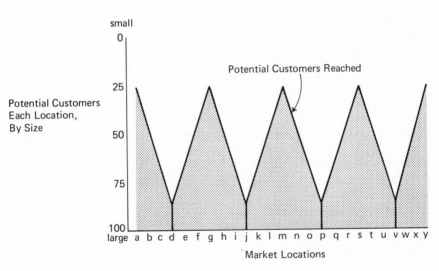

Figure 7–3. Market Coverage by Franchisees with Territorial Restrictions.

The presence or absence of competitive distributors in the market has no impact on the model. If the customers are rational, their selection of one good reflects their preference for it over available alternatives, including the alternative of saving their money in the absence of other viable alternatives.

The model shows territorial and customer restrictions having implications for the procompetitive objectives of extending market access by making it easier for franchisors to obtain new franchisees, increasing exposure of the franchised product to potential customers, and motivating franchisees to increase their depth coverage of narrowly defined markets rather than skimming customers over a wider geographic area.

The model also shows that the welfare of final customers is not clearly improved by a prohibition of restrictions on intrabrand competition. The gains to those customers attaining price reductions or service improvement must be weighed against the loss of market alternatives by those customers desirous of purchasing but shifted beyond the franchise break-even point by changes in franchisee net profits. Even where these customers are reached by suppliers of similar products, Preston points out that the provision of an additional market alternative cannot be dismissed as having negligible importance. Since the maximization of the number of outlets will involve a higher average retail price, some consumers must certainly be worse off. A maximum number of outlets may also involve an overcommitment of resources to distribution.

As suggested earlier, the conclusions of the Preston model, and of similar spatial models, are dependent on one highly restrictive assumption made to simplify the analysis. This is not, as might be assumed, the distribution of market locations, or the variable cost structure of each franchisee, but rather the seemingly innocuous assumption that each franchise, regardless of capacity or location, requires a single amount of capital investment. As Preston recognized, if this assumption is relaxed to permit a continuum of franchisee sizes (and investments) capable of serving viable optimum markets, then the spatial span-number of franchisees result disappears,[f] the procompetitive effects of territorial restrictions do not hold under all cost assumptions, and the analysis becomes sufficiently complex that required assumptions of linearity at several important steps reduce the return from the model to a simple display of analytical elegance. A good example of such assumptions is found in the article by Mills and Lav, mentioned earlier.

A more elegant and detailed treatment of the market location problem, placed in the context of product differentiation and starting with the classic Hotelling argument, has been formulated by Michael Lovell of Wesleyan University.[17] Lovell discusses a wide range of situations, for example the case where a franchisee is faced with territorial restrictions but in the absence of resale price maintenance; and the case where there is potential entry of rival franchisees, and the franchisor must develop a market strategy intended to forestall such competitive entry.

The Criteria of Least Necessary Restraint Applied

The quality control/goodwill and lowered barriers to entry cases introduced in the last chapter are probably not relevant to the discussion of

---

[f] Even so, free entry with variable franchisee size will not necessarily fill the market space.[16]

territorial and customer restrictions. One might defend a franchisor's attempt to keep the franchised product out of the hands of discount or similar outlets in terms of quality control/goodwill, but even here it is clear that the franchisor's objective would be equally served by imposing a restriction on sale to an identified account, to unauthorized outlets, or to one classification of customer, each of which is a least restraint alternative to the imposition of a closed territory.

The newcomer/infant industry case is very relevant to the discussion of territorial and customer restrictions, and it is presented below. In addition a further concept, the failing company case, is introduced.

The Newcomer/Infant Industry Case

It has been established that a potential franchisee may be willing to risk capital to introduce a new product (or an old product into a new market) only if he can be given some assurance of obtaining sufficient future returns to cover his initial set-up and promotion expenditures. This may require protection against other franchisees taking advantage of his promotional expenditures to enter the territory and undersell him.

Thus, at the time of entry when a newcomer is at a disadvantage not related to his economic efficiency or future potentials, protection from intrabrand competition may be merited. Through the imposition of closed territories, a small franchisor may thus be able to command sufficient franchisee efforts to challenge the market position of established firms and to precipitate price competition in an oligopolistic industry. The intrabrand competition which society foregoes may be more than offset by increased interbrand competition in the market for the good.

As the previous chapter pointed out, the relevant question is not simply whether some procompetitive result arises from the imposition of a restraint, but whether a given restraint is more severe than is necessary to achieve the business purpose which it is claimed to serve. Given the assumption that it is procompetitive to stimulate new businesses and product or service innovations by keeping entry barriers at low levels, it is also necessary to consider the alternatives to closed territories that might be available to the newcomer franchisor.

The most obvious alternative would be for the franchisor to integrate forward into the franchisee phase of his own business. If such integration were carried out through internal expansion rather than through acquisition there would be no antitrust problems unless the company came within the monopoly restriction of Section 2 of the Sherman Act. However, there are numerous managerial difficulties created in areas such as taxation, and increased management supervision. Also, vertical integration on a large scale is such an extreme undertaking that most franchisors, and certainly most market newcomers, could not afford it. (For new products, the initiator may be forced into vertical integration, at least long enough to demonstrate the saleability of the product. With this evidence, he can obtain franchisees or other dealers and expand his distribution system with low capital outlay.)

Following the decision in *Schwinn,* the franchisor also has the alternative of setting up agency or consignment arrangements with his franchisees, and then imposing territorial restrictions on the agents. According to *Schwinn* and the earlier *General Electric* case,[18] this would probably remove the danger of an antitrust violation, but it would impose stringent conditions that must be met to ensure that a true agency relationship existed between franchisor and franchisee. As Charles E. Stewart, Jr., has pointed out, citing the General Electric decision:

Extremely important to the validity of the agency agreement is the retention by the supplier of title to the product. In this respect, mere designation of title is not enough. The economic burdens of ownership must remain on the supplier. For example, payment by the supplier of casualty insurance premiums and property taxes on the goods; payment by the agent to the supplier for the goods only after sale to the ultimate consumer; the right of the distributor to return unsold goods; shipment by the supplier of goods sold by the agent directly to the purchaser; and the absence of competition between agent and principal; all point toward a true agency relationship. On the other hand, failure to police agents properly; failure of the agent to account to the principal for its products; and payment by the agent for the product prior to delivery to the ultimate consumer may give an argument that no true agency agreement exists.[19]

Use of an agency method of distribution thus shifts to the franchisor very substantial economic burdens, including the entire cost of maintaining inventory, and substantial accounting costs. This may prove an unacceptable burden, especially for the newcomer franchisor.

An alternative which tempers the conflict between the franchisor's good business purpose and the public's desire for intrabrand competition is the franchisor's use of an area of prime responsibility agreement rather than a closed territorial agreement. There are two major disadvantages in creating areas of prime responsibility. The first is that it tends to give an advantage to those franchisees who can meet their quotas easily, or who were franchised first and have had a longer period of time in which to develop their own territories. In either situation the franchisor cannot complain if the franchisee sells in adjacent territories, including those of newcomer franchisees.

The second disadvantage arises in enforcement if a franchisee violates the prime responsibility clause by selling beyond his territory when he has failed to meet his own territorial quota. It is clear under the Colgate doctrine and under the consent decrees which the Government has allowed, that if a franchisee does violate a prime responsibility clause, the franchisor's only recourse is to discontinue the franchise. The franchisor may not cut off the franchisee and then reinstate him after a pledge of compliance, nor may he simply warn him. The action must be unilateral and final. If surveillance is necessary to implement the clause, the franchisor must do it himself without any prompting or assistance from other franchisees. A violation of any of these conditions goes beyond a mere refusal to deal, and may result in an agreement which is in violation of the Sherman Act.

These two disadvantages may be more than enough to deter the small franchisor, or the newcomer franchisor, from the use of a prime responsibility clause. If they do not, then prime responsibility can be a convenient means for a franchisor to evade the current uncertain legal status of territorial arrangements.

One further alternative exists for the franchisor who wishes to restrict cross-selling without using the threat of franchisee termination. The franchisor may require the cross-selling franchisee to pay a high proportion of his profit on the sale to the franchisee in whose territory the sale was made. The passover payment could be made equal to the entire gross profit on the transaction, with a decreasing percentage as the newcomer franchisee becomes better established. In contrast to the case where termination is threatened, the selling franchisee has the option of deciding whether a particular sale is of sufficient importance to warrant making it at no profit, or at a slight loss. For example, he might be induced to make such a sale where the purchaser is a chain of retail outlets, most of which were in the selling franchisee's own territory. The newcomer franchisee initially receives a windfall return, but this would decrease in time to zero (or to the cost of local servicing of the account) as he becomes established in the market. The procedure is feasible, although accounting for the various passovers might become onerous in some types of franchise systems.

Overall, a strong argument can be presented that the problems of a newcomer franchisee in gaining a market foothold justify a temporary tolerance of territorial or customer arrangements to encourage him to make the necessary investments in equipment and promotion. The protection from intrabrand competition should not extend for a period longer than necessary to recoup initial expenses. The franchisee who cannot operate without protection after a relatively short period of time should not be preserved through artificial restrictions.

The Failing Company Case

The idea of a failing company case suggests the premise that territorial restrictions might be justifiable where they are the only method by which a weak firm can obtain dealers. The argument is immediately suspect. First, it is improbable that such situations occur very frequently. Second, while it is good economic policy to foster new entry, it is in most cases certainly not good policy to provide artificial support for those firms that have run the competitive race and have been fairly beaten.

In the absence of recourse to closed territories, there nevertheless do exist situations in which a franchisor who should be preserved in the marketplace is unable to attract or to retain franchisees to keep his product in competition. In this regard, the facts surrounding the *Sandura* case[20] are particularly interesting and illustrate the kinds of circumstances that might justify a failing company defense to territorial or customer arrangements.

The Sandura Case. In 1947–48, the Sandura Company developed a new process for manufacturing vinyl plastic floor covering which produced a significantly better product than those available in the industry at the time. The new covering was marketed under the trade name "Sandran."

The hard surface floor covering industry in which Sandura competed included products from inexpensive enamel surface, feltbase floor coverings to expensive rubber tile and high-grade vinyls. Soft surface floor coverings were also regarded by consumers as substitutes for Sandran in some cases. Sandura was the twenty-first largest firm in the industry, with a share of market that ranged from 1.1 percent in 1954 to 4.8 percent in 1958. The hard surface floor covering industry was dominated by three large integrated firms, Congoleum-Nairn, Pabco, and Armstrong Cork, which among them owned 80 percent of the industry's assets in 1958. The court cited Sandura as owning 1.5 percent of the industry's assets in the same year.[21] Thus, Sandura was not a major competitive force in its industry, and there was no danger of it monopolizing any portion of its market.

Sandran was introduced in 1949, with Sandura expecting a strong consumer demand for the new product. Initial acceptance was good, but within a year it was discovered that Sandran had two serious technical defects. One was that it turned yellow under heavy usage. A more serious defect was its tendency to delaminate between the paper and the felt backing, with the result that the paper would slide along the backing. Researchers discovered that this cold flow could be remedied by switching from an asphalt adhesive to a rubber one, but immediately after the changeover in 1951 rubber was rationed as a result of the Korean War. A substitute adhesive was found, but it tended to crystallize on aging, with the result that after Sandran had been used for six to eight months there was a complete separation of layers.

Both defects were remedied by 1953, but only after a period of extreme customer and dealer dissatisfaction that saw the company lose half of its sales volume over the three-year period. Sandura's sales from 1950 through 1955 show the response to its product difficulties.

1950 (Sandran introduction completed)	$7,126,000
1951 (Yellowing problem cured)	4,427,000
1952 (Cold flow problem serious)	5,353,000
1953 (Cold flow problem remedied)	3,842,000
1954 (Dealer reorganization undertaken)	3,557,000
1955 (Distributorships begin to be closed)	4,763,000

In 1954 and 1955, Sandura was unable either to meet bank overdraft payments or to pay raw material suppliers. It was heavily in debt to its distributors as a result of a price reduction in 1954 for which it had contracted to reimburse distributors for price losses on existing inventories. The company was also involved in buying back inventories of defective, unsalable Sandran. In 1955, Sandura described itself as being *de facto* bankrupt, in spite of the fact that it was producing a floor covering that was technically superior to any competing good on the market.

Because of its lack of capital, Sandura had been unable to finance any national advertising from 1951 to 1953. Without capital for either advertising or warehousing, Sandura was unable to consider marketing directly to floor covering retailers. The company's unstable history combined with its lack of national advertising made it unattractive to established wholesalers, who wanted a floor covering with some public acceptance. A further problem was that Sandura produced only two products, while a large company like Armstrong Cork could offer its distributors twelve different products. Sandura's sales manager testified before the F.T.C. that the company had reached a position where "the distributor who could handle our lines and pay his bills, who was a floor covering distributor, knew the market, was not interested in us. We had nothing to offer him that he didn't already have. . . ."

In 1953, Sandura began to change its distribution structure of multiple distributorships in each market by giving franchises to selected retail dealers, and permitting its distributors to resell only to such franchised dealers. In 1955 (at the point of near bankruptcy), Sandura introduced a system of closed territories under which each franchisee was not only the sole outlet in a city, but also the sole outlet in a predetermined territory surrounding it. Under the system of closed territories, Sandura sales rose from $4.7 million in 1955, to $8.7 million in 1956, to $11.8 million in 1957, to $19.6 million in 1958, and to $24.0 million in 1959. Sandura's financial position also improved substantially with the improved sales picture, and it succeeded in developing, with the aid of closed territories, an elaborate and successful system of franchised dealers.

Christopher D. Stone has indicated several reasons why a system of closed territories worked so well for Sandura:

Consider, for example, the position of a distributor who handles Kentile, Pabco, Wilson, and Goodrich floor covering as well as Sandura's. In trying to sell a dealer on one of these brands, the distributor must take into account the fact that making a convincing pitch for one line or another is only half the sale. He may persuade the dealer that Kentile is his best buy, but, even so, he may only be inducing the dealer to hold out for a better offer from a neighboring Kentile distributor. Knowing, however, that Sandura's closed territories preclude a neighboring Sandura distributing rival from taking his sale, the distributor knows that if he "sells" a dealer on Sandran, the account will be his. The distributor is thus encouraged to trade the dealer over towards Sandran rather than towards other goods in his inventory. The concomitant effect, that each distributor may be able to advance the price of Sandran a little above the competitive level, and for this reason dampen output, may be overcome by the impact of expanded sales effort.

A similar argument is claimed by Stone to apply to the dealer, who is freed from having to worry about intrabrand price competition:

Insofar as a dealer has power to influence the purchaser towards one product rather than another, he is not apt to emphasize one brand as his "best buy" if the dealer knows the customer will cross the street in a few minutes and find that "best buy" selling ten cents per yard cheaper, or remember that he saw it advertised for less across town.[22]

A final return to Sandura from closed territories was the increased incentive for distributors to promote Sandran. The company had been able to undertake no advertising at all from 1951 to 1953, and a total of only $24,000 was spent in 1954. By comparison, the average advertising expenditure per distributor for Sandran in 1956 was $28,044. Sandura undoubtedly carried part of the cost of this advertising through a lower manufacturer price than it would have charged had it done its own advertising. But given its extremely low credit rating, the cost to Sandura of closing territories to elicit advertising monies was almost certainly lower than the cost of borrowing money to finance the advertisements itself.

In 1962 Sandura, still with its system of closed territories, was charged by the Federal Trade Commission with violating section 5 of the F.T.C. Act. Sandura argued that its closed territories served a valid business purpose. The F.T.C. examiner agreed that there had been no lessening of competition as a result of the closed territories, but still found the company in violation of section 5. The Commission upheld the decision.

Under the criteria of least necessary force, Sandura was clearly not justified in maintaining closed territories in 1962. It is unlikely that it took Sandura distributors seven years to recoup their investments in facilities and promotion to handle Sandran. Also, less restrictive alternatives to closed territories were available to the company in 1962. It could have combined area of prime responsibility agreements with resale price maintenance, where available, to maintain distributor and franchisee enthusiasm. It could have instituted restrictions on sales to unauthorized accounts, or utilized a hands off period whereby distributors would refrain from selling or soliciting new franchised dealers for a period of time after another distributor had done so. It could have entered into cooperative advertising agreements with its distributors and franchised dealers to retain the level of Sandran advertising and promotion.

A more relevant question is whether, given the facts, Sandura's closed territories should have been legal in 1955, when no less restrictive alternatives were available. All the facts indicate that, had Sandura not been able to close territories after its drastic product failures, the company would have gone out of existence or have been merged into one of its larger competitors. Whatever arguments can be mustered against closed territories, the permanence and inflexibility of a merger makes that more objectionable still. If the Supreme Court is willing to allow a failing firm to enter into an otherwise unacceptable merger, perhaps some option should remain open for a failing firm in an already-concentrated industry to opt for closed territories if it feels that is the only way it can remain as a viable competitor. The closure would, of course, be strictly limited in time.

If the failing company case is permitted, a great many problems are raised. What criteria should permit a company that has run the competitive race and been fairly beaten to invoke contractual restrictions to prolong its business life? Are guidelines possible to allow the enforcement agencies to administer such cases, or must the courts be subject to a rule of reason determination every time a failing company wishes to impose restrictions? Finally, what role does the size of the franchisor, the structure of the industry, and the competitive performance of existing firms play in determining whether the failing company defense may be invoked?

8   Exclusive Franchising and Exclusive Dealing in Franchise Systems

This chapter discusses the two interrelated but separate concepts of exclusive franchising and exclusive dealing in franchise systems. The concepts are quite distinct; exclusive franchising does not require the granting of a reciprocal exclusive dealing arrangement, although the two are often found together.

Exclusive Franchising

As defined earlier, exclusive franchising is an agreement, by a market supplier or franchisor with a franchisee, that he will not sell his product to any other franchisee or user within the first franchisee's territory. Less extreme forms are also commonly found. The franchisor may retain the right to sell directly (but not exclusively) to certain governmental or national accounts. Or, the franchisor may grant exclusivity only for the franchisee's particular type of outlet, reserving the right to sell to other types of retailers or wholesalers within the territory. The franchisor may also agree to appoint no more than a stated number of franchisees per unit of population in a metropolitan area, but make no assurance as to where those franchisees will be located.

Exclusive franchising, while normally thought of as being applied at the retail level, may also be employed at the wholesale level even in those areas where it is not used at retail. This is done in a majority of manufacturer-wholesaler franchise systems. National manufacturers of beverage syrups, including Coca-Cola, Pepsi-Cola, and Seven-Up, offer exclusive franchises to independent bottling companies which in turn service nonexclusive retail and institutional accounts.

Some manufacturers, because of a desire for as broad a geographic coverage as possible, have eliminated exclusives completely. In the automobile tire industry, manufacturers have even denied exclusive franchises to their vertically integrated retail outlets. Other manufacturers have eliminated exclusives at the retail level but have retained them at the wholesale level as a means of obtaining and keeping good distributors.

Many exclusives are limited in duration, the time span depending on the reason for adopting this method of distribution. Commonly, exclusiveness is introductory; that is, limited to a period of one or two years to give the franchisee an opportunity to recoup his initial investment in advertising and sales promotion. At the other extreme, exclusive franchises may run as long as ten years. An example of the latter is the metropolitan outlet having a lease for that period of time on premises that cannot be adapted for other purposes. Another alternative, which is becoming less common for reasons relating to the legal status of the terminated franchisee, is the issuance of a franchise for an indefinite term, making it cancellable on notice and providing that territorial boundaries may be revised at any time. The franchisor generally prefers to keep the term of the exclusive short, so that he may reassess the franchisee's performance at regular intervals.

The Court's Analysis of Exclusive Franchising

The Court has permitted a franchisor to grant the right to use his trade name to whom he pleases, so long as he does not engage in any unfair act, enter into a contract in unreasonable restraint of trade, or seek to monopolize. In the *Schwing* case, the Court held that: "Unless the manufacturer dominates the market, he has a right to give a dealer an actual monopoly, let alone a 'virtual' monopoly, in the sale of his particular make or brand in a particular territory."[1] The franchisor may also assure his franchisee that he has been selected on an exclusive basis, and that he will be supplied as an exclusive outlet.[2]

There is no question that exclusivity is potentially detrimental to competition. When a franchisor appoints an outlet, three forces operate to restrict the price that the franchisee can charge for the franchised good. The first is the possibility of interbrand competition from substitute goods. The second is the possibility of intrabrand competition from other franchisees outside the territory; this is operative only when the franchisee's price rises sufficiently to overcome the transportation and other cost disadvantages (to the seller) of interterritorial competition. The third is the possibility of intrabrand competition from within the territory, either from another franchisee or from the franchisor selling there directly. The possible anticompetitive effect of exclusive franchising arises from its elimination of the last check. (Note that exclusive franchising is less anticompetitive than closed territories, which result in the elimination of the last two checks.) If the franchisee has an entrenched position in the local market because of his location or has the benefits of recognition in the eyes of the actual and potential customers, an exclusive franchise may act to reinforce the monopoly power which already exists.

Business Justification for the Use of Exclusive Franchising

In view of the potential detrimental effect on competition of exclusive franchising, it is useful to inquire whether a franchisor who would go beyond a unilateral decision to practice selective distribution, and bind himself by the promise of an exclusive franchise, has a good business justification for such behavior.

A franchisor can attain several significant economies from a selective (not necessarily exclusive) distribution policy. By restricting the number of buyers, he may reduce his selling and other costs, and by choosing only the most financially solvent dealers, he may minimize his credit risks. A system of large, experienced franchisees is better able to make accurate estimates of future demands for the franchised good—and thus allow the franchisor to better plan his own future production. Also, the franchisor may derive a certain prestige from association with only the best outlet in each territorial market. For a production without a well-known brand name, such an association may be an effective substitute for extensive franchisor advertising.

Richard H. Holton has suggested that the desire for exclusivity might be explained in terms of the franchisor's assessment of the price elasticity of demand for a good relative to the service elasticity. If a franchisor feels that the market is sensitive only to the price of the franchised good, he will desire a maximum number of franchised locations to encourage price competition. If he feels that final demand is more sensitive to service variables such as the franchisee's ability to fill orders out of current inventory, then the franchisor will attempt to maximize his profits by utilizing some form of exclusive franchising.

A franchisor can attain most or all of these economic benefits simply by enforcing a highly selective distribution policy. Why will he go the further step of binding himself not to appoint competing franchisees in each market? The answer most often given by franchisors is that they are required to offer exclusivity in order to obtain high quality franchisees. The franchisor can attain the advantages mentioned without a corresponding drop in franchisee sales only if the limited number of franchisees chosen are well qualified, well financed, well equipped, and aggressive. An increasing number of franchisors compete for such franchisees. Franchisors and other manufacturers claim that it is particularly difficult to avoid granting an exclusive in those cases where the franchised good requires heavy franchisee investment in showroom and servicing facilities, inventory, or personnel training. "One manufacturer currently operating under a consent decree reports that because it interprets the decree as barring exclusives, it is unable to attract satisfactory wholesalers and as a result is reluctantly integrating forward into [the] distribution function."[3] An exclusive franchise may be particularly necessary where the franchisee must erect a building according to blueprints or designs supplied by the franchisor. This arrangement is commonly found with petroleum service stations and food service franchises such as McDonald's Hamburgers. A building which is strongly identified with one franchise prevents the franchisee from selling it easily, or from converting it to alternative uses at reasonable cost. Thus, the franchisee may be locked into the franchise for as long as the franchisor wishes to keep him.

Under some circumstances, the franchisor may grant the franchisee an exclusive selling right in order to extract from him certain contractual undertakings that ensure his satisfactory handling of the franchised good. The franchisee may be required to make a large capital investment in the franchised location in service facilities, equipment, and in maintaining minimum levels of inventory or in retaining a minimum number of maintenance and service employees. The franchisee may also be required to keep his books according to a uniform accounting system, and his selling, servicing, and advertising facilities may be subject to continued scrutiny and change by the franchisor.

A franchisor with sufficient bargaining power may be able to obtain these concessions without granting exclusivity. This is clearly the case with franchising in the automobile industry, where franchisors control the behavior of their dealers in virtually every area of decisionmaking. The need for exclusiveness is thus attributable either to the franchisor's weak market supplier position, or to the franchisee's strong retail market strength. Since a very strong market position may tend to be harmful to competition, it is not clear whether franchisee bargaining power should justify an exclusive franchise. On the other hand, exclusiveness which is needed to overcome supplier weakness may result in increasing competition in that industry in the long run. The difficult analytical problem is to determine when the supplier's weak market position justifies the grant of an exclusive franchise, and when it is in the public interest to retain such a supplier in the market — and for how long.

Virtually all the business justifications put forth by a franchisor to justify his grant of exclusiveness also appear as reasons presented by franchisees for needing it, particularly where the franchisor is introducing a new product without customer acceptance. In return for his efforts in achieving market distribution for the good, the franchisee wants at least a temporary protection from newcomers who might wish to exploit his investment in the new market.

Economic Explanations for the Use of Exclusive Franchising

Given these justifications for the use of exclusive franchising, it is of interest to ask what formal economic analysis has to contribute to defining the conditions under which a franchisor might choose to offer exclusiveness to franchisees operating in separate markets. The question has been considered in some detail by Bedros Pashigian in his study of the distribution of automobiles,[4] and much of the analysis which follows is directly attributable to him. A more formal exposition of the argument is presented in Appendix E.

In a perfect retail market (if one existed), a franchisor would select that number of franchisees which minimize his distribution cost for any given volume of franchise system sales — where each franchisee operates at the minimum point of his long-run average cost curve. New franchises would be granted until competition eliminated the economic profits accruing to each franchisee. Thus, in a perfect retail market there is no reason for a franchisor to want exclusive franchising and the adoption of the practice in a perfect market implies nonprofit maximizing behavior.

In place of a probably nonexistant perfect retail market, assume a large, local market with a number of competing franchisees, each of whom is a differentiated seller (if only by virtue of location), and each of whom thus faces a downward-sloping demand curve.

The demand for the franchised good from the franchisor is a derived demand, being composed of the separate demand curves facing each franchisee. When marginal revenue from this derived demand curve equals marginal franchisor cost, an optimal output and an optimal franchisor price can be determined, and an optimal number of franchisees may be calculated by applying the marginal zero profit condition. The profit maximizing franchisor will only refuse to sell to a potential franchisee — for example, impose exclusive franchising — if his total sales to the franchise system as a whole are increased by so doing. It can be shown that total sales *will* increase under certain assumptions, essentially those of economies of scale in retailing, and customers who consider franchisees to be differentiated sellers. If these assumptions hold, the profit maximizing franchisor will have an economic incentive to use exclusive franchising.

The analysis is dependent, however, on a measurement of the slopes of each franchisee's marginal cost curve, and on the presence of explicit or implicit franchisor-imposed sales quotas for franchisees. The assumptions as to market size and competitiveness, of the differentiated nature of franchisees, and the measurement requirements make the analysis of primarily academic value in evaluating the justifications put forward for exclusive franchising.

There is another line of reasoning which might explain why a franchisor would go beyond merely adopting a highly selective marketing system. This argument states that a franchise system may develop consumer-franchisee attachments, and thus consumer-franchised good attachments, at a lower cost to the franchisor than any other type of sales promotion. Pashigian has claimed that officials in the automobile industry are in general agreement with this position.

... brand attachments may be more efficiently developed in the automobile industry by maintaining a stable group of dealers who remain in business year in and year out than by spending more on advertising. . . . the consumer must rely on the dealer to provide the necessary service to correct defects, to keep the auto in operating condition, and not to deceive him by selling him a 'lemon.' The automobile is a major capital expenditure. A poor selection means a large loss. Under these conditions, the consumer may be a risk averter, preferring to purchase from a dealer who has been in business for a period of years and with whom he has had previous experience.[5]

If the maintenance of consumer-franchised good attachments is best accomplished by maintaining a stable group of franchisees, then the franchisor is not indifferent to the loss of an established and successful franchisee. Pashigian asked the question: "What types of representation policies are likely to maintain a stable dealer organization over time in an industry as cyclical as the automobile industry?" He concluded that this could be accomplished by restricting the entry of new franchisees. The best way to restrict entry, and to assure franchisees that it will be restricted, is through a contractual agreement to exclusive franchises.

Exclusiveness can thus be thought of as a risk premium which the franchisor offers to franchisees to minimize the likelihood of a loss through unexpected shifts in demand. If we use the analogy of a risk premium, it can be argued further that exclusivity is more likely to be found in industries where output is concentrated among a few major producers. Bain claimed that it is in such oligopolies that wholesale price is likely to be most rigid, and short-range price adjustments to cushion the impact on franchisees and other dealers are least likely to be made.

This is in part because when price is controlled by agreement or price leadership, every change in price places some strain on the controlling mechanism and increases the probability of defections from the agreement. By maintaining a relatively rigid price, the oligopolists lessen the possibility that open price rivalry or price cutting will emerge.[6]

Thus, in a franchise system with supply price rigidity, the franchisor who seeks maintenance of consumer-franchised good attachments will seek to protect his franchisees from a probability of high loss if predictions of consumer demand for the franchised good are not accurate. Where entry into the franchisee sector is restricted, the franchisor can utilize a price for the franchised good which permits economic profits to the franchisee if demand has been correctly forecast, and which lessens the probability of zero or negative profits if demand is incorrectly forecast. Even if the price of the franchised good is set at a level which provides zero franchisee economic profit at forecast levels of demand, franchisees are still less likely to sustain any given loss under an exclusive franchising system which permits them to operate at higher sales volumes than they would with free entry at the franchisee level. The actual impact of restricted entry will depend on the aggressiveness of the franchisees, and on the structure of the market.

A Market Segmentation Basis for
Exclusive Franchising

The essence of an exclusive franchise, as it has been discussed so far, is that there is a geographic distance between franchisees in the same franchisees in the same franchise system, and that some physical measurement unit, perhaps customer travel time, is appropriate as a means of evaluating the state of franchisee protection from intrabrand competition.

This concept of travel time is made less operational by the widespread ownership of automobiles, and the proliferation of new freeways and other high-speed arterial traffic routes. Thus, a consumer located near a main traffic artery may find that it is as easy to travel five miles in one direction as five blocks in another. What then is the effect of the building of a new freeway on existing exclusive franchises and on the granting of new ones?

Even if a concept of exclusive franchising based on travel time or some other measure of geographic distance could be made more operational, it is not clear that it would be the correct one. The market segment that a franchisee hopes to serve may be a particular socioeconomic group rather than a spatial customer market. Sociologists have established that people associate themselves with a particular socioeconomic group, and that there are substantial differences in behavior, including purchasing behavior, that are related to the position of the individual on the socioeconomic scale.[7] The central finding of the studies that Pierre Martineau carried out for the *Chicago Tribune* was that the attraction of a particular retail outlet for a consumer was not based on his income-ability to shop there, but rather on his belief that he belonged in that store, that people similar to him were at home there. Those who feel at home in any one retail store (including, presumably, franchised outlets) tend to be clustered at a certain level on a socioeconomic scale that ranks groups from lower-lower to upper-upper. Martineau claimed that:

To assume that all persons would wish to shop at the glamorous, High Status stores in utterly wrong. People are very realistic in the way they match their values and expectations with the status of the store.[8]

There almost certainly are customers who will travel considerable distances to purchase a specialty good rather than shop in an outlet where discomfort would be caused by a conflict between their own status and the status of the outlet. Martineau states:

Economic factors will always be important. But unless the store image is acceptable to the shopper, price announcements are meaningless. The upper status woman cannot conceive of herself shopping in the subway store of a large department store . . . conversely, the wage earner's wife is not going to expose herself to the possibility of humiliation by shopping in the quality store . . . even if she has the money to buy something there.[9]

A franchisee's principal challenge may thus not be from the intrabrand competition of physically adjacent franchisees in the same system. To illustrate, there could exist two car-rental franchisees in the same block, one in the lobby of a high-status hotel, the second in a glassfront streetcorner location, and each franchisee would have a virtual exclusive in terms of his own clientele.

To make a concept of exclusive franchising based on socioeconomic differentiations operational, both the franchisor and franchisee must understand the appeal which each type of member of the franchise system has to the consumer. An error in judgement or empirical analysis would lead to duplicate coverage of one group and inadequate coverage of another, and to the franchisee losing his exclusivity.[a]

The Criteria of 'Least Necessary Restraint' Applied

It is probable that the quality control/goodwill, the lowered barriers to entry, and the failing company cases discussed in earlier chapters are not relevant to the discussion of exclusive franchising. A desire for exclusive franchising in other than the newcomer/infant industry case seems to arise almost solely from the franchisee's strong retail market strength and bargaining position. Since such retail strength may be detrimental to competition, it is not clear why a franchise restriction which leads to it should be permitted.[b] The newcomer/infant industry case is relevant to a discussion of exclusive franchising, and it is presented below.

The Newcomer/Infant Industry Case. It has been argued that a potential franchisee may be willing to risk capital to introduce a new product, or an old product into a new market, only if he can be given some assurance of

---

[a] Managerial problems under an exclusive franchising system based on socioeconomic factors are difficult to appraise. It might be difficult to convince a potential franchisee contemplating a large investment that he has an exclusive franchise, when another member of the same franchise system is located just down the street. It might also be difficult to convince the prospective franchisee that his promotional overflow would not directly benefit the adjacent franchisee who did not undertake the same kind of promotion.

[b] Michael Flicker has argued that a franchisee should be permitted an exclusive franchise in an established industry where there are requirements for substantial dealer investment and promotion, where the industry is highly concentrated, or where it shows signs of becoming oligopolistic. Unlike the newcomer situation where the public interest in introducing new products to the market is apparent, it is not clear that competition is promoted by allowing franchisees in established industries to use arrangements that are basically anticompetitive, particularly where the alternative of credit or other guarantees from a financially strong franchisor exist.[10]

obtaining sufficient future returns on his investment. A potential franchisee is understandably reluctant to handle the franchised good without some guarantee that he will not simply benefit competing franchisees in the same system through the product goodwill created by his investment and promotion. Such benefit would certainly occur when the franchised good is unknown in the market in which it is being sold for the first time. Thus, to attract the best franchisees it may be necessary to grant exclusivity, especially where the franchised good requires heavy investment in facilities, inventory, or training.

Given the assumption that it is beneficial to stimulate new businesses and product or service innovations, it is also necessary to consider alternatives to exclusive franchising that might be available to newcomer franchisees. A unilateral decision on the part of the franchisor to practice selective distribution (but without binding himself to a promise of exclusivity) is one such alternative. As indicated above, this is not sufficient in many cases to enable a new or comparatively weak franchisor to attract high quality franchisees.

Since the franchisee's long-run interest in securing an exclusive franchise may have anticompetitive effects, while the franchisor's interest is basically coincident with the public interest in higher volume and greater price competition, it might be argued that a second alternative is to presume exclusivity to be illegal whenever it is initiated by the franchisee, and to judge it on a rule of reason basis when initiated by the franchisor. But an approach which tries to determine which party's interest is being served encounters an obstacle. The most significant interests of the franchisor are themselves stated in terms of the interests of the franchisee, as in the case of a franchisor seeking contract conditions that will encourage franchisee entry, and leading to a viable franchisee existence coincident with franchisor profit maximization.

Overall, a sound argument can be presented for a temporary tolerance of exclusive franchise agreements to encourage new entry and adequate investment levels in new facilities. Exclusive franchises for very long terms are objectionable because of possible population or customer shifts, freeway construction and new shopping centers, or changes in socioeconomic group concentrations. A restricted term allows the franchisor all the benefits of selective distribution, but with the additional freedom of increasing franchisee representation, and perhaps competition, where justified. (It cannot be assumed that increased numbers alone will lead to increased competition. A few aggressive discount houses are likely more competitive than a large number of price-rigid franchisees.) Without the freedom to appoint new franchisees (and if existing franchisees refused to expand), a franchisor could find his franchised good seriously underrepresented in some markets.

Where the newcomer/infant industry defense is offered, the exclusive franchise should be limited in duration to a short period during which some or all of the initial investment can be recouped. This is the practice in most existing franchise systems. After the initial period, the franchisee should be able to rely on his established product identification and market acceptance to compete with any new franchisees that might be appointed. If advance estimation of the time required to establish the good is difficult, exclusivity could be granted for a maximum period, subject to earlier relinquishment when the franchisee achieves either a specified sales volume, or a certain profit or return on investment figure. A court confronted with an exclusive could then inquire whether the criterion of success was reasonable, and whether it had been met by the franchisee in question.

Finally, termination of an exclusive franchise at the end of a fixed or variable period would also serve to effectively terminate any policy of exclusive dealing with the franchisor which existed as a reciprocal grant by the franchisee.

Note that a time-restricted grant of exclusivity is itself a "least necessary restraint" alternative to the imposition of closed territories. If the grant of an exclusive franchise is sufficient to attract a good quality of market entrant, use of the control is preferable to the use of closed territories.

If the franchisor is dominant in the market, or if the franchisee attempts to achieve a monopoly position or market dominance, the concept of ancillary restraints as applied to exclusive franchising would require that the exclusiveness be deemed unreasonable, and the restraint be disallowed. Market dominance would normally never occur in the newcomer/infant industry case, but could occur in all other cases.

Exclusive Dealing

Exclusive dealing, which is normally found reciprocally with exclusive franchising, is the agreement by the franchisee to purchase, sell, or otherwise deal only in products supplied or approved by the franchisor. For example, an oil company may require franchisee-owned stations to sell only its brand of gasoline. Related to the exclusive dealing arrangement, but not as restrictive, is the arrangement whereby a franchisee or other dealer is permitted to purchase and deal in competitive goods, but agrees to push the supplier's brand. This was the situation in the *Schwinn* case. The exclusive dealing agreement may be express or implied. An implied agreement may be achieved through the granting of special prices, discounts, or other benefits to those franchisees who do not purchase competitors' products or services.

The Court's Analysis of Exclusive Dealing

The legal treatment of exclusive dealing arrangements has a long history marked by sharp swings between extreme positions of legality and illegality. Exclusive dealing requirements have not been considered illegal *per se* except when accompanied by an unlawful purpose such as an attempt to monopolize or to fix prices. The courts have inquired instead into the economic reasons for exclusive dealing, and its effect on competition, before determining the applicability of the antitrust laws. Generally, exclusive dealing has been upheld where there exists a valid business reason, and competing retailers are not foreclosed from a source of supply. The Supreme Court in the *Standard Stations* case[11] drew the line of illegality at what has been termed "quantitative substantiality." The Court framed the issue as whether the statutory prerequisite of potential competitive injury might be "met simply by proof that a substantial portion of commerce is affected or whether it must also be demonstrated that competitive activity has actually diminished or probably will diminish." Because *Standard Stations* is illustrative of the issues considered by the Court in evaluating exclusive dealing, it is discussed in some detail here.

The Standard Stations Case. In the 1946–1948 period, the Standard Oil Company of California sold petroleum products in Arizona, California, Idaho, Nevada, Oregon, Utah, and Washington. It sold through its own service stations, to the operators of franchised service stations, and to industrial sellers, and was the largest seller of gasoline in the area. In 1946 Standard's combined sales amounted to 23 percent of the total taxable gallonage sold in the territory that year. Sales by company-owned service stations constituted 6.8 percent of the total, and sales under exclusive dealing agreements with franchised dealers constituted 6.7 percent. The remainder were sales to industrial users. Retail service-station sales by Standard's six leading competitors accounted for 42.5 percent of total taxable gallonage, with remaining retail sales spread over some 70 smaller companies. Each of Standard's major competitors employed exclusive dealing arrangements; by 1948 only 1.6 percent of retail outlets sold the branded gasoline of more than one supplier.

Exclusive contracts with Standard had been signed, up to 1947, by the operators of 5,937 franchised stations, or 16 percent of the retail gasoline outlets in the territory. These outlets purchased from Standard $58 million worth of gasoline and $8 million worth of other products. One kind of exclusive agreement, covering 2,777 outlets, bound the franchisee to purchase all his requirements of gasoline, other petroleum products, and tires-batteries-accessories (TBA) from Standard. Another kind of exclusive agreement, covering 4,368 franchisees, bound the dealer only to purchase his requirements of Standard petroleum products. There also existed 742 oral agreements with franchisees by which they agreed to sell only Standard's gasoline. In some cases, these franchisees had also orally agreed to purchase their requirements of TBA items from Standard. Of the written agreements, most were of indeterminate length, terminable "at the end of the first 6 months of any contract year, or at the end of any such year, by giving to the other at least 30 days prior thereto written notice. . . ."

Between 1936 and 1946, Standard's sales of gasoline through franchised dealers remained at a constant proportion of the territory's total sales. Standard's sales of TBA goods rose slightly from 1936 levels, but never exceeded two percent of the total TBA sales in the area. (Since it is the preservation of competition which is at question, the significant territory was that where effective competition might reasonably exist — those states in which Standard itself sells.)

The Court refused to consider any economic justification for exclusive dealing. It held that the requirement of showing an actual or potential lessening of competition or a tendency to establish monopoly was adequately met by proof that the contracts covered a substantial number of outlets and amount of products. Given such "quantitative substantiality," the Court reasoned that the substantial lessening of competition was an automatic result, for the existence of exclusive dealing contracts denies franchisees the opportunity to purchase products from competing suppliers and excludes suppliers from access to those franchised dealers.

It is not clear from the Court's written opinion what tests were used to determine that the market foreclosed by the exclusive dealing was substantial. No comparison between the dollar volume of business done under exclusive contracts and the total dollar volume was made. Since the conclusion was reached that: "The affected proportion of retail sales of petroleum products is substantial," the inference could be reached that 6.7 percent of the total gallonage in the territory was the figure given critical weight in the decision. However, because the Court did not indicate an intention to overrule earlier cases, and because respect for legal forms or mathematical formulae is uncharacteristic of the Court's treatment of antitrust, it is unlikely that such an inference would be valid.

A significant element is found in the emphasis placed by the Court on the fact that Standard's major competitors, who had 42.5 percent of the total taxable gallonage in the territory, used similar exclusive dealing arrangements. The opinion stated that:

It would not be far-fetched to infer that their effect has been to enable the established suppliers individually to maintain their own standing and at the same time collectively, even though not collusively, to prevent a late arrival from wresting away more than an insignificant portion of the market.[12]

The Court gave no hint of what might have resulted had stations handling more than 55 percent of the total gallonage in the area not been tied to the seven major suppliers, with Standard's exclusive dealing agreements thus utilized as part of a system covering more than half of the market. The real significance of *Standard Stations* may lie not in the fact that contractual coverage of 6.7 percent of the market was regarded as substantial foreclosure, but rather in the shifting of the burden of proof to the defendant, and in the outlawing of a long-existing system of exclusive dealing contracts covering half of a substantial market.

In 1961 the Court again considered exclusive dealing in the *Tampa* case,[13] and this time indicated that it would consider justifications: for example, if only a small share of the market was involved, if the purpose of the agreement was to ensure to the buyer a sufficient supply of a commodity vital to the buyer's trade, or if the purpose was to ensure the market supplier of a market for his output where there was no trend toward concentration in the industry. *Tampa* lessened the severity of the mechanical foreclosure rule in *Standard Stations,* as the Court agreed that exclusive dealing is not *per se* prohibited where competitors are not foreclosed from a source of supply.

Business Justification for the Use of Exclusive Dealing

Exclusive dealing arrangements can be categorized under two distinct headings. The first type involves a franchisor prohibiting his franchisees from selling goods which are not directly competitive with the trademarked, franchised goods. A franchisor who permits his franchisees to associate other products under the franchise trademark, and who does not police adherence to minimum quality standards for those other products, runs a risk of diminution or loss of the value of the trademark. The franchisor who forbids such association usually argues that it is difficult or impractical for him to establish and enforce meaningful quality standards for nontrademarked items, as his product knowledge is limited to the goods in which the franchise system specializes. The franchisor also argues that association of other products with the franchised good will harm the image of outlet-uniformity which he has promoted, and may attract a class of customer which conflicts with the class the franchisor intends to reach.

The second type of exclusive dealing involves a franchisor who prohibits his franchisees from handling goods which are directly competitive with the franchised good. It should not be assumed that this is done simply to monopolize as many franchise outlets as possible. The purpose may be to reduce selling expenses, particularly salesmen's salaries. Another consideration is the franchisor's desire to ease production scheduling by obtaining an assured market for the term of the exclusive contract. By the use of medium term requirements contracts with staggered expiration dates, a franchisor is freed of many of the uncertainties of demand forecasting, especially where market requirements are fairly predictable. This may be illegal where staggered expiration dates are used to prevent franchisees from bargaining collectively with the franchisor for more advantageous terms.[14] The demand forecasting argument is most relevant in the case of the newcomer franchisor, where some assurance of an adequate return to market investment may be required.

The franchisor may also feel that exclusive dealing arrangements are necessary to assure a maximum and concentrated sales effort by franchisees, especially in the marketing of relatively expensive goods. In some cases, postservice sales to customers may be so important to the good will of the franchise system that the franchisor may decide that exclusion of competing goods is essential to ensure a sufficiently specialized franchisee service department.

Exclusive dealing arrangements can also be used by a franchisor to inhibit competing suppliers and to monopolize a large segment of the market. Regardless of its initial business purpose, exclusive dealing may have the effect of tying up so many of the best market outlets that a newcomer finds it difficult or impossible to enter the market. The effect on competing suppliers is most serious in a small local market which can support only a small number of dealers, but it may also be considerable in a large market when a number of the best dealers are tied to one or more suppliers.

Why would a franchisee agree to an arrangement that limited his freedom to purchase from competing suppliers? Where a requirements contract is not included, one of the strongest inducements to exclusive dealing is the reciprocal agreement by the franchisor to grant an exclusive franchise in an agreed territory. Or, the franchisee may simply be compelled to accept exclusive dealing by reason of a dominant franchisor's refusal to deal on any other basis — the petroleum service station case being an excellent example. There may also exist potential financial and other assistance which the franchisee expects to obtain from his exclusive supplier during the term of the contract.

Where a term requirements contract exists, incentives to the franchisee are somewhat greater. The principal inducement is probably the desire to obtain an assured source of supply. Where the good is critical to the franchisee's operation, a term requirements contract minimizes the danger of a supply failure which might restrict or suspend franchisee operations.

The franchisee may also desire to obtain the protection against price increases (or against price declines on existing inventories), that usually accompany a requirements contract. This is particularly important in seasonal businesses. If the term requirements contract enables the franchisor to spread his production more evenly over the year, he will be able to quote a stable (and perhaps lower) price. There also may be available a rebate or discount to franchisees who meet or exceed their sales quotas under the exclusive dealing arrangement.[15]

The Criteria of 'Least Necessary Restraint' Applied

From the franchisor's point of view, a regular exclusive dealing arrangement has all the benefits of a requirements contract,[15] but without the obligation to deliver the franchisee's requirements (except that it does not offer the same degree of sophistication in production scheduling based on franchisee sales estimates). From the franchisee's point of view, a requirements contract (even with 100 percent requirements) is preferable to a straight exclusive dealing arrangement, since it gives him some *quid pro quo* in terms of an assured supply, which is welcome in times of market shortage. Further, a requirements contract enables the franchisee to avoid either overstocking (with consequent storage charges and liquidation losses) or undertaking panic buying at a time of peak price. Because requirements contracts are more advantageous to the franchisee, and not more harmful to the franchisor—except perhaps in a period of market shortage—the criteria of least necessary restraint would seem to ban *per se* exclusive dealing without requirements contract provisions, and to concentrate attention on those circumstances in which a partial or full requirements contract may be consistent with the public interest.

Requirements contracts affect competition at both franchisee and franchisor levels. The effect at the franchisee level will not be considered, since any cost savings there offer only temporary benefit to the franchisee and consumer; eventually, the lack of price competition resulting from lack of competition at the franchisor level will harm *both* franchisee and consumer. The question of whether requirements contracts should be allowed then depends primarily on the extent of damage to competition at the franchisor level.[c] At this level the effects of requirements contracts depend on a number of factors, the combination of which determine whether they should be permitted.[16]

The first and most significant factor is the proportion of business done by those franchisees tied up by requirements contracts. Where a franchisor contracts with franchisees controlling 75 percent of the relevant market in a given territory, the effect on other suppliers will be more anticompetitive than where the franchisees control only a small portion of the market. This factor will be of less importance where exclusive franchising accompanies requirements contracts, in which case the number of franchisees tied up in each market area will be smaller than otherwise. This factor would be of no significance in the newcomer case, where the initial proportion of business tied up is zero.

The second relevant factor is the extent to which other suppliers are also using exclusive dealing or requirements contracts. If a large proportion is using them, as was the case in *Standard Stations,* the anticompetitive effect on newcomers and on existing suppliers will be correspondingly greater, since such newcomers and suppliers are excluded from a larger share of the potential market. (The question arises as to whether a new-

---

[c]There will always be some damage. In making a term requirements contract, a supplier consciously excludes all competitors from as much of the market as is represented by that customer's purchases. It must be recognized that a substantial portion of all business is transacted by or by means of vertically integrated companies on the one hand, and a multitude of favored-supplier arrangements on the other, with percentage requirements contracts falling somewhere in the middle of these two forms.

comer franchisor should be able to adopt requirements contracts automatically, as a defensive measure, when entering a market where they are in general use.)

The third relevant factor is the time duration of the requirements contract. The longer the term of the contract, the greater the anticompetitive effect. Even a contract with a very short term may be anticompetitive.

> . . . an automobile dealer may be free to stop selling a well-known make of car on 60 days notice, but he may be very reluctant to risk his entire business by switching to the cars of a newcomer. He might prefer to continue to handle the well-known car in large quantities, while buying a few of the new cars on an experimental basis. But an exclusive dealing arrangement, no matter how short its duration, will prevent him from doing this, and will increase the difficulty of the newcomer in finding outlets for its car.[17]

The fourth relevant factor is the likelihood that other suppliers may be able to establish their own distribution outlets, or set up their own franchise systems. If any analysis of the first three factors indicates that serious anticompetitive effects may arise, the possibility that suppliers can establish new competing outlets must be considered. This in turn depends on the type of good, the availability of managerial and other personnel, and the capital requirements for the new outlets. Lockhart and Sacks suggest that the effect will be most serious when, for example, a supplier ties up wholesale outlets which handle a variety of products and which require large amounts of capital to duplicate.

The fifth factor is that the onus should be on the franchisor to indicate the effect of the requirements contract on reducing his costs and to indicate that the cost saving has been passed on to franchisees. This is necessary because the only justification in allowing a franchisor to exclude competitors from part of the market is that, in the long run, competition in the whole industry may be aided. But exclusive dealing/requirements contracts can result in a degree of market control sufficient that the franchisor does not have to pass on his cost savings in order to retain his exclusive arrangements.

Finally, it is clear that the anticompetitive effect of requirements contracts will depend on the degree of competition existing in the market, and whether the firm using the device is a newcomer trying to establish a foothold, an established firm trying to expand, or a dominant firm seeking to preserve or extend its position. Because the latter two do not support the need for a requirements contract, only the newcomer/infant industry case is relevant.

The Newcomer/Infant Industry Case. The argument usually put forward for allowing the newcomer/infant industry to use requirements contracts is that it does not result in a substantial lessening of competition, since without the contract there would be no newcomer or infant industry, and no competition. The view fails to consider that a foreclosure does exist, since potential entrants are deterred even where there are no existing competitors. A justification for the newcomer/infant industry case does exist, but it is based on a policy of encouraging new entry, and not on the lack of foreclosure of competition.

Even so, the newcomer who substantially forecloses competition through a requirements contract (as determined by the five factors listed above) is justified only if current industry structure is highly concentrated. The rationale is that new entry should not be deterred where an industry is tending towards oligopoly. Where a concentrated industry structure does exist, the use of a requirements contract must be further justified by the franchisor showing a good business purpose: either a demonstrable and substantial reduction in selling expenses or investment, or a need for a concentrated selling effort by franchisees.[d] Moreover, the validity of the contract is strictly limited in time. This limitation can be accomplished by setting an arbitrary time limit on its duration, making it nonrenewable, and perhaps providing for decreasing proportional requirements during the life of the contract.

Thus, the criteria of 'least necessary restraint' suggests that a requirements contract is always preferable to a straight exclusive dealing arrangement, and the latter should be *per se* forbidden. A number of factors should be evaluated to determine whether requirements contracts are overly anticompetitive at the franchisor level. Where they are so found, the only justification for them should be in the newcomer/infant industry case, and only where the structure of existing industry tends toward oligopoly, and where the exclusive dealing arrangement is strictly limited in time.

The criteria apply only to the situation of a franchisor prohibiting his franchisees from handling goods which are directly competitive to the franchised good. A franchisor must be allowed to forbid his franchisees to handle noncompetitive goods in situations where there is a danger of diminution or loss of the value of the franchise trademark.

---

[d]The need of a guarantee of assured supply in order to attract franchisees can be met through the least restraint alternative of a contract provision which guarantees a minimum quantity shipment to the franchisee, but leaves the franchisee free to purchase from alternative suppliers if desired.

9

Conclusion

Summary

In spite of being the subject of a large number of articles in the popular and trade presses, the business relationship called franchising has been relatively undefined as to its size and characteristics. Thus the first part of this study, comprising Chapters 2–4, has dealt with the "what, where, and why" of franchise operations.

The definition which I have adopted for franchising is based on four aspects which make the franchise concept unique and identifiable: (1) legal independence of the franchisee from the franchisor; (2) a business operated with the name and standardization of the franchisor accruing to the franchisee; (3) a business that came into being in its existing form as a franchise outlet; and (4) the existence of a formal agreement. Two distinct classes of franchising, with six identifiable types, were discussed. Each type shows a reliance on certain kinds of controls in the franchise agreement, and each encounters different antitrust problems and emphases in its operations. Several types, notably trademark licensor association—association member systems, have not previously been identified in the literature as being part of franchised business, although from the standpoints of legal and economic analysis they have the same characteristics and problems as members of other franchise systems.

I have indicated that, while franchise systems gained their first substantial dollar volume and strategic importance with the growth of the automobile industry and the related growth of retail operations in the petroleum industry, the most recent and dynamic growth has come in cooperative and wholesaler-sponsored groups and, in particular, with trademark licensor franchise systems. At present, contractually integrated marketing systems, including franchise systems, are a more rapidly growing segment of vertical market organization than either their corporate or administered system counterparts.

This study has also established a point that has not been articulated well in the literature—the importance of franchised business to the total economy. Franchising is of substantial importance, both in its qualitative contributions and because of its quantitative size. Of particular qualitative interest are the social values implicit in the independent ownership of one's own business as opposed to being an employee of an integrated firm. Through franchising, many potential entrepreneurs have been enabled to enter their own businesses with a minimum of capital, knowledge, or experience, yet with a high probability of a viable operation.

141

Another qualitative aspect which requires much more investigation is the opportunity which franchising potentially holds for members of minority groups seeking to establish themselves in business. Relatively little attention has thus far been paid to the possibilities, and several large-scale experiments which have been carried out yielded mixed and generally unencouraging results. Still, it is obvious that the managerial assistance, lower financial requirements, and consumer acceptance of the trade-marked good in a franchise system can aid substantially in bringing non-whites into the entreprenurial class.

The quantitative size of franchised business is also of considerable significance. The projection of a dollar sales volume for franchised business of $124 billion is considerably above any estimates which have previously appeared in the literature, although my estimate still probably understates the true figure. The projected growth rate of 13,000 new franchisees per year, and the number of new franchisors coming into the field, suggests that franchising may still be in the growth stage of its development cycle.

In emphasizing the size and importance of franchised business, the first part of this study sets the stage for the second part, a discussion of the status of franchising under the antitrust laws. Franchising may be the only form of business in America today which is almost totally dependent for its future form (and perhaps existence) on the trend of Supreme Court decisions in interpreting existing statutes. An increased interest in the antitrust aspects of the controls in franchise agreements is shown in the sharp rise in activity by the Justice Department and the F.T.C., and by the increased number of suits initiated by private parties. That some of the controls involved, particularly tying, territorial and customer restrictions, exclusive dealing, and exclusive franchising are in widespread use and are seen as being critical to franchised operations is undeniable.

The threat to franchising in its present form arises because the courts, and federal and state enforcement agencies, seem inclined to condemn a variety of franchise system controls in the name of the rule of competition. The Supreme Court, in its ruling in the *Schwinn* case, said that it may not even be sufficient to demonstrate sound business reason and intent by a franchisor who would impose controls. The franchisor must also demonstrate that the impact of his controls on franchisees is pro-competitive.

In the light of these requirements by the Court, franchisors have, to date, made little effort to justify the controls they seek to impose, based on the managerial and economic realities of modern distribution. Chapters 6–8 of this study discuss the above mentioned controls, the commonly cited business justifications for their use, and present an economic analysis of the several possible functions which such controls may serve. It is shown that there are several legitimate functions for each control which satisfy the Court's requirement for sound business purpose, and that each control may have a procompetitive impact in the sense of encouraging new entry to franchised business. Thus, there are a number of possible defenses to the use of franchise system controls which are quite different from those that have actually been placed before the courts.

Perhaps the most important aspect of this study comes in its third part, where several criteria for antitrust enforcement are recommended which are analogous to the criminal law principle of least necessary force. It is shown that procompetitive results may stem from a following of these criteria. The final sections of Chapters 6–8 introduce the concept of 'least necessary restraint,' which is based on asking whether there are less restrictive ways whereby legitimate business objectives associated with the controls in franchise systems might be attained. Four cases exist in which controls may be acceptable for a restricted period of time: (1) quality control/goodwill; (2) newcomer/infant industry; (3) lowered barriers to entry; and (4) the failing company case. It is my contention that application of these criteria in evaluating franchise system controls will produce a result more in accord with the goal of a competitive economy than will the application of increasingly rigid criteria of *per se* illegality, and I have suggested that the criteria of 'least necessary restraint' are deserving of careful consideration in future antitrust enforcement.

Some Unresolved Issues

A number of important but unresolved issues reoccur in many of the cases testing franchise system controls. Is the relationship between franchisor and franchisee such that the controls imposed may be considered vertical restraints, or is the real relationship existing among the various franchisees and with the franchisor such as to bring about horizontal restraints? More important, should the answer to this question have any bearing upon the outcome of litigation and the direction of antitrust enforcement?

As the *White Motor* case showed, it is difficult to draw vertical-horizontal distinctions in terms of effect, so any distinction must be drawn in terms of differing purposes when controls are imposed by the franchisor, or agreed upon by the franchisees. But it is terribly difficult to draw such distinctions; even where conclusions can be reached as to the origin of a restriction, it remains difficult to make distinctions as to its legality. Thus, in the *General Motors* case, the District Court examined the evidence and held that GM had acted unilaterally to enforce a legitimate contract clause. The Supreme Court reviewed the same record and concluded that GM had acted conspiratorially with its dealers. Such difficulties lead me to conclude that there are many more significant factors than the vertical-horizontal dichotomy—the particular franchise program, its purpose, and its effect upon competition in the industry involved—that the Court might consider.

Closely related to the vertical-horizontal question is the issue of whether specific controls should be treated as *per se* illegal, tested by the rule of reason, or tested by some intermediate criteria such as that of 'least necessary restraint.' If a test is to be applied, at what point past the mere existence of the control is the burden of proving its reasonableness shifted to the franchisor? Consider even the seemingly obvious case of vertical price fixing. For years, McDonald's Hamburgers prescribed a 19¢ maximum selling price for hamburgers, and focused much of its national advertising on this apparent *per se* violation. Similarly, any customer of International House of Pancakes is aware of the multipage menu provided by the franchisor, and prescribing (apparently maximum) resale prices, again an apparent *per se* violation.

A related question is how to treat interbrand and intrabrand competition. Here, the basic issue is how the established, dominant brands can be kept under effective competition. In many situations, there will be and should be a variety of alternatives, including other dominant brands with heavy advertising support and strong market position, less well-known brands with greater relative reliance upon dealer cooperation, and private brands of mass distributors and other large buyers. The issue in public policy should not be to argue over the merits of interbrand and intrabrand competition, but to guarantee that there will be genuine alternatives for buyer choice, and hence effective competition.

Given these questions, the problem arises as to whether (once the newcomer phase is ended) the answers should differ in the case of large versus small franchisors, or in the case of product franchisors versus trademark licensing franchise systems. I have not considered such a differential treatment in this study, because I believe that difficulties in measurement and the cost of burdening antitrust enforcement with evaluating the subtleties of such arrangements would outweigh any possible benefits. The criteria of 'least necessary restraint' was proposed as an alternative to requiring such differential treatment, and it would seem to be applicable to all classes of franchisees. However, many members of the franchise industry (and, I suspect, of the antitrust bar) would disagree with such a stand. The whole problem of differential treatment for different sizes or types of franchisors does deserve to be discussed at much greater length than it has been here.

On a broader scale, a number of questions remain to be answered. Have the Court's decisions pointed the way to legally viable franchise programs? Is the approach being taken by the Court most conducive to continued growth and development of the small business sector of the economy, or should (or will) contractual integration give way to ownership integration as a sacrifice to ease of administration and lack of discrimination in the enforcement of the antitrust laws?

The issue of whether or not antitrust enforcement encourages vertical ownership integration is one of the most significant questions raised in this study, but the answer is far from clear. Manufacturers frequently con-

145

tend that unless they are permitted to establish restrictions on distributors, they will be compelled to take over the distribution function themselves—and thus eliminate a number of small independent businessmen and further the concentration of economic power. For example, if exclusive dealing were banned, would this lead to an abandonment of franchising? In the *Standard Stations* case, Mr. Justice Douglas stated that "elimination of these requirements contracts sets the stage for Standard and other oil companies to build service station empires of their own, either through agencies or through ownership acquisition of stations by subsidiary corporations."[1] In spite of this prediction, made almost 20 years ago, most major oil companies have maintained their franchise systems.

On the other hand, it is interesting to note what has happened to Schwinn since the Court's ruling. After an intensive study of the compliance problems involved, as well as the problems of raising adequate capital, Schwinn developed a multistep program of compliance which focussed on the remaining 18 independent Schwinn distributors. In August 1967, Schwinn publicly announced to its dealers and distributors that it planned to distribute its products nationally through company-owned sales subsidiaries. At the same time, Schwinn notified nine of its distributors that it was terminating their distributorships as of December 31, 1967, and asked the remaining nine to temporarily enter into a new form of agency agreement on bicycles to cover an area of prime responsibility equal to or slightly larger than the area they had previously served. Thus, the end of jobber franchising and the substitution of vertical ownership integration was Schwinn's permanent answer to the Court's ruling.[2]

A dangerous precedent may have been established with the *Sealy* case, in which the Court ignored the fact that the existing Sealy franchise arrangement was a 'least necessary restraint' solution to a competitive need. Given a market in which the ability to sell a nationally advertised line of products confers a competitive advantage over local or regional producers, and in which three or four large national companies dominate the industry, there were several alternatives available to small producers such as Sealy. Each might overcome its disadvantage through a merging of ownerships, or each might enter into a joint venture for the promotion of one or more nationally advertised lines of products. The joint venture is a 'least necessary restraint' alternative to the problem as compared with a full merger.

Considering this, it is truly anomalous that the partial territorial restrictions of the Sealy system were condemned, whereas both price fixing and territorial restrictions could be lawfully reinstated if some or all of Sealy's franchisee-shareholders merged into a single national company. Under the current antimerger doctrines of the Sherman and Clayton Acts, it is doubtful whether such a merger would be illegal. Since Sealy's licensees are widely scattered geographically, the relevant market in a merger case would have to be the whole United States. As there are about 500 member companies in the Bedding Manufacturers Association, and the industry is dominated by giants such as Simmons, it is likely that Sealy comprises substantially less than the 7.5 percent of the relevant market which was condemned in the *Von's Grocery Co.*[3] case.[a]

Such an ownership integrated distributor—be it Schwinn, Sealy, or Standard Oil of California—can with legal impunity fix prices, and can determine in detail how, when, where, and what to sell. If we concede that it is socially desirable that small business exist and succeed, and that small business should be able to successfully compete with ownership integrated distributors, then it must be argued that small businessmen should not be deprived of the tools to do so. In the case where newcomer status has ended and the franchisor has reached maturity, what should be permitted if there is a strong tendency in the industry to vertical ownership integration? Should a small-sized franchisor entering a highly oligopolistic industry, or even a larger, mature company in a concentrated industry, be permitted to impose contractual controls on franchisees without time limitation, because of the existing structure of the industry? I have argued that they should not, but the question is sufficiently complex and important that it requires a great deal of further study. For example, E. T. Grether has suggested, based on his investigations, that it is becoming increasingly difficult for even mature suppliers in some industries to attract and retain viable, independent dealer systems. If this is true, and if this is a widespread phenomenon, there may be a sound argument for extending the validity of contractual controls beyond what is permissible at present.

An important question relating to the large-size or dominant franchisor is whether, given his substantial bargaining power, he should be allowed to terminate agreements with franchisees pursuant to their contract, but without cause?[4] In the automobile industry, the Dealer's Day in Court Act gives the automobile dealer a cause of action where none previously existed, for damages where the automobile manufacturer has failed to act in good faith. Temporary injunctions have been granted enjoining termination of automobile franchises in cases of bad faith. The avowed purpose of this legislation is to alleviate the imbalance of bargaining power between automobile dealers and manufacturers. Such imbalance appears to exist in other segments of the franchise industry, notably with petroleum service stations in their relationships with major oil companies. For several years prior to 1970, Congress had considered extending similar protection to all franchisees, and hearings were conducted during 1966 and 1967 on such legislation by the Senate Subcommittee on Antitrust and Monopoly.[5] The proposed legislation is known as the "Fairness in

---

[a] E. T. Grether has pointed out that the argument as to legality might not hold if the Court strictly considered the trend of concentration rather than the quantitative substantiality involved, or if there were geographic areas of the country where Sealy was the dominant producer.

Franchising Act," and would require franchisors engaged in interstate commerce to show good cause in terminating or failing to renew franchise agreements. Good cause is defined as failure by the franchisee to comply with reasonable contract provisions, or the use of bad faith by the franchisee in carrying out the terms of the franchise. A number of states are also considering franchise legislation similar to the proposed federal legislation. Such special legislation would be required if there were an imbalance of franchisor-franchisee power, because under general contract principles and in the absence of special circumstances, courts will not interfere with contractual obligations freely entered into by the parties concerned. Every man is presumed to be capable of managing his own affairs, and whether his bargains are wise or unwise is not ordinarily a subject of inquiry by a court of either legal or equitable jurisdiction.

In conclusion, it is worth reiterating that in urging the legality of some restrictions imposed by a franchisor on franchisees, I am not arguing for a substantial antitrust exemption in favor of small business. I think there would be wide agreement that if protection of the small businessman were to require the discarding of the entire philosophy of competition as the principal regulator of business affairs, the price would be too high for society to pay. But it is possible to uphold these restrictions without denying society the fruits of competition. It is my thesis that the restrictions I have discussed strengthen the franchise system of business and the competitive economy, when applied with discretion and with a time constraint on their use. They restrict or may even eliminate intrabrand competition, but with the benefit of expanding interbrand competition. Are the anticompetitive consequences resulting from this restriction or elimination of intrabrand competition more than balanced by the pro-competitive effects of a more vigorous interbrand competition? The principle of 'least necessary restraint' looks at such a balance not in terms of forbidden-allowed, but in terms of the needs of the franchisor and of society, in what might be called a rule of economic reason approach.

Appendixes

Provisions of Selected Antitrust Statutes

**Sherman Antitrust Act
Sections 1–3
(15 U.S.C. 1–3)**

Section 1. Every contract, combination in the form of trust or otherwise, or conspiracy, in restraint of trade or commerce among the several States, or with foreign nations, is hereby declared to be illegal: Provided, That nothing herein contained shall render illegal, contracts or agreements prescribing minimum prices for the resale of a commodity which bears, or the label or container of which bears, the trademark, brand, or name of the producer or distributor of such commodity and which is in free and open competition with commodities of the same general class produced or distributed by others, when contracts or agreements of that description are lawful as applied to intrastate transactions, under any statute, law, or public policy now or hereafter in effect in any State, Territory, or the District of Columbia in which such resale is to be made or to which the commodity is to be transported for such resale, and the making of such contracts or agreements shall not be an unfair method of competition under section 5, as amended and supplemented, of the Act entitled "An Act to create a Federal Trade Commission, to define its powers and duties, and for other purposes," approved September 26, 1914: Provided further, that the preceding proviso shall not make lawful any contract or agreement, providing for the establishment or maintenance of minimum resale prices on any commodity herein involved, between manufacturers, or between producers, or between wholesalers, or between brokers, or between factors, or between retailers, or between persons, firms, or corporations in competition with each other. Every person who shall make any contract or engage in any combination or conspiracy hereby declared to be illegal shall be deemed guilty of a misdemeanor, and, on conviction thereof, shall be punished by fine not exceeding fifty thousand dollars, or by imprisonment not exceeding one year, or by both said punishments, in the discretion of the court. [July 2, 1890, Chap. 647, Sec. 1, 26 Stat. 209] [As amended, 15 U.S.C. 1]

Section 2. Every person who shall monopolize, or attempt to monopolize, or combine or conspire with any other person or persons, to monopolize any part of the trade or commerce among the several States, or with foreign nations, shall be deemed guilty of a misdemeanor, and, on conviction thereof, shall be punished by fine not exceeding fifty thousand

151

dollars, or by imprisonment not exceeding one year, or by both said punishments, in the discretion of the court. [July 2, 1890, Chap. 647, Sec. 2, 26 Stat. 209] [As amended, 15 U.S.C. 2]

Section 3. Every contract, combination in form of trust or otherwise, or conspiracy, in restraint of trade or commerce in any Territory of the United States or of the District of Columbia, or in restraint of trade or commerce between any such Territory and another, or between any such Territory or Territories and any State or States or the District of Columbia, or with foreign nations, or between the District of Columbia and any State or States or foreign nations, is hereby declared illegal. Every person who shall make any such contract or engage in any such combination or conspiracy, shall be deemed guilty of a misdemeanor, and, on conviction thereof, shall be punished by fine not exceeding fifty thousand dollars, or by imprisonment not exceeding one year, or by both said punishments, in the discretion of the court. [July 2, 1890, Chap. 647, Sec. 3, 26 Stat. 209] [As amended, 15 U.S.C. 3]

Clayton Antitrust Act
Section 3
(15 U.S.C. 14)

Section 3. That it shall be unlawful for any person engaged in commerce, in the course of such commerce, to lease or make a sale or contract for sale of goods, wares, merchandise, machinery, supplies or other commodities, whether patented or unpatented, for use, consumption or resale within the United States or any Territory thereof or the District of Columbia or any insular possession or other place under the jurisdiction of the United States, or fix a price charged therefore, or discount from, or rebate upon, such price, on the condition, agreement or understanding that the lessee or purchaser thereof shall not use or deal in the goods, wares, merchandise, machinery, supplies or other commodities of a competitor or competitors of the lessor or seller where the effect of such lease, sale, or contract for sale or such condition, agreement or understanding may be to substantially lessen competition or tend to create a monopoly in any line of commerce. [October 15, 1914, Chap. 323, Sec. 3, 38 Stat. 731] [As amended, 15 U.S.C. 14]

Federal Trade Commission Act
Section 5(a) (1)
(15 U.S.C. 45)

Section 5(a) (1). Unfair methods of competition in commerce, and unfair or deceptive acts or practices in commerce, are hereby declared unlawful. [September 26, 1914, Chap. 311, Sec. 5, 38 Stat. 719] [As amended, 15 U.S.C. 45]

B The Auto Dealer's Day in Court Act

The growth of retail automobile distribution through franchise systems over the past fifty years has brought with it a number of conflicts between franchisors and their franchisees. The bargaining strength of automobile manufacturers by the early 1950s was so great that a typical relationship between manufacturer and franchised dealer left the latter without remedy in the courts because of exculpatory clauses contained in the franchise agreement. The situation induced Congress to enact the Auto Dealer's Day in Court Act,[1] which attempted to balance the bargaining position of franchisor and franchisee by allowing the latter to recover compensatory damages incurred by reason of the failure of the franchisor to act in good faith in complying with the terms of the franchise, or in terminating or not renewing franchises with his dealers. The Act has relevance to all franchise systems, both because its good faith provisions have become accepted through a series of cases as being applicable to much of franchising, and because there have been a number of attempts in the Congress to introduce a bill which would extend the Act to all franchisees. For example, Representative Klyczynski reintroduced such a bill as H.R. 2818 during the First Session of the 90th Congress. Representative Klyczynski had introduced such a bill in two previous sessions.

The Act creates a cause of action where none previously existed in that, irrespective of contractual provisions, it grants a right of review in the federal courts for disputes between automobile franchisors and their dealers involving the good faith of the franchisor in dealing with franchisees.[2]

The relevant sections of the Act are as follows:

I The term "franchise" shall mean any agreement or understanding between a manufacturer and a dealer which involves a continuing commercial relationship between them and which grants to the dealer the right to distribute goods or commodities manufactured, processed, or distributed by the manufacturer. Any commercial relationship in effect for more than eighteen months shall be deemed a "continuing commercial relationship."

The term "good faith" shall mean the duty of each party to any franchise, and all officers, employees, or agents thereof to act in a fair and equitable manner toward each other so as to guarantee the one party freedom from coercion, intimidation, or threats of coercion or intimidation from the other party; provided that recommendation, endorsement, exposition, persuasion, urging, or argument shall not be deemed to constitute a lack of good faith.

II Any dealer may bring an action against a manufacturer with whom he has, or had, a franchise and who is engaged in commerce, in any district court of the United States in the district in which said manufacturer resides, or is found, or has an agent, without respect to the amount in controversy, and shall recover the damages by him sustained and the cost of suit by reason of the failure of said automobile manufacturer from and after passage of this Act to act in good faith in performing or complying with any of the terms or provisions of the franchise, or in terminating, cancelling, or not renewing the franchise with said dealer; provided, that in any such suit the manufacturer shall not be barred from asserting in defense of any such action the failure of the dealer to act in good faith.

The courts have construed the provisions of the Act in an extremely narrow fashion, and lack of good faith has taken on so strict a meaning as to make the franchisee's burden of proof difficult. In the first ten years since the passage of the Act, only one case, *Volkswagen*,[3] resulted in a judgment for the franchisee on the issue of lack of good faith.

The courts have held that a franchisor has wide latitude in his choice of methods to improve an inadequate franchisee. The franchisor still has the right to expect the dealer to provide a suitable outlet for the franchised product,[4] to protect the trademark or trade name,[5] and to compete effectively.[6] The courts have allowed a number of activities even where "couched in terms of coercion, or threat thereof."[7] Coercive actions which have been allowed include: insistence upon performance of franchise terms under threat of termination;[8] establishment of a competing franchisee close to the existing one;[9] and requests that the franchisee abandon his franchise in order to receive benefits to which he would not be entitled if he were terminated.[10]

The poor record of franchisees in court suggests that the Act has not helped those dealers who have had to resort to litigation. However, the Act has almost certainly had a positive influence on franchisor-franchisee relations in that it has induced the former to alter their franchisee agreements and to remove some of the more objectionable requirements. Dealer review boards were established as a result of hearings prior to the passing of the Act. In addition, it is likely that the Act has deterred some franchisor practices which were common in the automobile industry prior to its passage.

C

The Profitability of Nonmarginal Cost Pricing[1]

Given a product or good A, and sellers and buyers X and Y, with X a franchisor and Y a franchisee, we have the following cost and demand functions for sellers of a differentiated product.[2]

In subscripts, the letter preceding A designates the seller, the letter following designates the buyer. Thus, DD_{xay} is the demand facing X when selling A to $Y_1, Y_2, \ldots, Y_n$, the amount that Y_i will pay for successive units of A. DD_{xay}, MR_{xay}, and MC_{xay} are total functions. MC_{xay} does not,

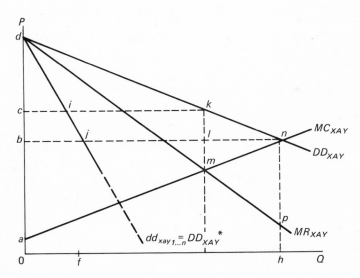

Figure C–1. Cost and Demand Functions for Sellers of a Differentiated Product.

Source: Adapted with permission from The Yale Law Journal Company and Fred B. Rothman & Company, from Richard S. Markovits, "Tie-ins, Reciprocity, and the Leverage Theory," *Yale Law Journal* 76 (1967), p. 1400.

156

however, include marginal pricing and promotional costs. We assume that all Y's have identical demand curves dd_{xay}, although this assumption can be relaxed without changing the conclusions of the analysis.

If X were a monopolist, or if X could induce Y_i to purchase A or its close substitutes only from X, then we would substitute DD^*_{xay} for DD_{xay}. Transaction surplus (TS) is defined as the difference between the marginal cost of a given quantity of product and the amount that buyers are willing to pay for that quantity, for example, the area between DD_{xay} and MC_{xay}.

$$\frac{d(TS)}{dP} > 0 \qquad \text{if } DD > MC$$

and

$$\frac{d(TS)}{dP} = 0, \quad \frac{d^2(TS)}{dP^2} < 0, \qquad \text{if } DD = MC, \quad \text{and } \frac{d(DD)}{dP} < 0$$

at the maximizing price $= Ob$, $TS = adn$
$TS =$ seller surplus (SS) + buyer surplus (BS)
at Ob, $SS = abn$, and $BS = bdn$.[a]

We assume that X's buyers incur no fixed cost (FC) in using A. Thus, X can remove all of the BS without affecting the viability of the long-run trading arrangement. Clearly, if $FC > 0$, Y would not be a viable organization in the long run.

Nonmarginal Cost Single Pricing

While TS is maximized using MC pricing, this does *not* maximize X's profits when $\frac{d(DD)}{dP} < 0$, because $P > MR$ where $MR = MC$. By way of illustration, given a non-MC price $0c$ at quantity $0g$; TS is reduced by kmn, but SS is *increased* by $(bckl - lmn) > 0$, with BS decreased by $bckn$. $0c$ (where $MC = MR$) is the maximizing price for X, but is *not* jointly maximal for X and Y.

Nonmarginal Cost with Lump Sum Pricing

Clearly, even at the maximizing price $0c$, there still exists $BS = cdk$, which is potentially available to X through a lump-sum charge levied on Y_i for the right to buy and/or resell A. Thus, if X charges the non-MC

---

[a] The area *bdn* will overstate consumer surplus if the good is superior. The difference arises because real income is not held constant along DD_{xay}.[3]

price 0*b*, and also charges each Y_i a franchise fee of *bdj* (and can prevent buyer arbitrage), he can increase *SS* from *ackm* to the maximum *TS* of *adn*. This regains both *BS* = *cdk*, plus that part of *TS* = *kmn* which could not be obtained using *MC* pricing. Note that

$$bdj = \int_0^f dd_{xay_{1...n}} - 0bjf$$

However, non-*MC* pricing can be used profitably with lump-sum pricing if and only if

    cdk + *kmn* > pricing and enforcement (or nonenforcement)
             costs of operating the tying arrangement
             which must accompany lump-sum pricing where
             the tied good is sold in a competitive market

Whether lump-sum pricing will actually be used will depend on a number of factors. The higher the $\frac{SS}{max^{TS}}$ ratio generated by single pricing, the less likely the use of lump-sum pricing, *ceteris paribus*. Thus, the greater the absolute slope of DD_{xay} and the less the absolute slope of MC_{xay} to the left of the relevant volume, the less likely is lump-sum pricing to be used.

Even with a favorable $\frac{SS}{max^{TS}}$ ratio, the use of lump-sum pricing will depend on *X*'s relative bargaining strength vis-à-vis Y_i. Even where *X* demands no more than *bdj* from Y_i, there is no certainty that he will get it. Y_i will always recognize that *X*, however much he would like to increase *SS*, will always prefer to make sales at *MC* than lose Y_i's patronage altogether. Thus, depending on the law and taking into consideration pricing and buying costs, *X* and $Y_{1...n}$ play either an *n*-person nonzero-sum game or a two person nonzero-sum game. The outcome of either is indeterminate, and will be a function of the relative bargaining strengths of *X* and each Y_i.

Nonmarginal Cost Pricing under Imperfect Information

In order to correctly estimate the (expected) value of the right to purchase and/or resell *X*'s product, *Y* must know the probability distribution over the possible shapes of DD_{xay} at each relevant price, producing an estimated demand DD_{xay}^E. The greater the average variation in $Y_{1...n}$'s demand for *A*, the greater the risk (and the greater the possible monetary loss) that the actual value of the right to purchase *A* — the franchise fee — will be less than its expected value.

Under imperfect information as to the probability distribution over the possible shapes of DD_{xay}, *X* will determine his optimal pricing strategy and Y_i will determine the highest franchise fee that he will pay to purchase A at X's marginal cost by calculating the expected value and discounting this sum according to the value of the risk that $DD^E_{xay} < DD_{xay}$. By lowering his lump sum franchise fee below bdn (say, to cdk) and using non-MC pricing, X can transfer the risk that $DD^E_{xay} < DD_{xay}$ to himself. The smaller the franchise fee and the higher P, the smaller Y_i's expected loss and the higher X's. Again, in this case as in the previous ones, non-MC pricing can only be used for a good sold in a competitive market *if* a tying arrangement is involved.

By lowering his franchise fee and using non-MC pricing, X's risk is increased less than the sum of the weighted average of Y_i's is decreased. For example, where Y resells to an ultimate user Z, X's rise under non-MC pricing is less than the sum of Y_i's risks under MC lump-sum pricing, X is concerned only with changes in industry-wide demand for A, while Y_i must also consider possible variance in his individual share of $\sum_1^n Y_i$ sales. Also, because of his (probable) greater ability to sustain short-run losses, X will be less adverse to risk taking than will Y_i. Non-MC pricing will reduce the discount demanded by X even where it does *not* decrease the actual risk.

Similarly, where X has difficulty estimating DD_{xay} and planning for production facilities, and so on, he can increase his expected return by substituting non-MC pricing for part of his lump-sum franchise fee — and thus provide a cushion for possible short-run upward shifts in his average-cost curve.

D
The Profitability of Price Discrimination[1]

It can be shown that, if elasticity of demand at the single profit maximizing price is not the same for Y_i and Y_{i+1}, and the seller wishes to increase gross profits, he will discriminate even if elasticities are equal at all other prices. If elasticities at the single profit maximizing price are the same in each market, MR's will also be equal. This follows from the fact that

$$MR = \text{Average Revenue } \frac{e-1}{e}$$

where e is the point elasticity of demand, with

$$e = \frac{\dfrac{\Delta Q}{Q}}{\dfrac{\Delta P}{P}}$$

Assume, for simplicity in drawing a diagram showing the sum of individual cost curves, that we have a constant cost situation with horizontal MC functions.

Clearly, X's single profit maximizing price $= 0g$, which corresponds to the intersection of $MR_{XA(Y_1+Y_2)}$ and $MC_{XAY_{1,2}}$. Similarly, in selling only to Y_1 the single profit maximizing price $= 0h$; in selling only to Y_2 the single profit maximizing price $= 0i$, where

$$0i < 0g < 0h$$

If X can raise $0g$ to $0h$ for Y_1, gross profit is increased by jkn (assuming of course that X would agree to sell A to Y_1 even past the point where $mr_{xay_1} < mc_{xay_1}$).

If X can lower $0g$ to $0i$ for Y_2, gross profit is increased by opq. X has two alternate ways of using a tying arrangement to enhance the advantages of price discrimination. He can offer to sell A to Y_1 and Y_2 for $0h$ per unit, and offer Y_2 the option to purchase an equal amount of some good B for ih below the current market price. Or, he can offer to sell A to Y_1 and Y_2 for $0i$ per unit, but condition has sales to Y_1 on the latter's agreement to purchase an equal amount of some good B for ih above the current market price.

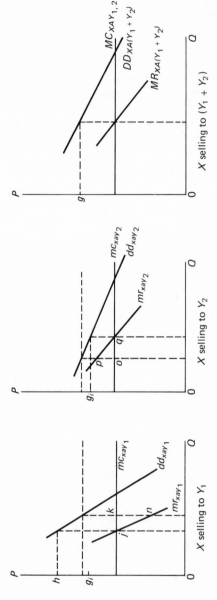

Figure D–1. Cost and Demand Functions for Sellers Facing Separate and Combined Buyers.

Source: Adapted with permission from The Yale Law Journal Company and Fred B. Rothman & Company, from Richard S. Markovits, "Tie-ins, Reciprocity, and the Leverage Theory," *Yale Law Journal* 76 (1967), p. 1446.

Economic Explanations for the Use of Exclusive Franchising

Perfect Retail Markets

In a perfect retail market distribution costs are minimized by selecting enough franchisees so that each operates at his minimum long-run average cost (LRAC) point. The franchisor subtracts from the cumulative franchisee demand curve a franchisor distribution-cost markup. The franchisor then maximizes his profits with respect to this net demand function. Thus:

$$P_f = MC_1^* + w$$

where P_f = retail price

$MC_1^* = AC_1^*$ is the minimum per unit cost of distribution, excluding the cost of the franchised good to the franchisee

w = wholesale price charged franchisee by franchisor

The demand relationship is in equilibrium only where each franchisee operates at the minimum of his (LRAC) curve. A profit maximizing franchisor will issue new franchises so long as a demand exists for them. The adoption of an exclusive franchising system in a perfect retail market implies nonprofit maximizing behavior on the part of the franchisor.

Small Retail Markets with Collusive Behavior

Each franchisee faces a demand curve

$$P_f = f(nq)$$

where q = the sales of each other franchisee, and
n = number of franchisees in the market, as determined by the franchisor

The profit of each franchisee is

$$\pi_f = f(nq)q - C(q) - wq$$

161

where $C(q)$ = franchisee's long-run distribution cost

$$\pi_f \geqslant 0$$

$$\frac{d\pi_f}{dq} = qnf' + f - C' = 0$$

and

$$f' = \frac{df}{d(nq)}, \quad C' = \frac{dC}{dq}$$

The profit for the franchisor is

$$\pi_{f'} = wqn - F(nq)$$

where $F(nq)$ = franchisor's long-run distribution cost differentiating with respect to n and q, and substituting, we have

$$C''(q) = 0$$

which implies that the franchisor will add franchisees only to the point where MC_f is horizontal; thus, the franchisor will offer exclusive franchises.

Large Retail Markets with Differentiated Franchisees

Given n differentiated franchisees in an imperfect market, the demand curve facing the kth franchisee is

$$P_k = A_k - a_{kk}q_k - \sum_{\substack{i=l \\ i \neq k}}^{n} b_{ki}q_i$$

where $k = (1 \ldots n)$
q_i = sales of the ith franchisee
$b_{ki} = b$, for all b and i except $i = k$
$a_{kk} = a$, and $A_k = A$
$c_k(q_k) = C(q_k)$ for all k
the a's and b's are assumed not to change with changes in n.

For any w, the franchisee will determine q_k so that $MR_f = MC_f$

$$A - 2aqk - b \sum_{\substack{i=l \\ i \neq k}}^{n} q_i = C'(q_k) + w$$

because of symmetry, $q_k = q_i$, and

$$A - [2a + b(n - 1)]\, q_k = C'(q_k) + w$$

Given his derived demand curve, the franchisor determines an optimum price for the franchised good equal to w^*, and the franchisee price becomes

$$P_k = w^* + AC_f$$

where $AC_f =$ franchisor's processing cost

Now, $(n^* - 1)$ franchisees can sell more total units than (n^*) franchisees only if

$$w^* = MR_{f'} > M'(nq)$$

where $MR_{f'} = $ the franchisor's marginal revenue
$M'(nq) = $ the franchisor's marginal cost

which implies that the sum of franchisee sales gains exceeds the sales of the excluded franchisee;

$$n\frac{dq}{dn} < -q$$

substituting into the equilibrium condition where $MR_f = MC_f$, we have

$$\frac{nb}{2a - b + nb + C''(q)} > 1$$

which will occur, as Pashigian shows, if the slope of $MC_{f'}$ satisfies

$$-2a < C''(q) < -(2a - b)$$

The franchisor is economically justified in using exclusive franchising given the existence of appropriate conditions for (1) the slope of MC_f; (2) the effect on P_f as price is increased; and (3) the effect on P_f as other franchisees increase sales.

Selected
Bibliography*

The Environment of Franchising

Governmental Regulation

American Bar Association, *Symposium – Antitrust Limits on Distribution Policies and Programs,* 26 A.B.A. Antitrust Section (1964).

Austin, A. D., "Tying Arrangement: A Critique and Some New Thoughts," *Wisconsin Law Review* (Winter, 1967), 88.

Averill, Lawrence, "Antitrust Considerations of the Principal Distribution Restrictions in Franchise Agreements," *Corporate Counsel's Annual 1966,* Albany, New York: Matthew Bender and Company, Inc., 1966, 428–482.

Axelrod, Norman D., "Practicing Law Institute – Franchising and Dual Distribution," *The Antitrust Bulletin,* XI, No. 3 (May–June, 1966), 533–540.

Caldwell, J. T., and Rhodes, R. S., "Antitrust Aspects of Dealer Licensing and Franchising," *Northwestern University Law Review,* 62 (March–April, 1967), 1 ff.

Covey, Frank M., Jr., "Franchising and the Antitrust Laws," *Notre Dame Lawyer,* 42 (June, 1967), 605–626.

Eckmann, James K., "Antitrust Ramifications of Trademark Licensing and Franchising," *Stanford Law Review,* 17 (May, 1965), 926–941.

"Franchising + Antitrust = Confusion: The Unfortunate Formula," *Santa Clara Lawyer,* 9 (Spring, 1969), 266.

Jordan, Robert L., "Exclusive and Restricted Sales Areas Under the Antitrust Laws," *U.C.L.A. Law Review,* 9 (January, 1962), 111–155.

McLaren, R. W., "Marketing Limitations on Independent Distributors and Dealers – Prices, Territories, Customers, and Handling of Competitive Products," *Antitrust Bulletin,* 13 (Spring, 1968), 161.

McLaren, R. W., "Territorial and Customer Restrictions, Assignments, Suggested Resale Prices, and Refusals to Deal," *ABA Antitrust Law Journal,* 37 (1968), 135.

---

* A more extensive bibliography on franchise systems may be found in Donald N. Thompson, "Franchising and Franchise Systems: The Marketing, Management, and Economic Literature," *Franchising Today 1967–68* (Part I); *Franchising Today 1968–69* (Part II); *Franchising Today 1969–70* (Part III) (Charles L. Vaughn and David B. Slater, eds.), New York: Matthew Bender (1968, 1969, and 1970).

Pearson, R. N., "Tying Arrangements and Antitrust Policy," *Northwestern University Law Review,* 60 (November–December, 1965), 626.

Rudnick, Lewis G., "Franchisor Liability and Susceptibility to the Jurisdiction of the Courts of States where Its Franchises Do Business," *Franchise Management Institute Legal Session,* Chicago: International Franchise Association, 1965.

Rudnick, Lewis G., "The Franchiser's Dilemma: Can He Satisfy the Legal and Commercial Requirements of a Trademark Licensing System without Exposing Himself to Other Legal Risks," *The Trademark Reporter,* 56, No. 9 (September, 1966), 621–642.

State Antitrust Laws, 29 A.B.A. Antitrust Section (1965), 258–300.

Stewart, Charles E., Jr., "Antitrust Considerations Involved in Product Distribution," *Business Law,* 19 (1964), 967 ff.

Thompson, Donald N., *Contractual Marketing Systems,* Lexington, Mass.: Heath Lexington Books (1971).

Timberg, Sigmund, "Territorial Exclusives," *The Business Lawyer,* XXI (November, 1965), 59–71.

Turner, Donald F., *Cooperation Among Competitors,* an address before the Fifth Annual Corporate Counsel Institute Meeting, Chicago, Illinois (October 13, 1966).

Turner, Donald F., "Some Reflections on Antitrust," *1966 N.Y. State Bar Association Antitrust Law Symposium,* New York, 1–9.

Turner, Donald F., "The Definition of Agreement under the Sherman Act: Conscious Parallelism and Refusals to Deal," *Harvard Law Review,* 75 (1962), 655 f.

Turner, Donald F., "The Validity of Tying Arrangements under the Antitrust Laws," *Harvard Law Review,* 50 (1958), 62.

Van Cise, Jerrold G., *Guiding Principles of Antitrust Law,* New York, mimeographed by author (May, 1966).

Zeidman, Philip F., "Antitrust Aspects of Franchising – Some Recent Developments," *Michigan State Bar Journal,* XLV (May, 1966), 27–37.

Public Policy and the Effects of Regulation

Baldwin, W. L., and McFarland, David, "Tying Arrangements in Law and Economics, *"The Antitrust Bulletin,"* VIII (1963), 743–780.

Bock, Betty, *Antitrust Issues in Restricting Sales Territories and Out-*

lets, New York: National Industrial Conference Board Studies in Business Economics #98, 1968.

Bork, Robert H., "The Rule of Reason and the Per Se Concept: Price Fixing and Market Division," *The Yale Law Journal,* Part I, 74, No. 5 (April, 1965), 775–847; Part II, 75, No. 3 (January, 1966), 373–476.

Bowman, Ward S., "Tying Arrangements and the Leverage Problem," *Yale Law Journal,* 67 (1957), 19–36.

Bridges, S. P., "New Concepts in Customer and Territorial Restrictions – the Schwinn and Sealy Doctrines," *Duke Law Journal* (December, 1967), 1156.

Burstein, M. L., "A Theory of Full-Line Forcing," *Northwestern University Law Review,* 55 (1960), 62 ff.

Burstein, M. L., "The Economics of Tie-In Sales," *Review of Economics and Statistics,* 42 (1960), 68–73.

Dixon, Donald F., "Impact of Recent Antitrust Decisions upon Franchise Marketing," *Business Topics,* 17 (Spring, 1969), 68–79.

Edwards, Corwin D., "Control of the Single Firm: Its Place in Antitrust Policy," *Law and Contemporary Problems,* XXX (Summer, 1965), 465–487.

Federal Trade Commission, "Statement," *Small Business Administration Hearing on Small Business Franchise Size Criteria* (March 10, 1966).

"Final Schwinn Judgement," *Legal Bulletin* (1968-I), 12–18.

Flicker, Michael R., "Newcomer Defenses: Reasonable Use of Tie-Ins, Franchises, Territorials and Exclusives," *Stanford Law Review,* 18 (1966), 457–474.

Hale, G. E., and Hale, Rosemary, Market Power: *Size and Shape under the Sherman Act,* Boston: Little, Brown and Company (1958), 53.

Handler, Milton, "Statement Before the Small Business Administration," *The Antitrust Bulletin,* XI, No. 3 (May–June, 1966), 417–438.

Hewitt, Charles M., "Termination of Dealer Franchises and the Code-Mixing Classified and Coordinated Uncertainty With Conflict," *The Business Lawyer,* 22 (1967), 1075 ff.

Kaysen, Carl, and Turner, Donald F., *Antitrust Policy, an Economic and Legal Analysis,* Cambridge: Harvard University Press (1959).

Keck, R. D., "Alternative Distribution Techniques – Franchising, Consignment, Agency, and Licensing," *Antitrust Bulletin,* 13 (Spring, 1968), 49.

Keck, R. D., "The Schwinn Case," *The Business Lawyer* (April, 1968), 669–687.

Kulp, F. Bruce, Jr.,"Tying Arrangements under The Antitrust Laws:The Integrity of the Product Defense," *Michigan Law Review,* 63 (1964), 1413–1424.

Markham, Jesse W., "The New Antitrust Policy and the Individual Business Firm," *Law and Contemporary Problems,* 30 (Summer, 1965), 607–620.

Markovits, Richard S., "Tie-Ins, Reciprocity, and the Leverage Theory," *The Yale Law Journal* 76 (1967), 1461.

Narver, John C., *Some Aspects of Public Policy and Conglomerate Mergers, Franchising, and Dominant Firms,* paper presented at the Fall Conference, American Marketing Association, Cincinnati, Ohio (August 25, 1969).

Report of the Attorney General's National Committee to Study the Antitrust Laws. Washington, D.C.: U.S. Government Printing Office (March 31, 1955).

Robinson, Stanley D., "Restraints on Trade and the Orderly Marketing of Goods" *Cornell Law Quarterly,* 45 (1960), 254–287.

Rudnick, Harry L., and Rudnick, Lewis, "Some Solutions to the Problems of Maintaining Quality Standards, Eliminating Unethical Practices, Supervising Promotions and Ensuring Successful Management of Franchised and Nonfranchised Retail Outlets," *The Antitrust Bulletin,* XI, No. 3 (May–June, 1966).

Rudnick, Lewis G., "Schwinn and Sealy" (International Franchise Association) *Legal Bulletin* (1967-II), 173.

Rudnick, Lewis G., "The Sealy Case: The Supreme Court Applies the Per Se Doctrine to a Hybrid Distribution System for Trademark Bedding Products," *The Trademark Reporter,* 57 (July, 1967), 459–467.

Small Business Administration, *Hearings on Franchises* (March 10, 1966), Washington, D.C.: Ace-Federal Reporters, Inc., 1966.

Stedman, John C., "Tying Arrangements," *22 A.B.A. Antitrust Section* (1964), 64–75.

Stone, Christopher D., "Closed Territorial Distribution: An Opening Question in the Sherman Act," *University of Chicago Law Review,* 30 (1963), 286–317.

Thompson, Donald N., "Franchise Operations and Antitrust Law," *The Journal of Retailing,* 45 (Winter, 1969), 39–53.

Thompson, Donald N., *Legislation and the Regulation of Franchise Systems,* Marketing Science Institute Working Paper (April, 1968).

Thompson, Donald N., "French Regulation Concerning Exclusive Distribution Agreements and Refusal to Sell," *McGill Law Quarterly,* 3 (1968), 6.

Travers, A. H., and Wright, T. D., "Restricted Channels of Distribution under the Sherman Act," *Harvard Law Review,* 75 (1962), 795.

Wilson, Rufus E., *How to Control the Purchases of Franchisees,* remarks before the Franchise and Antitrust Symposium, International Franchise Association, Washington, D.C. (May 3, 1968), mimeographed.

Zimmerman, Edwin M., "Distribution Restrictions after Sealy and Schwinn," *Legal Bulletin* (1968-I), 79–84.

Zimmerman, Edwin M., *Some Legal Issues Raised by Distribution Restrictions in Franchise Agreements—Department of Justice View,* an address to 1967 Federal Bar Association Convention, San Francisco, California (July 28, 1967).

Congressional Hearings

U.S. Congress, Senate, Subcommittee on Antitrust and Monopoly, Committee on the Judiciary, *Hearings on Automobile Dealer Franchises,* 84th Congress, 2nd Session, 1956.

U.S. Congress, Senate, Subcommittee on Antitrust and Monopoly, Committee on the Judiciary, *Distribution Problems Affecting Small Business,* Part 3, 89th Congress, 2nd Session, 1966.

U.S. Congress, Senate, Subcommittee on Antitrust and Monopoly, Committee on the Judiciary, *Distribution Problems Affecting Small Business*—(Part I, Franchising Agreements), 89th Congress, 1st Session, 1965; (Part II), 89th Congress, 2nd Session, 1966; (Part III), 89th Congress, 2nd Session, 1966.

U.S. Congress, Senate, Subcommittee No. 4, Select Committee on Small Business, *Hearings, The Impact upon Small Business of Dual Distribution and Related Vertical Integration,* I–IX, 88th Congress, 1st Session, 1963.

U.S. Congress, Senate, Subcommittee on Patents, Trademarks and Copyrights, Committee on the Judiciary, *Registration and Protection of Trademarks,* Part I, 87th Congress, 1st Session, 1961; Part II, 87th Congress, 2nd Session, 1962.

170

U.S. Congress, Senate, Subcommittee on Urban and Rural Development, Select Committee on Small Business, *The Impact of Franchising
on Small Business,* Part I, 91st Congress, 2nd Session, 1970.

Managerial Aspects of Franchising

Development and Organization

Atkinson, J. F., *Franchising: The Odds-On Favorite* (Chicago: International Franchise Association, 1968).

Bond, Robert J., *BDSA Franchise Programs for Equal Opportunity in
Business,* address to the Third Annual Boston College Management
Conference on Franchising (mimeographed), 5.

Hall, William P., "Franchising—New Scope for an Old Technique,"
Harvard Business Review (January–February, 1964), 60–72.

Kursh, Harry, *The Franchise Boom,* Englewood Cliffs, N.J.: Prentice-
Hall, Inc., rev. ed., 1968.

MacIntyre, Everette, *Statement on Franchising Developments* before
the Conference of the International Franchise Association, Washington, D.C., May 8, 1969.

Modern Franchising Magazine, Des Plaines, Ill.: Modern Franchising
Magazine (bimonthly).

Oxenfeldt, A. R., and Thompson, D. N., "Franchising in Perspective,"
Journal of Retailing, (Winter, 1969), 3–13.

Rahl, J. A., "Overseas Distribution, Franchising, and Licensing—Comparison With Domestic Techniques," *Antitrust Bulletin,* 13 (Spring,
1968), 193.

Sherwood, Rogers (publisher), *National Franchise Reports,* Chicago:
National Franchise Reports (monthly).

Sherwood, Rogers (publisher), *The Franchise Annual,* Chicago: National
Franchise Reports (yearly).

Slater, David, "Some Socio-Economic Footnotes on Franchising," *Boston University Business Review,* II, No. 1 (Summer, 1964), 19.

Task Force For Equal Opportunity in Business, *Franchise Companies—
Business Opportunities for Minority Groups* (a report to Secretary

Luther H. Hodges by Franklin D. Roosevelt, Jr., Undersecretary of Commerce). mimeo (December 1964).

Thompson, Donald N., "The One Foot Shelf–Franchise Systems," *California Management Review* (Fall, 1968), 94–96.

United States Department of Commerce, *Franchise Company Data for Equal Opportunity in Business,* Washington: United States Government Printing Office, 2nd ed., 1966; 3rd ed., 1967, 4th ed., 1969.

Woll, M., "Sources of Revenue to the Franchisor and Their Strategic Implications," *Journal of Retailing,* 44 (Winter 1969), 14–20.

Zeidman, Philip F., "The Growth and Importance of Franchising–Its Impact on Small Business," *Legal Bulletin* (1968-I), 46–59.

Franchisee Aspects

Bernstein, L. M., "Does Franchising Create a Secure Outlet for the Small Aspiring Entrepreneur?" *Journal of Retailing,* 44 (Winter, 1969), 21–38.

Brown, Harold, *Franchising: Trap for the Trusting* (Boston: Little Brown, 1969).

International Franchise Association, Inc., *Franchise Opportunity Handbook,* Chicago: International Franchise Association, 1966 (published yearly).

Lewis, Edwin, and Hancock, Robert, *The Franchise System of Distribution,* Minneapolis: Division of Research, Graduate School of Business Administration, University of Minnesota (November, 1963).

"Minority Group Franchise Financing Can Benefit From New SBA Plan," *Continental Franchise Review* (September 23, 1968), 5.

Seltz, D. D., *How To Get Started with Your Own Franchised Business,* New York: Farnsworth Publishing Co., 1967.

Weiss, E. B., "Corporate Chains are Franchising Independent Retailers" *Advertising Age,* 38 (February 6, 1967), 77–78.

United States Department of Commerce, *Bibliography on Marketing to Low Income Consumers,* Washington: U.S. Government Printing Office, 1969.

Van Cise, Jerrold G., "The Boston College Center's Special Committee On Unfair And Deceptive Practices in Franchising: The Chairman's Final Report," in Charles L. Vaughn, ed., *Franchising Today 1969,* Lynbrook, N.Y.: Farnsworth Publishing Co. (1969), 185–194.

172

Franchisor Aspects

Curry, J. A. H., Morris, T. R., Larkworthy, J. S., et al., *Partners for Profit: A Study of Franchising,* New York: American Management Association, Inc., 1966.

Fels, Jerome L., "Franchising — Some Legal and Financial Considerations" *Legal Bulletin* (1968-I), 12–18.

Lifflander, Matthew L., "Types of Franchises and Legal Considerations," in Charles L. Vaughn and David B. Slater, eds., *Franchising Today 1967–1968,* Lynbrook, N.Y.: Farnsworth Publishing Co. (1968), 262–276.

Loscocco, S. Joseph, "Location Analysis and Selection," in Charles L. Vaughn and David B. Slater, eds., *Franchising Today 1967–1968,* Lynbrook, N.Y.: Farnsworth Publishing Co. (1968), 262–276.

Rudnick, Harry L., "Arbitration of Disputes between Franchisors and Franchisees," *Franchise Management Institute Legal Session,* Chicago: International Franchise Association, 1965.

Rudnick, Lewis G., *Exporting American Franchises,* an address to 1967 Federal Bar Association Convention, San Francisco, California (July 28, 1967).

Timberg, Sigmund, "Some Working Antitrust Rules in Distributing through Franchised and Non-Franchised Outlets," *Remarks* before the Symposium on Franchising of the Practising Law Institute, New York City (December 3–4, 1965).

Wilson, Rufus E., "Current Legal Problems in Franchising as Seen by the Enforcement Agencies," in Charles L. Vaughn, ed., *Franchising Today 1969,* Lynbrook, N.Y.: Farnsworth Publishing Co. (1969), 154–161.

Vaughn, Charles L., *Franchise Industry Training 1967–1968: A Demonstration Project Of Franchise Industry Training and Work Experience for Youth Who Have Not Completed High School,* Chestnut Hill, Massachusetts: Center for the Study of Franchise Distribution, Boston College, 1968.

Zeidman, Philip F., "An Ounce of Prevention: Legal Aspects of the Selection of a Franchisee," in Charles L. Vaughn and David B. Slater, eds., *Franchising Today 1967–1968,* Lynbrook, N.Y.: Farnsworth Publishing Co. (1968), 150–163.

Franchising in Selected Industries

American Institute of Food Distribution, Inc., *Fast-Food Franchising* (1969), Fair Lawn, New Jersey: A.I.F.F.D.

Assael, Henry, "Dealer Reactions to Factory Policies and Actions: A Case Study of the Automobile Dealer," in Peter D. Bennett, ed., *Marketing and Economic Development,* 1965 Fall Conference of the American Marketing Association, Chicago: American Marketing Association (1965), 672–673.

Henderson, Ernest III, "The Evolution of a Franchise Division," in Charles L. Vaughn and David B. Slater, eds., *Franchising Today 1967–1968,* Lynbrook, N.Y.: Farnsworth Publishing Co. (1968), 189–193.

Hewitt, Charles M., Jr., *Automobile Franchising Agreements,* Homewood, Ill.: Richard D. Irwin, Inc., 1956.

McLean, John G., and Haigh, Robert W., *The Growth of Integrated Oil Companies,* Boston: Division of Research, Graduate School of Business Administration, Harvard University, 1954.

Weiner, J. B., "Coca-Cola: The Greatest Franchise of All," *Dun's Review and Modern Industry,* 88 (October, 1966), 31 f.

Economic Aspects of Franchising

Franchise Systems and Restraints

"Business Justification for Tying Agreements: A Retreat from the Per Se Doctrine," *Western Reserve Law Review,* 17 (October, 1965), 257.

Burstein, M. L., "The Economics of Tie-In Sales," *The Review of Economics and Statistics* XLII (1960), 68–73.

Ferguson, James M., "Tying Arrangements and Reciprocity: An Economic Analysis," *Law and Contemporary Problems,* XXX (Summer, 1965), 552–580.

Gillespie, Samuel M., *An Analysis of Control in Franchise Distribution Systems* (Masters of Science in Marketing Thesis), Urbana: University of Illinois, 1966.

Hilton, George W., "Tying Sales and Full-Line Forcing," *Weltwirtschaftliches Archiv,* 81 (1958), 265–276.

174

Ingraham, S. Michal, *Management Control Potentials and Practices of Franchise Systems,* Ann Arbor: University Microfilms, 1963.

Lockhart, William B., and Sacks, Howard R., "The Relevance of Economic Factors in Determining Whether Exclusive Arrangements Violate Section 3 of the Clayton Act," *Harvard Law Review,* 65 (1952), 913 ff.

Markovits, Richard, "Tie-Ins, Reciprocity, and the Leverage Theory," *The Yale Law Journal,* 76 (1967), 1399–1443.

Pashigian, Bedros P., *The Distribution of Automobiles: An Economic Analysis of the Franchise System,* Englewood Cliffs, N.J.: Prentice-Hall, Inc., 1961.

Preston, Lee, E., "Restrictive Distribution Arrangements: Economic Analysis and Public Policy Standards," *Law and Contemporary Problems,* XXX (Summer, 1965) 506–529.

Scitovsky, Tibor, "Some Consequences of the Habit of Judging Quality By Price," *The Review of Economic Studies,* 811 (2), No. 32, 1944–45.

Singer, Eugene M., *Antitrust Economics: Selected Legal Cases And Economic Models,* Englewood Cliffs, N.J.: Prentice-Hall Inc. (1968).

Thompson, Donald N., *Franchising, A Public Policy Dilemma: Comment,* Paper Presented At the 1969 Fall Conference, American Marketing Association, Cincinnati, Ohio (August 25, 1969).

Vertical and Contractual Integration

Bowersox, Donald J. and McCarthy, E. J., *Strategic Planning of Vertical Marketing Systems,* paper presented at the Vertical Marketing Systems Workshop, Northwestern University (November 6, 1968).

Bucklin, Louis P., *The Economic Analysis of Channel Structure,* paper presented at the Vertical Marketing Systems Workshop, Northwestern University (November 6, 1968).

Comanor, William S., *Vertical Mergers, Market Power, and the Antitrust Laws* (mimeo, Department of Economics, Harvard University, 1968).

Hewitt, Charles M., *The Changing Role of Contracting as a Device for Market Control,* paper presented at the American Marketing Association Annual Meeting, Washington, D.C. (December 27, 1967).

Mills, Edwin S., and Lav, Michael R., "A Model of Market Areas with Free Entry," *Journal of Political Economy,* 72 (1964), 278–288.

Wedding, Nugent (ed.), *Vertical Integration in Marketing,* Urbana: University of Illinois, Bureau of Economic and Business Research, 1952.

Related Marketing Literature

Evolution and Change in
Marketing Channels

Clewett, Richard M., and Stasch, Stanley F., *Progress and Opportunities in the Study of Distribution Channels,* paper presented at the Vertical Marketing Systems Workshop, Northwestern University (November 6, 1968).

Martineau, Pierre, "Social Classes and Spending Behavior," *Journal of Marketing,* XXIII (October, 1958), 121 f.

McCammon, Bert C., Jr., "Alternative Explanations of Institutional Change and Channel Evolution," in Steven A. Greyser, ed., *Toward Scientific Marketing,* 1963 Winter Conference of the American Marketing Association, Chicago: American Marketing Association (1963), 477–490.

McCammon, Bert C., Jr., "The Emergence and Growth of Contractually Integrated Channels in the American Economy," in Peter D. Bennett, ed., Marketing and Economic Development, 1965 Fall Conference of the American Marketing Association, Chicago: American Marketing Association (1965), 496–515.

Oxenfeldt, A. R., and Kelly, A. O., "Will Successful Franchise Systems Ultimately Become Wholly Owned Chains," *Journal of Retailing,* 44 (Winter, 1969), 69–83.

Warner, W. Lloyd, Meeker, Marcia, and Eells, Kenneth, *Social Class in America,* Chicago: Science Research Associates, Inc., (1949).

Weale, W. Bruce, "Measuring the Customer's Image of a Department Store," *Journal of Retailing* XXXVII (Summer, 1961), 40 f.

Theoretical Aspects of Marketing Channels
and Channel Selection

Balderston, F. E., "Communication Networks in Intermediate Markets," *Management Science,* 4 (January, 1958), 154–171.

Baligh, Helmy H., "A Theoretical Framework for Channel Choice," in

Peter D. Bennett, ed., *Marketing and Economic Development,* 1965 Fall Conference of the American Marketing Association, Chicago: American Marketing Association (1965), 631–654.

Bucklin, Louis P., *A Theory of Distribution Channel Structure,* Berkeley: Institute of Business and Economic Research Special Publications, University of California, 1966.

Granbois, Donald H., and Willett, Ronald P., "Patterns of Conflicting Perceptions among Channel Members," in L. George Smith, ed., *Reflections on Progress in Marketing,* 1965 Winter Conference of the American Marketing Association, Chicago: American Marketing Association (1965), 86–100.

Losch, August, *The Economics of Location,* New Haven, Conn.: Yale University Press (1954).

Mallen, Bruce, "Conflict and Cooperation in Marketing Channels," in L. George Smith, ed., *Reflections on Progress in Marketing,* 1965 Winter Conference of the American Marketing Association, Chicago: American Marketing Association (1965), 65–85.

Mills, Edwin S., and Lav, Michael R., "A Model of Market Areas with Free Entry," *Journal of Political Economy,* 72 (June, 1964), 278–288.

Marketing Channel Management

Macaulay, Stewart, "Non-Contractual Relations in Business: A Preliminary Study," *American Sociological Review,* 28 (1963), 55.

Raffel, Forrest R., "Analyzing Franchise Locations," in Charles L. Vaughn and David B. Slater, eds., *Franchising Today 1967–1968,* Lynbrook, N.Y.: Farnsworth Publishing Co. (1968), 199–202.

Ridgeway, Valentine P., "Administration of Manufacturer-Dealer Systems," *Administrative Science Quarterly,* I (March, 1957), 464–483.

Notes

Chapter 1
Introduction

1. See Harry Kursh, *The Franchise Boom* (rev. ed.), Englewood Cliffs, N.J.: Prentice-Hall, Inc. (1968); Edwin Lewis and Robert Hancock, *The Franchise System of Distribution,* Minneapolis: Graduate School of Business Administration, University of Minnesota (1963); and J. A. H. Curry, T. R. Morris, J. S. Larkworthy *et al., Partners for Profit: A Study of Franchising,* New York: American Management Association, Inc. (1966).
2. *White Motor Company* v. *United States,* 372 U.S. 253 (1963).
3. *U.S.* v. *Arnold, Schwinn & Co.,* 388 U.S. 365 (1967), at 366.

Chapter 2
The Nature of Franchising

1. Grant Mauk, quoted in J. A. H. Curry, et al., *Partners For Profit: A Study of Franchising,* New York: American Management Association, Inc. (1966), p. 12.
2. Monte E. Pendleton, *Statement* before U.S. Congress, Senate, Subcommittee on Antitrust and Monopoly, Committee on the Judiciary, *Distribution Problems Affecting Small Business — Part I,* 89th Congress, 1st Session, 1965, pp. 47–48.
3. From *Changing Times — The Kiplinger Magazine,* quoted in Harry Kursh, *The Franchise Boom,* Englewood Cliffs, New Jersey: Prentice-Hall (1962), p. 14.
4. Philip F. Zeidman, *Antitrust Aspects of Franchising — Some Recent Developments,* remarks before a meeting of the Antitrust Law Section, State Bar of Michigan considering the Antitrust Problems of Small Business, April 29, 1966. Essentially the same definition is found in the various editions of United States Department of Commerce, *Franchise Company Data for Equal Opportunity in Business.*
5. Charles M. Hewitt, Jr., *Automobile Franchise Agreements,* Homewood Illinois: Richard D. Irwin, Inc. (1956), pp. 189–206.
6. I am indebted for an early form of this classification to William P. Hall, "Franchising — New Scope for an Old Technique," *Harvard Business Review* (January–February, 1964), pp. 60–72.
7. Leonard J. Konopa, "What is Meant By Franchise Selling?," *Journal of Marketing* (April, 1963), pp. 35–37.
8. See "Note," *Yale Law Journal* 72 (1963), pp. 1171, 1182–1186.
9. Argued in *Susser* v. *Carvel Corp.,* 206 F. Supp. 636 (S.D.N.Y. 1962), *aff'd* 332 F. 2d 505 (2d Cir. 1964).
10. Argued in *Denison Mattress Factory* v. *Spring Air Co.,* 308 F. 2d 403 (5th Cir. 1962).

11. Walter J. Schob, "Statement," *Registration and Protection of Trademarks, Part I,* 87th Congress, 1st Session (1961), p. 41.

12. U.S. Congress, Senate, Subcommittee on Antitrust and Monopoly, Committee on the Judiciary, *Administered Prices, Study of Administered Prices in the Bread Industry,* 86th Cong., 1st Session, June 16, 1959, part 12, p. 6038.

Chapter 3
The Development and Contributions of
Franchised Business

1. Ernest Henderson, Sr., "Franchising Yesterday," *Franchising Today 1966–67,* Albany, New York: Matthew Bender (1967), p. 239.

2. Andrew B. Jack, "The Channels of Distribution for an Innovation: The Sewing Machine Industry in America, 1860–1865," *Explorations in Entrepreneurial History* (February, 1957), pp. 113–141.

3. Charles Mason Hewitt, Jr., *Automobile Franchise Agreements.* Homewood, Illinois: Richard D. Irwin, Inc. (1956), p. 19. The material in this section has been drawn from Hewitt's analysis of the early automobile industry.

4. An example of Ford Motor Company franchisees being forced to share the financial problems of the parent company through purchase of inventory overstock is given in Edward D. Kennedy, *The Automobile Industry,* New York: Reynal and Hitchcock (1941), pp. 126–127.

5. "In Autos: Volume vs. Markup?," *Business Week* (February 5, 1955), p. 54.

6. The material in this section has been drawn from an extensive research report by John C. McLean and Robert Wm. Haigh, *The Growth of Integrated Oil Companies.* Boston, Mass.: Graduate School of Business Administration, Harvard University (1954), especially pp. 57–330.

7. "Grocery Business Annual Report," *Progressive Grocer* (1950 and 1968 editions). Further statistical breakdowns appear in U.S. Department of Commerce, *Facts About Grocery Wholesaling* (1968).

8. From a survey by the editors of *American Druggist.* See also U.S. Department of Commerce, *Facts About Drug Wholesaling* (1969).

9. *Dun's Review and Modern Industry* (April, 1964), p. 36.

10. *New York Times* (October 6, 1963), Section 3, p. 46.

11. *New York Times* (July 9, 1967), Section 3, p. 1.

12. "Franchising, No End To Its Growth," *Printers Ink* (August 13, 1965), p. 3.

13. David B. Slater, "Some Socio-Economic Footnotes on Franchising," *Boston University Business Review* (Summer, 1964), p. 23; J. F. Atkinson, *Remarks* to Sixth Annual International Management Conference on Franchising, Boston College, April 3, 1970.

179

14. J. F. Atkinson, *Franchising: The Odds-On Favorite*, Chicago, Illinois: International Franchise Association (1968).

15. Arthur S. Dewing, *The Financial Policy of Corporations* (Volume IV), New York: The Ronald Press Company (1920), p. 4. Dewing's ideas have found support in much of the modern literature. See for example Chapter 3 of Richard M. Cyert and James G. March, *A Behavioral Theory of the Firm*, Englewood Cliffs, New Jersey: Prentice-Hall Inc. (1963); and M. W. Reder, "A Reconsideration of the Marginal Productivity Theory," *Journal of Political Economy* (October, 1947), pp. 450–458.

16. Robert L. Grover, *Statement* before U.S. Congress, Senate, Subcommittee on Antitrust and Monopoly, Committee on the Judiciary, *Distribution Problems Affecting Small Business—Part I*, 89th Congress, 1st Session, 1965, p. 63.

17. J. A. H. Curry et al., *Partners for Profit: A Study of Franchising*, New York: American Management Association (1966), p. 95.

18. S. Michal Ingraham, *Management Control Potentials and Practices of Franchise Systems*, Ann Arbor, Michigan: University Microfilms, Inc. (1963), pp. 91–94.

19. *Susser* v. *Carvel Corp.*, 206 F. Supp. 636 (S.D.N.Y. 1962) at 640; *aff'd.* 332 F. 2d 505 (2d Cir. 1964).

20. Federal Trade Commission, "Statement," *Small Business Administration Hearing on Small Business Franchise Size Criteria* (March 10, 1966).

21. Philip F. Zeidman, "Antitrust Aspects of Franchising—Some Recent Developments," *Michigan State Bar Journal* XLV (May, 1966), p. 29.

22. Senator Philip A. Hart, "Statement," *Distribution Problems Affecting Small Business—Part II*, 89th Congress, 2nd Session, 1966, pp. 696–699.

23. U.S. Congress, Senate, Subcommittee on Antitrust and Monopoly, Committee on the Judiciary, *Concentration Ratios In Manufacturing Industry*, 86th Congress, 2nd Session, 1963, p. 2.

24. For a more complete discussion of the problem of conversion of franchise systems to wholly owned ones, see Alfred R. Oxenfeldt and Anthony O. Kelly, "Will Successful Franchise Systems Ultimately Become Wholly Owned Chains?", *Journal of Retailing* (Winter 1968–1969), pp. 69–83.

25. Quoted in Philip F. Zeidman, "The Growth and Importance of Franchising," *Remarks* at the 1967 Federal Bar Association Convention, San Francisco, California (July 28, 1967), and Small Business Administration statistics.

26. Figures from Office of Minority Business Enterprise, United States Department of Commerce.

27. Figures from U.S. Department of Commerce, cited in Ross B.

Baxter, *Address* before annual meeting of the Center for the Study of Franchise Distribution and Smaller Business, Boston College (April 4, 1970). "Minority" includes black, Mexican-American, Puerto Rican, American Indian, Eskimo, and Aleut.

28. Fred C. Allvine, "Black Business Development," *Journal of Marketing* 34 (April, 1970), 4.

29. U.S. Department of Commerce, *Franchise Company Data for Equal Opportunity in Business,* Washington, D.C.: Department of Commerce (published approximately annually). About 85,000 copies had been distributed as of June, 1970.

Chapter 4
Market Organization and Vertical
Channel Relations

1. For a fuller discussion of the four forms of vertical organization, see D. N. Thompson, "Contractual Marketing Systems: An Overview," in D. N. Thompson, ed., *Contractual Marketing Systems,* Lexington, Mass.: Heath Lexington Books, D. C. Heath and Company (1971).

2. William R. Davidson, "Changes in Distributive Institutions," *Journal of Marketing* 34 (January, 1970), p. 7.

3. The earliest comprehensive discussion of administered channels, and the most cited, is Valentine F. Ridgeway, "Administration of Manufacturer-Dealer Systems," *Administrative Science Quarterly* (March, 1957), pp. 464–467.

4. William R. Davidson, *op. cit.,* p. 8.

5. *Chicago Board of Trade* v. *United States,* 246 U.S. 231, at 238.

6. For a classification of the range of systems involved, see Bert C. McCammon, Jr., "The Emergence and Growth of Contractually Integrated Channels in the American Economy," in Peter D. Bennett, ed., *Marketing and Economic Development,* Chicago, Illinois: American Marketing Association (1965), p. 499.

7. Edwin Lewis and Robert Hancock, *The Franchise System of Distribution,* Minneapolis: Division of Research, Graduate School of Business Administration, University of Minnesota (1963).

8. J. A. H. Curry *et al., Partners for Profit: A Study of Franchising,* New York: American Management Association, Inc. (1966).

9. S. Michal Ingraham, *Management Control Potentials and Practices of Franchise Systems,* Ann Arbor, Michigan: University Microfilms, Inc. (1963).

10. Itemized Rating Scales are also known as Specific Category Scales and are discussed in Claire Sellitz et al., *Research Methods in Social Relations* (rev. ed.), New York: Henry Holt & Co., Inc. (1960), p. 347.

11. Samuel M. Gillespie, *An Analysis of Control in Franchise Distri-*

bution Systems (Master of Science in Marketing Thesis), Urbana, Illinois: Graduate College, University of Illinois (1966).

12. An extensive discussion of these concepts of control is found in Richard A. Johnson, Fremont E. Kast, and James E. Rosenzweig, *The Theory and Management of Systems,* New York: McGraw-Hill Book Company, Inc. (1963), especially pp. 57–88. A discussion of optimum control within a distribution channel structure is found in Almarin Phillips, *Market Structure, Organization, and Performance,* Cambridge: Harvard University Press (1962).

13. E. Barry Nann, *Summary of Questionnaire Responses* (from the Curry study), Concord, Mass.: mimeographed (n.d.), p. 11.

14. Lewis and Hancock, *op. cit.,* p. 22.

15. U.S. Congress, Senate, Subcommittee on Antitrust and Monopoly, Committee on the Judiciary, *Distribution Problems Affecting Small Business* (Parts I, II, III), 89th Congress, 1st Session, 1965. See especially Part I (Franchising Agreements).

16. E. Barry Nann, *op. cit.,* p. 10.

17. Nann, *op. cit.,* p. 11.

18. See A. R. Oxenfeldt and D. N. Thompson, "Franchising In Perspective," *Journal of Retailing* (Winter, 1968–69), pp. 1–7.

19. Lewis B. Sappington and C. G. Browne, "The Skills of Creative Leadership," in William Lazar and Eugene J. Kelley, eds., *Managerial Marketing,* rev. ed., Homewood, Illinois: Richard D. Irwin (1962), p. 350.

Chapter 5
Legislation and the Regulation of
Franchise Systems: An Overview

1. *Snap-On Tools Corp.* v. *F.T.C.,* 321 F. 2d 825 (7th Cir. 1963).
2. *Sandura Co.* v. *F.T.C.,* 339 F. 2d 847 (6th Cir. 1964).
3. *Simpson* v. *Union Oil Co.,* 337 U.S. 13 (1964).
4. *Osborn* v. *Sinclair Refining Co.,* 324 F. 2d 566 (4th Cir. 1963).
5. *Packard Motor Car Co.,* v. *Webster Motor Car Co.,* 243 F. 2d 418 (D.C. Cir. 1957), *cert. denied,* 355 U.S. 822 (1957).
6. *White Motor Co.* v. *United States,* 372 U.S. 253 (1963).
7. *Susser* v. *Carvel Corp.,* 206 F. Supp. 636 (S.D.N.Y. 1962), *aff'd.* 332 F. 2d 505 (2d Cir. 1964).
8. Robert L. Jordan, "Exclusive and Restricted Sales Areas Under the Antitrust Laws," *U.C.L.A. Law Review* 9 (January, 1962), p. 117.
9. J. G. Van Cise, *Guiding Principles of Antitrust Law* (mimeo by author), n.d., p. 2. Much of the material in the remainder of this section is found in this reference, pp. 2–4. The monopolization aspect is found in *Lorain Journal Co.* v. *United States,* 342 U.S. 143 (1951).

10. *Times Picayune Publishing Co.* v. *United States,* 345 U.S. 594 (1953); *United States* v. *Parke, Davis & Co.,* 362 U.S. 29 (1960).

11. *United States* v. *Bausch & Lomb Optical Co.,* 321 U.S. 707 (1944); *Lawlor* v. *National Screen Serv. Corp.,* 352 U.S. 17 (1957).

12. *Packard Motor Car Co.* v. *Webster Motor Car Co., op. cit., Schwing Motor Co.* v. *Hudson Sales Corp.,* 239 F. 2d 176 (4th Cir. 1956), *cert. denied,* 335 U.S. 823 (1957).

13. *Garvin* v. *American Motor Sales Corp.,* 318 F. 2d 518 (3rd Cir. 1963).

14. *United States* v. *Reading Co.,* 226 U.S. 324 (1912).

15. *Maryland Baking Co.* v. *F.T.C.,* 243 F. 2d 716 (4th Cir. 1957).

16. *Walker Distrib. Co.* v. *Lucky Lager Brewing Co.,* 323 F. 2d 1 (9th Cir. 1963).

17. *Eastern States Lumber Association* v. *United States,* 234 U.S. 600 (1914).

18 See in particular *Kiefer-Stewart Co.* v. *Joseph E. Seagram & Sons,* 340 U.S. 211 (1951).

19. *U.S.* v. *Colgate & Co.,* 250 U.S. 300 (1919), at 307.

20. *U.S.* v. *Parke, Davis & Co.,* 362 U.S. 29 (1960), at 46–47.

21. *George W. Warner & Co.* v. *Black & Decker Manufacturing Co.,* 277 F. 2d 787 (2d Cir. 1960).

22. *Ibid.,* at 790.

23. Van Cise, *op. cit.,* p. 5.

24. *F.T.C.* v. *Beech-Nut Packing Co.,* 257 U.S. 441 (1922).

25. Lewis G. Rudnick, "The Franchisor's Dilemma: Can He Satisfy The Legal and Commercial Requirements of a Trademark Licensing System Without Exposing Himself to Other Legal Risks," *The Trademark Reporter* 56 (September, 1966), pp. 623–4.

26. William B. Lockhart and Howard R. Sacks, "The Relevance of Economic Factors in Determining Whether Exclusive Arrangements Violate Section 3 of the Clayton Act," *Harvard Law Review* 65 (1952), pp. 920–922.

27. *Tampa Electric Co.* v. *Nashville Coal Co.,* 365 U.S. 320 (1960), at 335.

28. *Standard Oil Co.* v. *United States,* 337 U.S. 293 (1949); *Tampa Electric Co.* v. *Nashville Coal Co., op. cit.*

29. S. Chesterfield Oppenheim, "Antitrust Booms and Boomerangs," *Northwestern University Law Review* 59 (1964), 33–39.

30. *F.T.C.* v. *Brown Shoe Company, Inc.,* 384 U.S. 316 (1966), *reversing* 339 F. 2d 45 (6th Cir. 1964).

31. *Northern Pacific Railroad* v. *United States,* 356 U.S. 1 (1958), at 5.

32. Discussed in Ward S. Bowman, Jr., "Tying arrangements and the Leverage Problem," *Yale Law Journal* 67 (November, 1957), pp. 19–36, and W. L. Baldwin and David McFarland, "Tying Arrangements

in Law and Economics," *The Antitrust Bulletin* 8 (1963), pp. 767–771.

33. Charles E. Stewart, Jr., "Antitrust Considerations Involved in Product Distribution," *Business Lawyer* 19 (1964), p. 995.

34. *Susser* v. *Carvel*, op. cit., at 519.

35. *Carvel Corp.* F.T.C. Dkt. 8574 (July 19, 1965).

36. *Associated Press* v. *Taft-Ingalls Corporation,* 86 Sup. Ct. 47 (1965), *affirming* 340 F. 2d 753 (6th Cir. 1964).

37. *Denison Mattress Factory* v. *Spring-Air Co.,* 308 F. 2d 403 (5th Cir. 1962).

38. *Atlantic Refining Co.* v. *F.T.C.,* 381 U.S. 357 (1965); *Goodyear Tire & Rubber Co.* v. *F.T.C.,* 331 F. 2d 394 (7th Cir. 1964).

39. *F.T.C.* v. *Brown Shoe Co.,* 339 F. 2d 45 (6th Cir. 1964); *reversed* 384 U.S. 316 (1966).

40. *United States* v. *J. I. Case Co.,* 101 F. Supp. 856 (D. Minn. 1951).

41. *United States* v. *Jerrold Electronics Corp.,* 187 F. Supp. 545 (E. D. Pa. 1960), *aff'd.* 365 U.S. 567 (1961).

42. *United States* v. *Richfield Oil Corp.,* 343 U.S. 922 (1952).

43. I am indebted for the classification system used here and for many of the references and interpretations to Lawrence H. Averill, Jr., "Antitrust Considerations of the Principal Distribution Restrictions in Franchise Agreements," in H. Friedman and H. Schlagmann, eds., *Corporate Counsel's Annual 1966,* Albany, New York: Matthew Bender (1966), pp. 428–82.

44. *United States* v. *Bausch & Lomb,* 321 U.S. 707 (1944), *affirming* 45 F. Supp. 387 (S.D.N.Y. 1942).

45. *United States* v. *Sealy, Inc.,* 388 U.S. 350 (1967); *United States* v. *Arnold, Schwinn & Co.,* 388 U.S. 365 (1967).

46. *Report of the Attorney General's National Committee to Study the Antitrust Laws.* Washington, D.C.: U.S. Government Printing Office (March 31, 1955), p. 28.

47. *Boro Hall Corp.* v. *General Motors Corp.,* 124 F. 2d 822 (2d Cir. 1942), at 823.

48. *United States* v. *General Motors,* 384 U.S. 127 (1966), *reversing* 234 F. Supp. 85 (S.D. Cal. 1964).

49. Quoted in A. H. Travers and T. D. Wright, "Restricted Channels of Distribution under the Sherman Act," *Harvard Law Review* 75 (1962), p. 819.

50. *Roux Distrib. Co.* v. *F.T.C.,* 55 F.T.C. 1386 (1959).

51. See Travers and Wright, *op. cit.,* p. 822.

52. *Chicago Sugar Co.* v. *American Sugar Refining Co.,* 338 U.S. 948 (1950), *affirming* 176 F. 2d 1 (7th Cir. 1949).

53. *Dehydrating Process Co.* v. *Smith* 292 F. 2d 753 (1961).

54. *Denison Mattress Factory* v. *Spring Air Co.,* op. cit., at 406.

55. *Susser* v. *Carvel Corp.,* op. cit., at 640.

56. Jackson Brewing Co. v. Clarke, C.C.H. Trade Cases 71082

(Texas Court of Civil Appeals, 9th District, 1964). For an extensive discussion of cases see *State Antitrust Laws,* 29 A.B.A. Antitrust Section (1965), pp. 258–300.

Chapter 6
Tying Arrangements in Franchise
Systems

1. *United States* v. *Arnold, Schwinn & Co.,* 388 U.S. 365 (1967), at 366.
2. *Northern Pacific Railroad* v. *United States,* 356 U.S. 1 (1958).
3. *Brown Shoe Co.* v. *F.T.C.,* 339 F. 2d 45 (6th Cir. 1964): *reversed* 384 U.S. 316 (1966).
4. *Susser* v. *Carvel Corp.,* 206 F. Supp. 636 (S.D.N.Y. 1962), *aff'd* 332 F. 2d 505 (2d Cir. 1964).
5. *Morton Salt Co.* v. *Suppiger Co.,* 314 U.S. 488 (1942).
6. *United States* v. *Loew's, Inc.,* 371 U.S. 38 (1962), at 45.
7. *United States* v. *Jerrold Electronics Corp.,* 365 U.S. 567 (1961), *affirming* 187 F. Supp. 545 (E.D. Pa. 1960).
8. *Brown Shoe Co.* v. *United States,* 370 U.S. 294 (1962), at 330. See also *Harley-Davidson Motor Co.,* 50 F.T.C. 1047, at 1066.
9. *Atlantic Refining Company* v. *Federal Trade Commission,* 381 U.S. 357 (1965), at 371.
10. Rufus E. Wilson, *How To Control The Purchases of Franchisees,* remarks before the Franchise and Antitrust Symposium, International Franchise Association, Washington, D.C. (May 3, 1968), mimeographed, pp. 5–6.
11. *Report of the Attorney General's National Committee to Study the Antitrust Laws,* Washington, D.C.: U.S. Government Printing Office (March 31, 1955), p. 145.
12. Ward S. Bowman, Jr., "Tying Arrangements and the Leverage Problem," *Yale Law Journal* 67 (1957), pp. 19–20.
13. *Times-Picayune Publishing Company* v. *United States,* 345 U.S. 594 (1953), at 604.
14. G. E. Hale and Rosemary Hale, *Market Power: Size and Shape Under the Sherman Act,* Boston: Little, Brown and Company (1958), p. 53.
15. *Crawford Transp. Co.* v. *Chrysler Corp.,* 380 U.S. 959 (1965).
16. See generally F. Bruce Kulp, Jr., "Tying Arrangements Under the Antitrust Laws: The 'Integrity of the Product' Defense," *Michigan Law Review* 63 (1964), pp. 1413–1424.
17. *International Business Machines Corporation* v. *United States,* 298 U.S. 131 (1936).

18. *Heaton-Peninsular Button-Fastener Company* v. *Eureka Specialty Company,* 77 Fed. 288 (1896).

19. *Wilson* v. *Simpson,* 9 Howard 109 (1849).

20. *Henry* v. *A. B. Dick Co.,* 224 U.S. 1 (1912).

21. *International Salt Co.* v. *United States, op. cit.*

22. Bowman, *op. cit.;* George W. Hilton, "Tying Sales and Full-Line Forcing, *Weltwirtschaftliches Archiv* 81 (1958), pp. 265–276; W. L. Baldwin and David McFarland, "Tying Arrangements in Law and Economics," *The Antitrust Bulletin* 8 (1963), pp. 743–780.

23. A simple numerical example, in a slightly different context, is given in Eugene M. Singer, *Antitrust Economics: Selected Legal Cases and Economic Models,* Englewood Cliffs, N.J.: Prentice-Hall, Inc. (1968), pp. 177–180.

24. *F.T.C.* v. *A. & B. Gratz, et al.,* 1 F.T.C. 249 (1918).

25. W. L. Baldwin and David McFarland, *op. cit.,* p. 771.

26. Hilton, *op. cit.,* p. 274.

27. Richard S. Markovits, "Tie-Ins, Reciprocity, and the Leverage Theory," *The Yale Law Journal* 76 (1967), p. 1461.

28. This section, and Appendix C, have as academic antecedents the following: Robert L. Bishop, "Elasticities, Cross Elasticities, and Market Relationships," *American Economic Review* XLII (December, 1952), pp. 779–803; Mancur Olson and David McFarland, "The Restoration of Pure Monopoly and the Concept of the Industry," *The Quarterly Journal of Economics* 76 (1962), pp. 613–631; M. L. Burstein, "The Economics of Tie-In Sales," *The Review of Economics and Statistics* XLII (1960), pp. 68–73; and, especially, Richard Markovits, *op. cit.,* pp. 1399–1443.

29. F. Y. Edgeworth, "Railway Rates," *Papers Relating to Political Economy* I, London: Royal Economic Society Papers (1925), pp. 172 ff.; A. C. Pigou, *The Economics of Welfare,* 2nd ed., London: Macmillan & Co. Ltd. (1924), p. 254; Joan Robinson, *The Economics of Imperfect Competition,* London: Macmillan & Co. Ltd. (1933), pp. 200–202.

30. M. L. Burstein, "A Theory of Full-Line Forcing," *Northwestern University Law Review* 55 (1960), pp. 66–68.

31. Analysis of this situation is rather involved. A discussion can be found in Burstein, "Full Line Forcing," *op. cit.,* pp. 65–68; or Markovits, *op. cit.,* pp. 1448–1454.

32. *Henry* v. *A.B. Dick Co., op. cit.,* at 9.

33. An exception: see Donald F. Turner, "Some Reflections on Antitrust," *1966 N.Y. State Bar Association Antitrust Law Symposium,* New York: New York State Bar Association (1966), pp. 1–9.

34. *United States* v. *Columbia Pictures Corporation,* 189 F. Supp. 153 (S.D.N.Y. 1960), at 178.

35. *United States* v. *Jerrold Electronics Corp., op. cit.,* at 560.

36. *Dehydrating Process Co.* v. *A. O. Smith Corp.*, 292 F. 2d 653 (1st Cir.), *cert. denied*, 368 U.S. 931 (1961).

37. *Standard Oil Co.* v. *United States*, 337 U.S. 293 (1949), at 306–307 (dictim); *White Motor Co.* v. *United States*, 372 U.S. 253 (1963), at 263 (dictim).

38. *Federal Trade Commission* v. *Sinclair Refining Co.*, 261 U.S. 463 (1923).

39. Carl Kaysen and Donald F. Turner, *Antitrust Policy, An Economic and Legal Analysis*, Cambridge: Harvard University Press (1959), p. 157.

40. Donald F. Turner, "The Validity of Tying Arrangements under the Antitrust Laws," *Harvard Law Review* 72 (1958), pp. 60–62.

41. 365 U.S. 320 (1961).

Chapter 7
Territorial and Customer Arrangements
in Franchise Systems

1. Joe S. Bain, *Industrial Organization*, 2nd ed., New York: John Wiley & Sons, Inc. (1968), pp. 228–235.

2. *United States* v. *White Motor Co.*, 372 U.S. 253 (1963); see also 1964 Trade Cases par. 71, 195 (N.D. Ohio).

3. *Sandura Co.* v. *F.T.C.*, 339 F. 2d 847 (6th Cir. 1964); *Snap-On Tools Corp.* v. *F.T.C.*, 321 F. 2d 825 (7th Cir. 1963); *Denison Mattress Factory* v. *Spring-Air Co.*, 308 F. 2d 403 (5th Cir. 1962); *United States* v. *Arnold, Schwinn & Co., et al.*, Civ. 58-C-272(3) (E.D. Mo. trfd. to N.D. Ill.); *United States* v. *Sealy, Inc.*, Civ 60-C-844 (N.D. Ill.).

4. *United States* v. *Arnold, Schwinn & Co.*, 388 U.S. 365 (1967).

5. The background to the case is found in the Supreme Court and District Court decisions, and in the printed transcript in the Supreme Court. The latter is quoted in Robert C. Keck, "The Schwinn Case," *The Business Lawyer* (April, 1968), pp. 669–687.

6. Betty Bock, *Antitrust Issues in Restricting Sales Territories and Outlets*, New York: National Industrial Conference Board, Inc. (1968), p. 13.

7. Donald N. Thompson, "Franchise Operations and Antitrust Law," *The Journal of Retailing* 45 (Winter, 1969), pp. 39–53.

8. *Simpson* v. *Union Oil Co.*, 377 U.S. 13 (1964), at 22.

9. Betty Bock, *op. cit.*, p. 27.

10. *United States* v. *Sealy, Inc.*, 388 U.S. 350 (1967).

11. A detailed description of the *Sealy* case is found in Lewis G. Rudnick, "The Sealy Case: The Supreme Court Applies The Per Se Doctrine To A Hybrid Distribution System For Trademarked Bedding Products," *The Trademark Reporter* 57 (July, 1967), pp. 459–467.

12. 60 C 845 (N.D. Ill., May 31, 1960); 60 C 828 (N.D. Ill., May 27,

1960); 60 C 843 (N.D. Ill., May 31, 1960); 60 C 844 (N.D. Ill., May 31, 1960).

13. Christopher D. Stone, "Closed Territorial Distribution: An Opening Question in the Sherman Act," *University of Chicago Law Review* 30 (1963), p. 315.

14. The most important theoretical works are Harold Hotelling, "Stability in Competition," *Economic Journal* XXXIX (1929), pp. 41–57; August Lösch, *The Economics of Location*, New Haven, Conn.: Yale University Press (1954), especially pp. 105–114, and Edgar M. Hoover, *The Location of Economic Activity*, New York: McGraw-Hill Book Co. (1948). A model related to the one presented in this chapter is Edwin S. Mills and Michael R. Lav, "A Model of Market Areas With Free Entry," *Journal of Political Economy* 72 (1964), pp. 278–288.

15. Lee E. Preston, "Restrictive Distribution Arrangements: Economic Analysis and Public Policy Standards," *Law and Contemporary Problems* 30 (Summer, 1965), pp. 506–529.

16. See Mills and Lav, *op. cit.*

17. Michael C. Lovell, "Product Differentiation and Market Structure," a paper presented at the December, 1969 meetings of the Econometric Society, New York City. See also Michael C. Lovell, "Optimal Franchising in Theory," in Donald N. Thompson, ed., *Contractual Marketing Systems*, Lexington, Mass.: Heath Lexington Books (1971).

18. *United States* v. *General Electric*, 272 U.S. 476 (1926).

19. Charles E. Stewart, Jr., "Exclusive Franchises and Territorial Confinement of Distributors," *A.B.A. Antitrust Section* 22 (1963), pp. 39–40.

20. *Sandura Co.* v. *F.T.C.*, 339 F. 2d 847 (6th Cir. 1964).

21. The facts of the case are set out in *Sandura Co.*, F.T.C. No. 7042 (September 15, 1961). An excellent summary is found in Stone, *op. cit.*, pp. 293–297, 301–308.

22. *Ibid.*, p. 302–303.

Chapter 8
Exclusive Franchising and Exclusive
Dealing in Franchise Systems

1. *Schwing Motor Company* v. *Hudson Sales Corp.*, 138 F. Supp. 899, at 906–907; *cert, denied*, 355 U.S. 823 (1957).

2. See *Lawlor* v. *National Screen Serv. Corp.*, 352 U.S. 992 (1957), and *Standard Oil Co.* v. *United States*, 337 U.S. 293 (1949).

3. A. H. Travers, Jr., and Thomas D. Wright, "Restricted Channels of Distribution Under The Sherman Act," *Harvard Law Review* 75 (1962), p. 806.

4. Bedros Peter Pashigian, *The Distribution of Automobiles, An Eco-*

nomic Analysis of the Franchise System, Englewood Cliffs, New Jersey: Prentice-Hall, Inc. (1961), especially pp. 25–51. The formulation follows James M. Henderson and Richard Quandt, *Microeconomic Theory,* New York: McGraw Hill Book Co., Inc. (1958), especially Chapter 6.

5. Pashigian, *op. cit.,* p. 38.

6. Joe S. Bain, *Price Theory,* New York: Henry Holt & Company, Inc. (1952), p. 294.

7. Early studies were W. Lloyd Warner, Marcia Meeker, and Kenneth Eells, *Social Class in America,* Chicago: Science Research Associates, Inc. (1949); Pierre Martineau, "Social Classes and Spending Behavior," *Journal of Marketing* XXIII (October, 1958), p. 121. A later approach is W. Bruce Weale, "Measuring the Customer's Image of a Department Store," *Journal of Retailing* XXXVII (Summer, 1961), p. 40.

8. Martineau, *op. cit.,* pp. 126–127.

9. Martineau, *loc. cit.*

10. Michael R. Flicker, "Newcomer Defenses: Reasonable Use of Tie-Ins, Franchises, Territorials, and Exclusives," *Stanford Law Review* 18 (January, 1966), p. 466.

11. *Standard Oil Co. of California* v. *United States,* 337 U.S. 293 (1949).

12. *Ibid.,* at 309.

13. *Tampa Electric Co.* v. *Nashville Coal Co.,* 365 U.S. 320 (1961), at 335.

14. See *United States* v. *Pullman Co.,* 330 U.S. 806 (1947), *affirming* 50 F. Supp. 123 (E. D. Pa. 1943).

15. See *Carter Carburetor Corp.* v. *F.T.C.,* 112 F. 2d 722 (8th Cir. 1940).

16. The discussion follows William B. Lockhart and Howard R. Sacks, "The Relevance of Economic Factors in Determining Whether Exclusive Arrangements Violate Section 3 of the Clayton Act," *Harvard Law Review* 65 (April, 1952), pp. 923–927.

17. Lockhart and Sacks, *op. cit.,* p. 925.

Chapter 9
Conclusion

1. *Standard Oil Co. of California* v. *United States,* 337 U.S. 293 (1949), at 320.

2. A discussion of Schwinn's compliance alternatives is given in Robert C. Keck, "The Schwinn Case," *The Business Lawyer* (April, 1968), pp. 683–687.

3. *United States* v. *Von's Grocery Co.,* 384 U.S. 270 (1966).

4. This situation is described in detail in the decision of the Honorable Joseph F. Gagliardi, Judge of the Supreme Court of the State of New

York, in *Eastchester Service Center* v. *Mobil Oil Corporation,* reprinted in the *Congressional Record,* Vol. 115, No. 190 (Tuesday, November 18, 1969), pp. S. 14511–S. 14514.

5. S. 2321, S. 2507 (1967); S. 1967, H. R. 12074 (1969).

Appendix B

1. 70 Stat. 1125 (1956); 15 U.S.C. 1221–25 (1958).

2. H.R. No. 2850.

3. *Volkswagen Interamericana, S.A.* v. *Rohlsen,* 35 U.S. Law Week 3150 (Oct. 25, 1966), *affirming* 360 F. 2d 437 (1st Cir. 1966).

4. *Staten Island Motors, Inc.* v. *American Motor Sales Corp.* 169 F. Supp. 378 (D.N.J. 1959).

5. *Woodward* v. *General Motors Corp.,* 369 U.S. 887 (1962), *affirming* 298 F. 2d 121 (5th Cir. 1962).

6. *Ibid.,* at 128.

7. *Leach* v. *Ford Motor Co.,* 189 F. Supp. 349 (N.D. Cal. 1960).

8. *Victory Motors, Inc.* v. *Chrysler Motors Corp.,* 357 F. 2d 429 (5th Cir. 1966).

9. *Garvin* v. *American Motors Sales Corp.,* 318 F. 2d 518 (3rd Cir. 1963).

10. *Fabert Motors, Inc.* v. *Ford Motor Co.,* 355 F. 2d 888 (7th Cir. 1966).

Appendix C

1. See M. L. Burstein, "The Economics of Tie-In Sales," *The Review of Economics and Statistics* XLII (1960), pp. 68–73, and Richard Markovits, "Tie-Ins, Reciprocity, and the Leverage Theory," *The Yale Law Journal* 76 (1967), pp. 1399–1443.

2. The analysis closely follows Richard Markovits, *op. cit.*

3. Milton Friedman, "The Marshallian Demand Curve," *The Journal of Political Economy* (1949), pp. 463 ff. We also assume that the marginal utility of money remains constant. Reference: J. R. Hicks, *Value And Capital,* 2nd ed., Oxford: The Clarendon Press (1946), pp. 38–41, 330–332.

Appendix D

1. Price discrimination is analyzed in most intermediate economics texts. See, for example, A. W. Stonier and D. C. Hague, *A Textbook of Economic Theory,* New York: John Wiley & Sons, Inc. (1964), pp. 172–181.

Appendix E

1. Adapted from Bedros Peter Pashigian, *The Distribution of Automobiles, An Economic Analysis of the Franchise System*, Englewood Cliffs, New Jersey: Prentice-Hall, Inc. (1961), especially pp. 25–51. The formulation follows James M. Henderson and Richard E. Quandt, *Microeconomic Theory*, New York: McGraw-Hill Book Co., Inc. (1958), especially Chapter 6.

About the Author

Donald N. Thompson is Fellow in Law and Business Administration, Harvard University and Associate Professor, The University of Alberta, and has been a Visiting Professor at Long Island University. He is a graduate of the University of California, Berkeley.

Professor Thompson is the editor of *Contractual Marketing Systems* (Heath Lexington Books, 1971) and has contributed articles on marketing and public policy to both legal and business journals. He has addressed a number of professional meetings dealing with the economic implications of governmental constraints on marketing decision-making. He was Chairman of the American Marketing Association's 1970 Workshop on Contractual Marketing Systems, and has served as an advisor to committees of the Canadian and United States governments.